Decoding Dylan

Decoding Dylan

*Making Sense of the Songs
That Changed Modern Culture*

JIM CURTIS

McFarland & Company, Inc., Publishers
Jefferson, North Carolina

LIBRARY OF CONGRESS CATALOGUING-IN-PUBLICATION DATA

Names: Curtis, James M., 1940– author.
Title: Decoding Dylan : making sense of the songs that changed modern culture / Jim Curtis.
Description: Jefferson, North Carolina : McFarland & Company, 2019 | Includes bibliographical references and index.
Identifiers: LCCN 2019008866 | ISBN 9781476678450 (paperback. : acid free paper) ∞
Subjects: LCSH: Dylan, Bob, 1941– —Criticism and interpretation.
Classification: LCC ML420.D98 C9 2019 | DDC 782.42164092— dc23
LC record available at https://lccn.loc.gov/2019008866

BRITISH LIBRARY CATALOGUING DATA ARE AVAILABLE

ISBN (print) 978-1-4766-7845-0
ISBN (ebook) ISBN 978-1-4766-3649-8

© 2019 Jim Curtis. All rights reserved

No part of this book may be reproduced or transmitted in any form or by any means, electronic or mechanical, including photocopying or recording, or by any information storage and retrieval system, without permission in writing from the publisher.

Front cover image: Bob Dylan, circa mid 1970s (Photofest)

Printed in the United States of America

McFarland & Company, Inc., Publishers
  Box 611, Jefferson, North Carolina 28640
  www.mcfarlandpub.com

Acknowledgments

This book would never have seen the light of day without the indefatigable editorial work of my wife Donna Curtis. With unwavering dedication, she applied herself for long periods of time to clarify what I had written and to make all the parts of the book consistent. I am deeply grateful to Donna for her work on this book, and for so many other things as well, including her unfailing love and support. That is why I dedicate the book to her.

I also want to acknowledge the role of the University of Missouri–Columbia, where I taught for 31 years. The University supported me in what must have seemed like a quixotic desire to teach a course on popular culture. I am also grateful to a student in that course, Rick Worland (who is now a professor of film at Southern Methodist University), with whom I have had ongoing conversations about music and film in American life for 40 years and counting.

Another professor, Walter Ong, of St. Louis University (who died in 2003), was also someone from whose friendship I benefited. I learned a great deal about the interaction of orality and literacy in the formation of culture during our conversations. Ong was a phenomenally productive scholar; he remains the epitome of someone who combined scholarly achievement and spiritual dedication.

Despite Donna's best efforts, some factual mistakes and stylistic problems may remain. They are solely my responsibility.

"Songs for Passersby"
by James M. Curtis

Things are they are
Were changed on Dylan's guitar.
Yes, and Bobby Zimmerman, a sweet-faced boy from afar,
That boy too was changed on Dylan's guitar.

Did Dylan, faux populist that he was,
Read not the beats but also Stevens?
He would of course deny it,
Why take him at his word?
What to do with a denial so absurd,
Louise, why not defy it?

Just think of Guthrie together with Stevens!
The stretch between them is enormous,
Yet Dylan could, would, flourish precisely there.
Though he would rather die than inform us.

With Picasso's help, Dylan learned to rearrange glum faces
Putting the blue guitar in unfamiliar places.
He dwelt among the fractured sixties,
And much, much more than they, he was a-changin'.
He was released one day—fated to transcend.
The formless yet tempting Johanna led him on
Das ewig webliche zieht uns hinan.

Society's ills, such as they are,
Were hardly changed on Dylan's guitar.
Bullies still clamor to build the big guns.
We may always have these men—the masters of war.
What then was truly changed on Dylan's guitar?

Not things, but songs, sung loudly in a bar.
Benefited most from Dylan's guitar.
Left alone beneath the diamond sky,
He sent back songs for passersby.

Table of Contents

Acknowledgments	v
"Songs for Passersby" by James M. Curtis	vi
Preface	1
Introduction	4

Section I: Theories and Practices

1. Bob Dylan: His Biography and His Career	7
2. The Early Years in New York	27
3. Affinities with Franz Kafka, T.S. Eliot and Pablo Picasso	51

Section II: Songs and Songwriting

4. Songs of Transcendence—*Highway 61 Revisited* and *Blonde on Blonde*	73
Table 1. Chronology of Songs	74
Table 2. Night Songs	87
5. Songs of Assimilation—*John Wesley Harding* and *Nashville Skyline*	95
6. "Putting a Certain Orderliness to the Chaos"	103
Table 3. Rhyme Forms in Dylan's Songs of the Early 1960s	106
Table 4. Rhyme Forms in Dylan's Songs of the Late 1960s	107
Table 5. Examples of Triple Rhymes in Tin Pan Alley Songs	112
Table 6. Triple Rhymes or More in Some American Songs (1968–1984)	114

Table of Contents

7. Dylan and Springsteen — 118

8. The Real Revolution of the 1960s — 129
    Table 7. Chronologies of Early Successes of Dylan, Barbra Streisand and Woody Allen by Approximate Age — 133

Conclusion: Dylan's Paradoxes — 148

Chapter Notes — 151

Bibliography — 157

Index — 161

Preface

"Popular music has no, whatever you call them, critics, that understand popular music in all of its dynamic fundamentalism."[1]

In 2016, the Nobel Prize Committee awarded the prize in literature to Bob Dylan "for having created new poetic expressions within the great American song tradition."[2] The awareness that Dylan innovated within tradition, and specifically within the great American song tradition, was long in coming. In the 1960s, Dylan's songs seemed startlingly and shockingly new. No one had ever sung such dense lyrics to the strident chords of an electric guitar before.

Corresponding to the dialectic between innovation and tradition in Dylan's work is the dialectic between high culture and popular culture in his work, a dialectic that has a modest equivalent in my own life. I grew up in Elvis Presley's hometown of Tupelo, Mississippi, and I saw Elvis perform live there in 1956. That experience gave me a lifelong fascination with rock and roll and with popular music in general. It was that unforgettable Elvis concert that inspired me to write my book *Rock Eras: Interpretations of Music and Society, 1954–1984*. This book incorporates some materials and ideas that I present in the long chapter on Dylan in that book.

But I have done other things in my life besides listen to rock and roll and write about it. I left Tupelo to go north to school—first to Vanderbilt University in Nashville, and then to Columbia University in New York, where I received a PhD in Russian literature. Odd as it may seem, I find Russian novels and rock and roll songs equally fascinating.

About a decade after I saw Elvis, I had a second formative experience that also informs this book—reading Marshall McLuhan's seminal book on media theory, *Understanding Media: The Extensions of Man*. McLuhan's work came as a revelation to me because it gave me a coherent (and, to me, persuasive) way to understand the social context of the culture of the two regions that have fascinated me for my entire life—Russia and the American South. I was so excited about the explanatory potential of McLuhan's work that I wrote the first analysis and justification of McLuhan's work, *Culture as Polyphony: An Essay on the Nature of Paradigms.* These three books, including this one, form a coherent trilogy of books that apply media theory to the interpretation of culture, and assume that both popular and high culture have equal validity.

While working on this book, from time to time I did informal surveys with friends and family, asking them how many Dylan songs they could name. It turned out that most people could name only two: "Blowin' in the Wind" and "Lay Lady Lay." These two songs form bookends, as it were, for the great songs of the middle period, such as "Highway 61 Revisited" and "Visions of Johanna." Songs such as these may be too long and too demanding for people who are accustomed to listening to songs written in couplets about the agony and ecstasy of young love. It is as though Dylan wrote these songs in a code for which they have no key.

I call this book *Decoding Dylan* because I am following the standard procedure of codebreakers and emphasize pattern recognition as a way of showing the coherence in passages that people have previously found puzzling. I show that, first of all, decoding Dylan involves relating him to the cultural environment that formed his sensibility, namely New York in the 1960s. It was in the tumultuous decade of the 1960s that Dylan revolutionized popular music while writing and performing the songs on which his reputation is based.

For all his complexity, Dylan is a profoundly American artist, and breaking the code of his songs involves doing what codebreakers do—identifying recurring patterns. That is why I rely on some essential recurring patterns in American life to relate Dylan's songs to his society, and no pattern occurs more frequently, or has greater emotional resonance in America, than the relationship between democracy and elitism. American artists have used this relationship in a variety of ways to inform their creative endeavors and have kept it current and vital.

Thus, identifying patterns by relating an individual song or an individual artist to the appropriate cultural text becomes a study that widens out and opens up into a study in American cultural history. In short, Dylan is too important to be studied in isolation.

Dylan is not the first artist in the history of Western civilization who left home as a teenager for the big city, where he would succeed beyond his wildest dreams. We enrich our understanding of Dylan if we study his life and career in terms of other similar lives and careers. We could say that he has the same significance for our time that William Shakespeare had for his. This statement does not mean that Dylan is as good as Shakespeare, because they are both comparable and incomparable. What the statement does mean becomes apparent in the opening of Stephen Greenblatt's *Will in the World: How Shakespeare Became Shakespeare*. Change a few names and dates, and everything that Greenblatt says about Shakespeare applies to Dylan:

> A young man from a small provincial town—a man without independent wealth, without powerful family connections, and without a university education—moved to London in the late 1580s and, in a remarkably short time, becomes the greatest playwright not of his age alone but of all time. His works appeal to the learned and unlettered, to urban sophisticates and provincial first-time theatergoers. He makes his audiences laugh and cry; he turns politics into poetry; he recklessly mingles vulgar clowning and philosophical subtlety.[3]

Dylan's great songs of the 1960s also derive from a mixture of sources and inspirations in both high and popular culture.

In presenting Dylan in his way, I take an essential methodological clue from an unlikely source—T.S. Eliot. Eliot wrote something in his famous essay "Tradition and the Individual Talent" that is key to his influential idea of criticism and to this book:

> No poet, no artist of any art, has his complete meaning alone. His significance, his appreciation is the appreciation of his relation to the dead poets and artists. You cannot value him alone: you must set him, for contrast and comparison, among the dead.[4]

It does not diminish great artists of any kind to "set them among the dead." On the contrary, it enhances them. This principle especially applies to Dylan, whose life and work has baffled so many people. I apply Eliot's ideas about criticism in ways that he never would have imagined to songs that he would never have considered worth his attention. Nevertheless, Eliot's work has great relevance for this book both because he was a major influence on Dylan and also because, as Eliot himself said, it is innovation that keeps tradition alive—even tradition in criticism.

It is also possible to integrate Dylan's songs with what he has said about them. When it comes to talking about his songs, the notoriously reclusive Dylan is not so much a Sphinx as an Ariadne. (In Greek mythology, Ariadne was the daughter of the Cretan king who gave the Athenian hero Theseus a ball of thread that enabled him to find his way out of a labyrinth.) If we listen to Dylan's songs carefully and read his writings attentively, we find that—like Ariadne—he gives us the clues we need to navigate the labyrinth of his work.

Introduction

The purpose of this book is to help the reader understand the often puzzling, confusing songs that Bob Dylan wrote during the 1960s. It does this by showing how he used ideas and images from songs, movies, books, and poems to create his songs. Such discussions help to define his place in American Culture. Songs and songwriting is what this book is about. It is not a biography of Dylan, such as Howard Sounes's *Down the Highway*; it is not about general cultural history, like Sean Wilentz's *Bob Dylan in America*; and it does not deal with a particular theme in Dylan's songs, such as Christopher Rick's *Dylan's Vision of Sin*.

Although this book does not deal with biography as such or with cultural history as such, it does touch upon those topics by following a method that I call "Dylan and…." This book analyzes Dylan's life and his songs, not as separate topics, but rather in the context of the lives of other high achievers in the arts, and other popular songs. It is a contextualized analysis. Although this book discusses the lyrics of Dylan's songs, it does not include them, and readers are encouraged to listen to Dylan's recordings or consult written lyrics such as those found in Dylan's *Lyrics: 1962–2001*.

The first section, "Theories and Practices," includes chapters on Dylan's evolution until about 1964. These chapters discuss some well-known facts about Dylan and relate them to some general theories about markers of creativity. Certain patterns, such as birth order and ethnicity, recur in the lives of high achievers in the arts, and it enriches our understanding of Dylan if we match these features of his life to analogous features in the lives of the small group of his peers. The influences of books he read and exposure to other cultural factors lead to an understanding of the place of his songs in popular culture. Also, Dylan has some affinities with major figures of High Modernism—Franz Kafka, T.S. Eliot, and Pablo Picasso. Picasso probably has greater importance for Dylan as an influencer and role model than any other single artist in any field.

The second section, "Songs and Songwriting," shows the overall coherence of songs by relating them to various themes and organizational principles and discusses his influence on later songwriters. The chapter on songs of transcendence deals primarily with "Mr. Tambourine Man," "Desolation Row," and "Visions of Johanna" as an internally coherent progression. Innovation gives way to assimilation and "putting a certain orderliness to the chaos," as Dylan said when he started making drawings. Alongside the image of Dylan as the rebel is Dylan as the careful craftsman and student of song writing. Finally, an analysis of Bruce Springsteen's complex and productive relationship completes this section.

Chapter 8 includes a discussion of Dylan's career in the context of two other important cultural figures who became prominent in the 1960s: Barbra Streisand and Woody Allen. Dylan and these two other geniuses with Jewish backgrounds have dominated American popular culture since the mid-1960s as no others have done.

SECTION I: THEORIES AND PRACTICES

1

Bob Dylan
His Biography and His Career

Don't Look Back (1967), the documentary film about Dylan's 1965 concert tour in England, features an unforgettable shot.[1] In it, a slender young man stands on a large stage in the glare of two small spotlights. He holds an acoustic guitar and wears a harmonica rack around his neck, and that is it. There are no backup musicians and no backup singers. With the exception of a few solo pianists, few performers had ever appeared on the stage of London's venerable Royal Albert Hall without any accompaniment at all. And surely none of them had ever looked so completely and utterly alone. As Joan Baez, who probably understands Dylan better than anyone, once commented in her wonderful memoir *And a Voice to Sing With*, "When he faces a crowd, he looks as though he'd rather be in a dark parlor playing chess. Perhaps in a sense he is."[2]

Nevertheless, it does not do justice to the complexity of Dylan's psyche to say that he is "very private" and "reclusive." The ever-thoughtful, ever-perceptive Baez comments that when she accompanied Dylan and his then wife Sara on the Rolling Thunder Revue in 1975–76,

> Bob and Sara were ill-equipped to handle the practical matters of life. I was forever handing them towels, bringing glasses of water and cups of coffee, lighting their cigarettes, looking after their kids and trying to get them seated together at dinner tables. I don't know what I meant to them. Sometimes I thought I was the male figure, or perhaps a caretaker for two floundering things from another space and time, slow-moving and strange beings, as out of place as wolves in the winter, whom the gods had thrown together to fend for themselves.[3]

Baez would appreciate something that the Richard Gere version of Dylan says in the 2007 quasi-biographical movie *I'm Not There*: "I don't know who I am most of the time."

Dylan's lack of a stable cultural identity means that his psyche simply is not connected to this world, and his relationships with his wives indicate as much. When he married Sara Lownds on November 22, 1965, he denied it to friends and did not appear in public with her.[4] Even more radically, he never so much as mentioned that a backup singer in his band, Carolyn Dennis, had given birth to his daughter, Desire Gabrielle Dennis-Dylan on January 31, 1986. He later married her in Los Angeles on June 4, 1986.[5] The astonishing fact that he has never so much as mentioned the birth of this child and his marriage to this child's mother would seem to go way beyond eccentricity and a celebrity's need for privacy.

Male celebrities often have trouble with the women in their lives, but Dylan has never been close to men, either. He has never had what earlier generations of American men would have called "pals." There has never been anybody in his life comparable to Bing Crosby's golfing buddy Bob Hope, or Frank Sinatra's "Rat Pack." He has never had flunkies at his beck and call, like Elvis Presley's "Memphis Mafia." To be sure, he toured with Robbie Robertson and The Hawks, and made the legendary basement tapes with The Band rock group, but he only played with them briefly, and then moved on. In any case, these sidemen were never collaborators, the way the E Street Band collaborates with Bruce Springsteen as an extension of Bruce's genius.

Dylan's intense introversion may explain why he never became a major movie star, as Bing Crosby, Frank Sinatra, and Elvis did. The tradition of the charismatic singer as movie star dies out with him. He has only appeared in one major Western film, *Pat Garrett and Billy the Kid* (1973), in which he co-starred with James Coburn and Kris Kristofferson. Film, however, is a notoriously collaborative medium, and Dylan does not collaborate well, which may help to explain why his film *Renaldo and Clara* (1978) got terrible reviews. Only the documentaries in which Dylan appears offer lasting interest to his fans, including *Don't Look Back* and *No Direction Home*.[6]

How do we understand and interpret a great performer, someone who defines our time, but who looks like he might "rather be in a dark parlor playing chess"? If we begin very generally, and think of Dylan's position in American culture as a whole, we can say that he belongs to what might be called the reclusive tradition, whose representatives include the poet Emily Dickinson and the painter Andrew Wyeth. But poets like Dickinson and painters like Wyeth create their work in private, and people usually experience it in private. We can state the dilemma that Dylan poses for us by saying that he is a performer with the mentality of a writer or a painter. With the exception of his concerts, he very rarely appears in public or on television, and he simply withdraws into his private world for long periods of time.

However—and it is a big however—it was Dylan's fate in life to play a major role in bringing about a key transition in American culture. With the advent of television, the private presentational arts of literature and painting ceded their former importance to the public performing arts of singing and acting, thereby creating the most important change in American culture in the second half of the twentieth century. Unlike the presentational arts, the performing arts are collaborative, because they require other people. And one must stand up in front of other people, either on a stage or on a screen, to do them.

Dylan's reclusiveness caused such frustration in the 1960s that his fans did many crazy things. When he lived in New York, they went through his garbage cans, and when he moved to Woodstock to get away from them, they followed him there as well—to his considerable annoyance. But there is a better way to decode Dylan than looking through his garbage cans or even interviewing him. To decode (i.e., make sense of) Dylan's often baffling songs we would be well advised to adopt the procedures of cryptographers, people who decode messages for a living.

Cryptographers know that the first thing to do when decoding is to look for patterns. Any given sequence in a coded message may seem incomprehensible by itself, and the tendency to isolate Dylan's work from that of other artists has often produced what might be called the drama of enigma. Thus, Greil Marcus comments in his book *The Basement Tapes*, "Out of some odd displacement of art and time the music seemed both transparent and inexplicable."[7] Marcus, like many other Dylan fans, gives the impression that the very fact that the songs are "inexplicable" proves how great they are. Yet in cryptography what is inexplicable in isolation often makes sense as part of a larger pattern. That is certainly the case with Dylan's songs.

We can do this by starting with some basic facts about Dylan's life, and then decode them by relating them to larger patterns in the lives of other creative people. The performer that we know as Bob Dylan was born Robert Allen Zimmerman into an observant Jewish family in Duluth, Minnesota, on May 24, 1941. In February 1946, another son, David, was born into the family, and the Zimmermans moved from Duluth to nearby Hibbing, where the boys' father Abraham Zimmerman, known as Abe, went into business with his brothers. This business was Zimmerman Furniture and Electric, and was located at 1925 E. Fifth Avenue in Hibbing, and Bobby Zimmerman grew up, went to high school, and had his bar mitzvah in Hibbing.

Taken by themselves, these facts are comparable to those of many other boys. We can ask ourselves then, if some biographical facts are more important than others, and if so, what are they? The people who have studied high achievers such as Dylan have identified what psychologist Dean Simonton calls "biographical antecedents of achieved eminence." I prefer the simpler term "markers of creativity." I will discuss here four major markers of creativity: cultural marginality, ethnicity, relationship to the father, and birth order. I will show how each of these applies to Dylan and other major figures in cultural history, beginning with the most general and proceeding to the specific.

In the documentary film *No Direction Home*, Dylan defines his cultural marginality by telling director Martin Scorsese, "I was born a long way from where I was supposed to be." Like many other creative people, young Bobby Zimmerman could have used "We Gotta Get Out of This Place," the title of a 1965 hit song by Eric Burdon and the Animals, as his theme song. No matter what amenities and advantages a place has, if it does not offer creative people opportunities to develop their abilities, it creates a situation of cultural marginality for them. Thus, a prodigiously gifted Italian boy named Leonardo grew up in the village of Vinci, but left home for the exciting opportunities offered by Florence, where he became known as Leonardo da Vinci. Young Will Shakespeare left Stratford-on-Avon for London, where he became known as William. These two boys, and many other talented boys like them, suffered from what Stephen Sondheim in the song "New York New York" called the "little town blues."

When we study the psychodynamics of creativity, it appears that growing up far from where you are supposed to be has some long term advantages that compensate for the obvious short-term disadvantages. For one thing, it sometimes forces people to define what they want in life, if only by forcing upon them the awareness that what is around them is not it. For another, the frustration caused by cultural marginality helps to build up energy and determination, a "head of steam," so to speak, that will help to overcome adversity in the future.

Issues of ethnicity have relevance for all aspects of American life, and especially for popular music, which has been primarily created by African-Americans, Italian-Americans, and Jews.[8] The topic of Jews and Judaism in connection with what Simonton calls "achieved eminence" has particular importance for Dylan. However, with the exception of a brief period in the 1970s, Dylan was not, and is not, an observant Jew and has had little interest in Judaism as a formal religion. What matters first and foremost here is not so much Dylan's religious practice, if any, but his genetic heritage. Intelligence and creativity seem to be prominent in the DNA of Jews, as Simonton suggests. He comments that "Jews make up only between 1% and 3% of the population of Europe and the United States. Yet their presence in the lists of the eminent exceeds statistical expectations by a factor of 10 or more."[9] Dylan's career makes sense as part of a distinct pattern in the lives of eminent Jewish high achievers.

In the late twentieth century, a consensus appeared that whatever it was that French poet Charles Baudelaire meant by "modernity," it was primarily created by Jews. Historian Yuri Slezkine has even called the twentieth century "the Jewish century."[10] The names usually mentioned in this connection are Sigmund Freud, Albert Einstein, and Franz Kafka. In psychotherapy, in physics, and in literature, Freud, Einstein, and Kafka changed the way we think by abandoning old concepts and creating new concepts as well as new terms to describe them. They created what we now call a paradigm shift. Outsiders such as these Jews, who had the considerable advantage of not growing up with the received categories that insiders took for granted, could thus perceive and employ alternatives.

And then there is the matter of the extraordinary verbal gifts of Jews. Although Freud was trained as a doctor, his therapeutic practice consisted mainly of verbal analysis (especially of dreams, of course). From the famous couch in Freud's consulting room, it is a logical step to Phillip Roth's novel *Portnoy's Complaint*, which presents the title character's monologue as the beginning of therapy. Roth himself belongs to the glittering array of Jewish-American novelists such as Nobel Laureate Saul Bellow and Bernard Malamud. As outsiders, such Jewish writers have had uncanny insights into the life of WASP Americans. The 1984 movie *The Natural*, in which Robert Redford's awesome star power found its purest expression, was based on a novel by Malamud.

Given the significance of painting in Dylan's life, the significance of Jewish painters in New York in the 1960s also deserves a few words. Graphic artist and political activist Ben Shahn did representational work that corresponds well enough to the style and activism of Dylan's acoustic period. It was Shahn, for example, who painted the portrait of Dr. Martin Luther King, Jr., which appeared on the cover of the March 19, 1965, edition of *Time*.

For Dylan's challenging electric period in the 1960s, Mark Rothko has particular relevance. Rothko did a series of black on black paintings that may have suggested to Dylan the title of *Blonde on Blonde*. Rothko's work, like Dylan's, has an intense spirituality.

We have eyewitness accounts of Dylan's fascination for another Jewish painter, Marc Chagall. When Dylan began painting with a neighbor, Bruce Dorfman, Dylan brought a book of Chagall's work to the studio one day. Dorfman says, "It was perfect, because you had all these multilayered images—things flying, things walking, clocks flying, rabbits with green faces. It was all there. Chagall was it. He made the connection."[11] In fact, Dylan has an enduring fascination with Chagall. The poet Michael McClure went to an exhibit at the Guggenheim Museum with Dylan, and said, "He had eyes for nothing but the Chagalls. Chagall was the meaningful world to him."[12] It is reasonable to suppose that what Dylan took away from Chagall was the freedom to include anything, even "things flying, things walking," in a song. In this sense, then, Chagall gave Dylan a vital precedent that liberated him to write his startlingly innovative songs.

Dylan's fascination with Chagall has a larger meaning as well. Although Dylan had grown up on popular music, soon after he got to New York he abandoned the widespread notion common in America that popular culture is exciting and high culture is boring. In his music, he is primarily interested in popular culture, whereas in literature and painting he is primarily interested in high culture. Nevertheless, he would never say that high culture is better than popular culture, or vice versa. I emphasize this point because none of Dylan's political opinions in the early 1960s were even remotely as radical and subversive as his acceptance of, and respect for, both high culture and popular culture.

Any book that even mentions ethnicity and popular culture must also mention the extraordinary role of Jews in creating American popular culture as we know it today. Two of the first big stars were Jews: Al Jolson (born Asa Yoelson) and Fannie Brice (born Fania Borach). In *An Empire of Their Own: How the Jews Invented Hollywood*, Neal Gabler showed how the Dream Factory (Hollywood) was originally the dream of some outsiders full of chutzpah. In New York, most of the great Tin Pan Alley songwriters were Jews: Jerome Kern, Harold Arlen (whom Dylan greatly admires[13]), Irving Berlin, Richard Rodgers, and Oscar Hammerstein. It was primarily these phenomenally gifted songwriters who married song to drama and created the American musical.

One might even say that Jewish composers and songwriters constitute a through line for American popular music in the twentieth century. Just consider the continuity from George and Ira Gerschwin to Leonard Bernstein to Stephen Sondheim. Bernstein is the pivotal figure and obviously has enormous importance for both popular and classical music in the twentieth century. Bernstein often played Gerschwin's "Rhapsody in Blue," and he collaborated with Sondheim on *West Side Story*.

However, the formative role of Jews in creating American popular culture probably mattered very little to Dylan in the turbulent 1960s. In the first years after he left Minnesota, Judaism became for him a matter of personal relationships rather than faith and rituals. His first wife, Sara Lownds, and his first business manager, Albert Grossman, were Jews. His favorite guitarist, Mike Bloomfield, who played on "Like a Rolling Stone" and other Dylan classics, was a Jew. What it comes to is that Dylan surrounded himself with Jews not out of religious conviction, but because they were people with whom he felt comfortable because of their shared backgrounds.

We all hope that boys will have warm, nurturing relationships with their fathers; however, such relationships rarely produce high achievers. Rather, the opposite is the case. High achievers usually have relationships with their fathers that psychologists call "impaired," a term that has as wide a range of meanings, as does "cultural marginality." At one extreme, impairment may mean no relationship with the father at all, as in the cases of Isaac Newton, Aleksandr Solzhenitsyn, and Bill Clinton, whose fathers died before they were born. Other gifted boys such as John Lennon, Willie Nelson, and Smoky Robinson were abandoned by their fathers when they were young. (President Barack Obama is the obvious example in politics.) And sometimes when the fathers remain at home, they abuse their sons, as the fathers of Brian Wilson and Michael Jackson did. Divorce is another form of impairment, of course. The parents of Billy Joel and Neil Young divorced when the boys were about 12. Although nothing as drastic as death, abuse, or divorce occurred in the Zimmerman family, Dylan did have an impaired relationship with his father, and it had a lasting effect.

Here is Dylan biographer Howard Sounes's account of what happened to Abraham Zimmerman about the time Dylan's younger brother David was born, in February 1946:

> ... Abe was stricken with polio.... After a week in the hospital he came home and crawled up the front steps "like an ape," as he described it. He stayed home for six months, and then lost his job at Standard Oil.... Without work, short of money, and needing relatives around to help them, the Zimmermans moved to Hibbing ... where two of Abe's brothers ran a business.[14]

Here is a first and early form of an impaired relationship with the father. Young Bobby Zimmerman could only have perceived his father as a cripple and a failure.

Once he got back on his feet, both literally and figuratively, Abraham Zimmerman, known to everyone in Hibbing as "Abe," seems to have been content running a small business in a small town. His first-born son, however, was not content to follow in his footsteps. Here is what Dylan writes about his father in *Chronicles*: "My father was the best man in the world and probably worth a hundred of me, but he didn't understand me. The town he lived in and the town I lived in were not the same."[15] As this telling quote indicates, Dylan was not so much alienated from his father as disconnected from him. And surely a boy's emotional disconnect from his father qualifies as impairment. This disconnect was so extreme that on June 5, 1968, when he received a phone call with the news that his father had died, he did not tell anyone.[16]

Boys who are disconnected from their fathers acquire the habit of living inside their heads. Dylan comments in *Chronicles* that after his father's funeral "there would be no way of saying what I was never capable of saying before."[17] Since they cannot tell anyone their hopes and dreams, they learn not to expect to make connections with others. We find in young Bobby Zimmerman, the boy who did not live in the same town as his father and was thus incapable of saying anything meaningful to him, an embryonic form of Bob Dylan, the adult recluse.

When Dylan writes, "My father was the best man in the world and probably worth a hundred of me," he is clearly overcompensating. No one can take this statement seriously, and it is a rare emotional slip on Dylan's part to give us such an obvious clue to his emotional state. I suspect that Dylan is revealing here his idealized version of the real father he could not and did not relate to. But that is all we have, and all we are going to get about this relationship; we are not going to get any significant help from Dylan about how an impaired relationship with the father affects gifted boys.

Dylan's impaired identity as a Jew is inseparable from his impaired relationship with his Jewish father, which is in turn inseparable from the "little town blues" that he experienced while growing up in Hibbing. Judaism, the impaired relationship with the father, and cultural marginality all came together for Dylan in a key song that he wrote as he was rising to greatness, "Highway 61 Revisited."

Before analyzing that song, I need to mention that autobiographical interpretations of Dylan's songs are usually both the most popular and least successful of interpretations. The problem is that for most people, doing autobiographical interpretations of Dylan's songs involves playing a matching game. They match references in songs to specific people, and let it go at that. What such people really want to know is an answer to questions such as, "Was Dylan really thinking of Echo Helstrom when he wrote 'Girl of the North Country'?"[18]

And even when Dylan himself tells us that the song has biographical significance, we cannot trust him. In *Revolution in the Air* Clinton Heylin says of "Sad-Eyed Lady of the Lowlands" that "for once, there can be little doubt that Sara Dylan is the immediate subject of this paean. Dylan says so, albeit in 1975's 'Sara'.... Who can forget the roar that greeted those lines...?"[19] The lines in "Sara" that fans greeted with a roar are those in which Dylan refers to writing the song in the Chelsea Hotel in New York. Unfortunately, Heylin adds, "In fact there is an overwhelming amount of evidence that suggests that Dylan did nothing of the sort." Heylin says that "he may have come up with that magnetic chorus at their Chelsea Hotel love nest, but the bulk of the song was written in Tennessee from February 15 [1966] through the wee hours of the next morning."[20] We know this because he wrote it in the studio, and studio musicians who were coming in and out watched him do it.

Nevertheless, the reaction of the audience, "the roar that greeted these lines," tells us something valuable about biographical interpretations. It gives confirmation that people find them gratifying, and it also tells us that they limit possible interpretations. They certainly tempt people to say, "Oh—'Sad-Eyed Lady of the Lowlands' is about Dylan's wife Sara. He wrote it about her." And since we have Dylan's word for the truth of this, who could dispute it? The serious interpreter of Dylan's songs does not so much want to dispute the truth of this, but rather to ask if there is anything else that anyone can say about the song. For example, one could ask such questions as: Why does the Sad-Eyed Lady have a "mercury mouth"? Why does the singer have "warehouse eyes"? The biographical interpretation gives us no answers for these and other possible questions that one might raise about the song.

The effect of autobiographical interpretations of Dylan's songs is to reduce them to something like musical diary entries. They lead us away from the songs, rather than enrich our understanding of them. That is why I offer here an autobiographical interpretation of "Highway 61 Revisited" that does not contract the meaning of the song by making it refer to a single individual. Rather, it expands the meaning of the song in a way that is consistent with Dylan's creative methods.

Interpreting songs in this way means relying again on pattern recognition. An integrated understanding of Dylan's statements and songs makes it possible to recognize thematic patterns as well as departures from those patterns, which appear as anomalies. These anomalies can then serve as aids to interpretation. It matters that "Highway 61 Revisited" is an anomaly in Dylan's work. It is his only song that refers to a specific incident in the Bible—and does so in the first verse, too! It begins with a slangy, ironic retelling of the famous incident in Genesis 22: 1–24, in which God orders Abraham to sacrifice his son Isaac. This passage is the Jewish version of the Oedipal complex, which implies that the father's jealousy of the son is so great that he could kill him. This song derives from Dylan's intuition that he could bring together two coincidences in a single work.[21]

The first coincidence is that Dylan's father was named Abraham, and was known as "Abe," which is the way God addresses Abraham in the first verse of the song. Autobiographically then, the first verse expresses Dylan's awareness that his father, and his father's mundane life at Zimmerman Furniture and Electric in Hibbing, meant death to him; not so much death in a literal sense, but death to his creativity and death to his spirit. However, if we care about the song as a song, and not just as a musical diary entry, then we do not stop with autobiography. Since this is a song by Bob Dylan, we want to know what other meaning it has, which is why we notice the second coincidence.

The second coincidence involves the actual Highway 61 itself. Since it ran through Hibbing, which represents the middle-class life of his father's appliance store, Dylan associates it with death in a series of Kafkaesque verses. And this association constitutes his use of a key song in Hank Williams's oeuvre, "Lost Highway." In that song Hank uses the phrase "a road of sin." If "Lost Highway" is about a sinner's lack of redemption, "Highway 61" is about a man child's awareness of violence in America, which is introduced by the story of Abraham—both the Biblical Abraham and the Hibbing Abraham—

and Isaac. Abraham's potential violence toward Isaac serves as an introduction to the potential violence on the road on the outskirts of town.

However, for Dylan, Highway 61 was not only, or even primarily, a road. When John Cohen and Happy Traum interviewed him for *Sing Out!* magazine in the fall of 1968, they asked, "Which [sic] and where is Highway 61?" Dylan replied: "I knew at one time, but at this time it seems so far away I wouldn't even attempt it. It's out there, it's a dividing line."[22] By calling Highway 61 a "dividing line," Dylan is doing something he was a master at; he is playing a deliberately obfuscating word game with naive interviewers in order to hide the song's mythic significance as a uniting line.

Highway 61 both divides and unites because it runs through Hibbing and continues southward for over a thousand miles, all the way to New Orleans. It meant so much to the African Americans who began leaving the South in the 1920s that they called it "Freedom Road."[23] As Dylan commented in his interview with Cohen and Traum, "A lot of famous people came off that highway."[24] When they fled the South to head north to St. Louis and Chicago, they took Highway 61. In Mississippi, Highway 61 goes through the heart of the Delta, and is thus associated with Delta blues music. That is why the Highway 61 Blues Museum is located in Leland, Mississippi.

In Minnesota, Highway 61 was all too familiar and threatened death to Dylan's artistic genius. In Mississippi, the same highway led people out of the South, which threatened them with literal as well as cultural death. It ultimately took blues greats like Muddy Waters, who was born in the Delta, out of Mississippi to Chicago, where the blues became a vital part of American music. There is no more powerful mythic archetype than the interrelatedness of life and death, and Dylan relies on the exceptional historic significance of this highway to hide that archetype in plain sight in "Highway 61 Revisited."

Dylan gave special prominence to "Highway 61" by choosing it as the title track of the album on which it appeared. He did so because the song served as his declaration of independence, very much as "Independence Day" would later serve as Bruce Springsteen's declaration of independence. In using the word "revisited," he was acknowledging that the version of the blues that he, a northern white boy, sang was tamer and more ironic than the genuine article, "Highway 61," which was sung by Mississippi Fred McDowell and other Delta bluesmen. (The question of whether a white man could sing the blues was hotly debated in the 1960s.) He was also acknowledging his distance from both ends of Highway 61, from both Mississippi and Minnesota. By the time he made this album, he had gained enough confidence to feel sure that he was not going back to Hibbing and work in his father's appliance store.

What was Hibbing like for a prodigiously talented, confused young man? What formative musical experiences did Bobby Zimmerman have? To answer these questions, we may say that it now seems to us that Hibbing in the 1950s, like so many small towns in America, was a cultural environment characterized by sensory deprivation. And young Zimmerman had a series of musical shocks whose effects were not immediately obvious. A useful way to think of the awakening of Bob Dylan's creative genius is to recall the image of the seed of the rose buried deep beneath the snow in Amanda McBroom's magnificent song "The Rose," which is best known in Bette Midler's performance of it in the movie of the same name. When Bobby Zimmerman was growing up in Hibbing, his genius was buried beneath the snow of the complacency of life in the 1950s, and of his father's indifference. Gradually, though, like the rays of Spring sunshine in the song, life-giving performers penetrated the cultural snow.

It is important to understand, though, that the mature Dylan *likes*, and probably *needs*, the snow. People who want to understand Dylan need to keep in mind a couple of things about him. First, he is an intense introvert who is made very uncomfortable by interactions with people. It is worth repeating that it is more common for painters such as Andrew Wyeth and poets such as Emily Dickinson to be introverts. It causes no problems for them, because they create in private, in front of an easel. Dylan, however, has needed to perform for people since he was a small boy. The ongoing irresolvable tension between his introversion and his need to perform explains a great deal about his career.

Since Dylan needs the snow that covers up the sources of his inspiration, he reveals them only reluctantly and gradually. Apparently, it took the effect of receiving the Nobel Prize for Literature to prompt him to reveal some key experiences. Although he could not be bothered to go to Stockholm and give a speech in public, like other Nobel Laureates, he did accept the award at a private ceremony—held at a secret location! And then on June 4, 2017, he recorded some remarks about literature; in them he mentions three works he presumably read in high school that affected him.[25] These were Herman Melville's *Moby Dick*, Erich Maria Remarque's *All Quiet on the Western Front*, and Homer's *The Odyssey*. Dylan speaks in detail and with uncharacteristic intensity about these works. In particular, he singles out *Moby Dick* as a work that affected his songs. In saying this, he was surely expressing his own subjective sense, because I find no overt trace of Melville's masterpiece anywhere in his work. My best guess about what he means is that reading Melville gave him license to include cultural references in some of his great songs, like "Desolation Row."

Although Dylan has what seems to an outsider like an obsessive need for secrecy about his life and work, he sometimes chooses to reveal something essential. A case in point is his revelation in his Nobel Prize talk that he somehow (in a borrowed car? with friends?) drove 300 miles, possibly in the snow (real, not metaphorical, snow this time), from Hibbing to Clear Lake, Iowa, to attend what turned out to be Buddy Holly's last concert on February 2, 1957.

Although he does not say so, it was probably the first rock concert he had ever attended. It was also presumably the first, but by no means the last, time when he responded to an inner prompting to leave Hibbing and go somewhere else. It also may well have been the farthest away from Hibbing that he had ever travelled, and thus an indication of how deeply he felt the need to go.

Dylan says that, at one moment in the concert, Buddy looked directly at him, and made a connection. Great performers do this with audience members, of course, but the moment of eye contact had a special meaning for Dylan; for him, it signified a passing of the torch, especially since Buddy died so soon afterwards. It is an indication of the lasting importance of this moment of empowerment that it is the first time, to my knowledge, that Dylan has ever mentioned in public what was obviously a deeply moving experience. We can only suppose that precisely because this connection with Buddy moved him so much was why he needed to keep it beneath the metaphorical snow. It is indicative that in his high school yearbook he said that his ambition was to join Little Richard, not to be like Buddy Holly.

Although he does not quite put it like this, Dylan also says that making the connection with Buddy began a series of life-giving encounters with singers that produced shocks in his culturally starved psyche. Very soon after seeing Buddy, he heard "Cotton Fields" by folksinger Leadbelly (pseudonym of William Huddie Leadbetter). Although this song, with its easy couplets, does not seem so remarkable now, for the young Zimmerman it came as a revelation. Dylan says that he must have played it 100 times.

Clearly, young Zimmerman was an impressionable boy. Some singers, like Buddy Holly and Leadbelly, made huge impressions on him because they revealed hitherto unexpected possibilities in vocal performance. Others, however, spoke to him more deeply, and did so for reasons that merge biography with ambition. Boys like Bobby Zimmerman who lack a close connection with their biological fathers tend to seek out artistic father figures. I offer this as the explanation for the overwhelming experience that he had when he heard Woody Guthrie for the first time.[26] It was like hearing Leadbelly for the first time, only more so. He had found the first man who could serve as his artistic father.

Zimmerman/Dylan was so taken with Guthrie that he used him as a role model, and even as a surrogate identity. Sounes says that during his student days at the University of Minnesota, "when he was drunk, or stoned on Dave Whitaker's marijuana, Bob would put on a hat and pretend to be Guthrie. It was partly Bob being goofy, but he took the joke a long way. 'If you didn't call him Woody, he wouldn't answer,' says Bonnie Beecher."[27] It is a reasonable but unverifiable guess that Bobby Zimmerman attempted to become Woody Guthrie as much as he could, both because he had no connection with his Jewish father, and also because becoming Woody Guthrie would have given him a white identity in a white world. As Dylan tells Scorsese in the documentary *No Direction Home*, "I went through Guthrie."

The infatuation with Guthrie has become part of Dylan lore, in part because Guthrie was still alive when Dylan arrived in New York, and Dylan was able to visit him in the hospital in New Jersey. The Dylan-Guthrie connection has been given more importance than it deserves because it was easy to understand; it was easy to categorize the young Dylan as Guthrie's heir. The connection between them seemed like the passing of the torch from an older generation to a younger one. It was thus very satisfying for those who had a vested interest in the lasting viability of American folk music. Guthrie, folk music, and social activism were key elements of his transition from being Bobby Zimmerman from Hibbing, to being Bob Dylan from New York. It turned out, though, that they were short-lived elements of his career as a whole.

When Bobby Zimmerman was still in Hibbing, before he had ever heard, or heard of, Woody Guthrie, he discovered two other white guitar-playing singers who made a far deeper and more lasting impression on him than Guthrie did—Hank Williams and Elvis Presley. Among other things, his connection with Hank and Elvis created the lasting connection between his Northern sensibility and Southern music that produced his album *Nashville Skyline* and his friendship and collaboration with Johnny Cash.

He was able to discover Hank and Elvis because the cultural marginality of Hibbing was not as complete as it may have seemed to him in moments of despair. He had some advantages that earlier artists such as Will Shakespeare, stuck inside of Stratford-on-Avon, for example, did not have: communications media. In particular, two key media, radio and television, allowed young Zimmerman to reach far beyond Hibbing into cultural centers that he had never visited.

Radio in the 1950s meant AM radio, and what interests us here is clear-channel AM radio. Those of us who grew up in the South at the time can remember the clear channel, high-powered (for the time) radio stations with late-night shows like Randy's Record Mart that played both country classics and what was then called "race music." On cold winter nights in Hibbing, young Bobby Zimmerman could stay up late and listen to clear-channel stations such as "WSM—Clear Channel 650, Nashville." And it was probably on WSM that he heard Hank Williams for the first time.

It is a measure of Dylan's life-long devotion to Williams that he does not engage in any of his usual verbal acrobatics when he writes about him in *Chronicles*: "When I hear Hank sing, all movement ceases. The slightest whisper seems sacrilege."[28] Hank Williams was probably the first great performer whom he heard, and it is obvious that the contrast between Hibbing and Nashville left an impression that remains vivid and unchanged over sixty years later. WSM radio and Hank Williams also gave Dylan his first connection with Music City (Nashville), where Dylan would record some of his greatest songs, and whose music he would profoundly affect.

But if Nashville seemed like it was a long way away from Hibbing, New York must have seemed like it was on another planet. Nevertheless, when television took the country by storm in the 1950s, it brought New York into the Zimmerman living room. And in particular, television brought to Hibbing, live from the Ed Sullivan Theater, that force of nature known as Elvis Presley.

Although Bobby Zimmerman wrote in his high school yearbook that he wanted "to join Little Richard," Elvis overwhelmed him. "Hearing him for the first time was like busting out of jail," he said.[29] Baez remembers that when Dylan was still a scruffy kid in New York, still a complete unknown, he told her that he would be "bigger than Elvis." Sounes comments about Dylan's song "Mixed Up Confusion" that "it sounded like a track from Elvis Presley Sun sessions, and it flopped."[30] Long after he had become rich and famous, Dylan visited Elvis's hometown of Tupelo, Mississippi, "to soak in the essence of Elvis," as Douglas Brinkley put it.[31] Radio and television thus connected Bobby Zimmerman with these two great Southern singers, who remain such an immediate presence in our lives that we know them by their first names.

Hank and Elvis both had impaired relationships with their fathers. Hank, a first-born child, grew up in Mobile, Alabama, without a father, and got his first radio gigs there. Elvis, an only child,[32] whose father served time in prison when he was young, grew up in Memphis, recorded the Sun sessions in Memphis, and bought a house in Memphis. Dylan avoided naming his heroes directly, but relied on the alliteration of the place names to express his remembered sense of inferiority in another autobiographical song, "Stuck Inside of Mobile with the Memphis Blues Again."[33] This song is not about his biological father, but about his musical fathers.

While young Bobby Zimmerman was stuck inside of Hibbing with the "small-town blues," Hank Williams and Elvis were, to use the title of one of Hank's great songs, "setting the woods on fire." The contrast must have seemed overwhelming. However, in order to make this interpretation and others like it still to come more persuasive, we need to pause here to present a theory of influence that will help to explain some of Dylan's other key cultural relationships as well.

When we speak of influence in popular culture, people often leave the matter abstract and general, as when people acknowledge that Bruce Springsteen was influenced by Dylan without ever taking the trouble to refer to specific songs and images that show Dylan's influence. In America, this general way of speaking about artistic influence is surely related to our fixation on originality as an expression of individualism. We tend to think that originality is good, and any overt sign of influence is a marker of imitation. However, if we wish to decode Dylan (and Bruce Springsteen and many other great performers as well), we must give up this simplistic opposition of originality on one hand and imitation on the other. To do that, we must reframe the relationships between artists in a more suggestive, and less reductive, way. Fortunately, critic Harold Bloom has proposed some exciting ways to do just that in his book *The Anxiety of Influence*. Applying Bloom's ideas to rock stars may serve as an ongoing illustration of the commonalities between high culture and popular culture.

Basically, what Bloom does is to take Freud's theory of the Oedipal complex, in which a son is jealous of his father and desires his mother, and apply it to poetry. Like T.S. Eliot, from whom his work derives in part, Bloom has no interest in biographical interpretation. What he does have an interest in, and what makes his ideas so exciting for popular culture, is analyzing connections between artists. Bloom writes in his book *A Map of Misreading* that, "insofar as a poet authentically is and remains a poet, he must exclude and negate other poets. Yet he must begin by including and affirming other poets, for there is no other way to become a poet."[34] In Bloom's scheme of things, an aspiring poet/artist/rock star seizes upon a father figure in the person of an accomplished poet/artist/rock star, the "precursor." In modeling himself on the precursor, an artistic father figure, the young man becomes his student, or spiritual son, or "ephebe." (Although Bloom has nothing to say about the pattern in which artists often have an impaired relationship with the father, it is surely obvious that such an impaired relationship gives artists a need to seek a relationship with a surrogate artistic father figure as compensation for the impaired relationship with the biological father.)

However, the precursor does not "influence" the ephebe in the usual sense of that word, which usually means the passing on of themes and images. Always the iconoclast, Bloom writes, "Influence, as I conceive it, means that there are *no* texts, only relationships *between* texts."[35] This statement represents another version of what I have called the "Dylan and..." method, a method that implies that major artists such as Dylan, and major works like "Like a Rolling Stone," cannot be understood in isolation, but are understood only as part of the evolution of artistic tradition, which consists of "relationships between texts."

Perhaps an analogy will serve to clarify the point. Let us suppose that Bloom's phrase "relationships between texts" actually constitutes what T.S. Eliot called tradition. If so, we may say, then, that tradition is to artists what water is to swimmers. Just as it is water that makes the act of swimming possible, so, in the same way, it is tradition that makes the act of creativity possible. And just as swimmers can swim different strokes in the water (back stroke, crawl, butterfly, etc.), in the same way, artists can use tradition in different ways as well. Even artists, who proclaim to all and sundry that they are rebelling against this or that tradition, are pushing off from tradition very much as swimmers push off against the wall of the pool when they make a turn.

Let us take the idea that Bloom is referring to the relationship between texts. If we substitute "songs" for "texts," and say that there are no songs, only relationships between songs, then we can ask what that means for popular music in general, and for Dylan in particular. More specifically, we can ask about the dynamics of these relationships between songs. What are they like?

Actually, Bloom is interpreting in artistic terms the contests by which men find their identity. Walter Ong says that these contests occur between men of wildly different interests and abilities. We know that athletes, for example, are intensely competitive, and there is no reason why artists should not be as competitive as athletes. In Ong's book *Fighting for Life: Contest, Sexuality, and Consciousness*, he writes that: "The only adversary who can enable one to establish male identity is another male."[36] Ong adds: "In real life across the world, ceremonial physical contest between father and son—wrestling, boxing, dueling—helps to bring sons to normal maturity, establishing the friendly agonistic distancing the male psyche needs."[37]

Clearly, then, men have a need to define themselves through contests with other men. Most frequently, of course, this process occurs when sons define themselves against their fathers. But as we know, gifted boys often have an impaired relationship with their biological fathers, who are physically absent or psychologically unavailable, and thus they must prove themselves in competitions with other artistic men.

We have a particularly clear musical example of this process in the "cutting contests" between jazz groups that Thomas Brothers describes in his book *Louis Armstrong's New Orleans*. Brothers says that when Armstrong was a young man, jazz groups would get on wagons and drive through the streets. When one jazz group encountered another, a cutting contest would begin. One group would play for the crowd that quickly assembled, and then the other one would play. The crowd would decide which one was better, and that group would get gigs in the neighborhood. Brothers says, "The musical cutting contests … could set either individually, soloist against soloist, or collectively, band against band. 'It seemed as though all the bands were shooting at each other with those hot riffs,' wrote Armstrong."[38] Brothers adds, "Without this kind of competitive drive—the same quality, of course, that has always propelled the great popular musicians onto the national stage—neither one of them [Armstrong and his mentor Joe Oliver] would have been able to overcome the obstacles against crossing Canal Street."[39] Armstrong and Oliver did cross Canal Street, and get lucrative gigs with Creoles that they had not gotten before. And, of course, Armstrong went on to become the intimidating precursor that everyone who wants to play jazz trumpet must come to terms with.

It is important to notice Brothers' phrase "competitive drive" in the description above. We often think of athletes as having competitive drive, but rarely think of musicians and performers in this way. The point of Bloom's theory of the anxiety of influence, as I apply it here, is that musicians and performers also compete with each other. Their competitions and struggles for artistic identity are made more complicated by the fact that their opponents/precursors aren't always alive. As Dylan and countless other artists can attest, dead precursors are just as threatening as living ones—sometimes more so—because history has confirmed their greatness.

To understand the history of popular music, and in particular Dylan's place in its evolution, we need to take into consideration another aspect of the analogy between athletes and performers. We commonly say of athletes and of sports teams that they are competing against each other. It is very helpful to apply this terminology to Dylan's songs, and say that he wrote them against other songs and other performers. That is to say, we understand the songs in depth once we understand that intended contrast between them and songs and precursors from the past. Since this contrast has some similarities with sports such as football, we can say that Dylan wrote certain works "against" other works.

If we take Dylan's statements about Hank and Elvis as clear evidence of his anxiety of influence, it becomes possible to interpret one of Dylan's key songs, "Stuck Inside of Mobile with the Memphis Blues Again," in a new way. We can say that it is a song written against the heritage of Hank and Elvis, and is thus a key marker of Dylan's artistic evolution. As an ephebe with the "little town blues," Bobby Zimmerman surely felt that he was stuck inside of Hibbing, and Dylan's song states the ephebe's ultimate fear, which is that he cannot escape. Escaping from Hibbing, and from the sense of inferiority that any ephebe experiences when stuck in a situation of cultural marginality, seems impossible to him. After all, deep affinities have drawn him to the precursors whom he admires, and their very accomplishments that cause him to admire them also make him feel not just inferior, but hopelessly so.

As if Hank and Elvis were not already intimidating enough as precursors, Dylan includes in his song the ultimate precursor for a poet who writes in English—Shakespeare. In the second stanza of "Stuck Inside of Mobile," Dylan puts Shakespeare, the consummate literary genius with biographical similarities to Dylan, in the alley and reduces him to a stage fool, complete with bells and pointed shoes.

We can, however, paraphrase Wordsworth's definition of poetry as "emotion recollected in tranquility," and say that "Stuck Inside of Mobile with the Memphis Blues Again" represents Dylan's anxiety of influence recollected in artistic maturity. After all, the song appears on *Blonde on Blonde*, along with such masterpieces as "Visions of Johanna" and "Sad-Eyed Lady of the Lowlands." He was no longer stuck inside of Hibbing, or anywhere else for that matter, and recorded the song in Nashville, the site of Hank's triumphs, where Hank was, and is, universally worshipped. The song thus represents, with rare explicitness, the moment when Dylan engaged in a dual process whose parts are hardly distinguishable. He was able to articulate his anxiety of influence, and by articulating it, purge himself of it. This did not mean, however, that he had "gone through" Hank and Elvis, as he had earlier "gone through" Woody Guthrie. Rather, in "Stuck..." he declares himself the equal of Hank and Elvis, and thus re-defines his life-long engagement with them.

He dealt with the threats that Hank and Elvis posed differently because he perceived them differently. He listened to Hank, and certainly to Elvis, too. But he also *saw* Elvis on television. For Dylan, Hank remained a singer-songwriter, but Elvis was the performer who electrified America—in more ways than one. Let us consider how Dylan responded to the creative challenges posed by each of these great performers.

As Dylan understands so acutely, Hank Williams's songs come as close to perfection as anything in American popular music. Their bare, stripped-down lyrics, as in "Your Cheatin' Heart," make Wordsworth-like poetry of the speech of the plain-talking, hard-working folk that Hank had grown up with. Their very plainness gave Dylan an opportunity to define himself as different from Hank, and he seized it. If Hank made disciplined poetic perfection out of plain speech, Dylan made disciplined poetic perfection of the opposite. He took the bizarre, provocative images of the French Symbolist poets and the long lines of the Beat poets while retaining the gift that Hank gave him, a gift that neither of those two groups of poets had: craftsmanship.

As usual, Bloom has a word for this particular kind of precursor-ephebe relationship, which is tessera. "In the tessera, the later poet provides what his imagination tells him would complete the otherwise 'truncated' precursor poet...."[40] Hank's simple language readily qualifies as "truncated," especially because it contrasts so strikingly with much modern poetry, so Dylan "completed" him with rich, baffling lyrics.

Hank sang exquisitely simple lyrics in a simple voice. Elvis was not simple, though. He tried on a variety of singing styles during the Sun sessions. The mature Elvis could sing as sweetly as anybody in America ever had ("Love Me Tender") and also as hot as anybody ever had ("Jailhouse Rock"). Moreover, he lived until 1977, so for about the first fifteen years of Dylan's career, Dylan was dealing not with the safely dead Hank, but with a living, breathing precursor who was constantly in the news and on the charts. Right up until his death, Elvis was filling convention centers and singing to sold-out posh venues in Las Vegas.

More than anything else, Elvis was for Dylan "Elvis the Pelvis"—the wild-eyed Southern boy who had never taken in the niceties and proprieties of middle-class life, and thus remained the force of nature that I once saw in Tupelo. As he had done with Hank, Dylan dealt with Elvis by going to the opposite extreme. With regard to Elvis, he resorted to what Bloom calls "kenosis." "In strong poets, the kenosis is a revisionary act in which an 'emptying' or 'ebbing' takes place *in relation to the precursor*."[41] Dylan, the lonely performer shown on the stage in the documentary *Don't Look Back*, is a performer who has performed kenosis on himself. If Elvis grabbed the microphone—and everyone's attention—and gyrated and flung his arms in the air, and overwhelmed the world with his force and passion, Dylan decided that he would just ... stand there. At concerts, he does not introduce himself or banter with the audience; he just comes out, sings his amazing songs, and leaves. Even in concerts with rock royalty—Ringo Starr on drums, Eric Clapton on guitar, and Mick Jagger on vocals—he just stands there. Lacking Elvis's amazingly versatile high baritone, Dylan stays within the limited range of his raspy baritone, and concentrates on phrasing.

In his performance style, and in much else as well, Dylan was also creating his persona and his songs in a manner consistent with trends in art during the 1960s. At the time when he was creating his stripped-down performance style, critics created the term minimalism for the simple, abstract forms in the work of artists like Ad Reinhardt and Ellsworth Kelly. Dylan dealt with Elvis, and created a place for himself on stage, by adopting a minimalist performance style and refusing to indulge in banter with the audience or even move.

Another key aspect of what psychologist Dean Simonton calls, in his book *Greatness*, "achieved eminence," and not just for artists, is birth order. Birth order is not destiny, and it has many nuances and complexities, but it does explain a great deal about success and creativity. We know that Dylan is a first-born with a younger sibling, for instance. So are Paul McCartney, Mick Jagger, and Brian Wilson, to mention only a few of Dylan's contemporaries who belong to the Rock and Roll Hall of Fame. Other high achievers are only children—always first-borns. The list of only children among 1960s rock stars includes John Lennon, Ringo Starr, Keith Richards, Paul Simon, Art Garfunkel, Jim Morrison, and Jimi Hendrix.

And it is not just rock stars who are often first-borns and only children. First-borns tend to become self-reliant high achievers, and the results are all around us. Simonton comments that "one recent inquiry found that nearly half of all notable creators, leaders, and celebrities in the 20th century were first-born children."[42] Birth order expert Kevin Leman adds, "Research bears out that first borns are more highly motivated to achieve than later borns ... of the first twenty-three Americans sent into outer space, twenty-one were first borns and the other two were only children. All seven astronauts in the original Mercury program were first borns."[43]

And what about the rock stars who are only children? Leman has something relevant to say: "Only children are excellent candidates for growing up to be ultra perfectionists. They want things to be just so and when things don't go their way they get frustrated, antsy, and even angry."[44] Doesn't that sound like the stereotypical behavior of rock stars? And then there are the positive aspects of perfectionism. When perfectionism is combined with talent, a person has the persistence it takes to master an instrument, the personality it takes to dominate a stage, and the patience it takes to produce great records in the studio.

As a case in point, Sounes describes Dylan's demeanor during the recording sessions for "Like a Rolling Stone" like this: "Standing at attention in the control room while the others slouched, he had the commanding presence of a general, and now that he was a genuine star he possessed real authority. He did not necessarily abuse his power in the studio, but he made sure that people did exactly what he wanted."[45] Dylan's authority in the studio, on stage, and elsewhere as well, was the authority of a genius at the height of his powers, to be sure; but it was also the authority of a genius who was a first-born and who grew up with a younger sibling.

If we think of a creative young boy whose markers of creativity compel him to set out on a mythic quest, the first test he must pass is to get to the place where he is "supposed to be," as Dylan put it. It is as though the frustration that the boy experiences when he is growing up in a situation of cultural marginality stands him in good stead. As his frustration with his limited circumstances mounts, it provides the energy that he needs to get from the place where he is to the place where he is supposed to be. In doing this, he also gathers the energy and the determination that he will need to deal with the challenges that face him as a complete unknown when he finally gets to the big city. This was Dylan's situation when he arrived in New York on January 24, 1961. This fateful date marked the beginning of his creative life; everything that had happened in Minnesota was "the beginning before the beginning," as he put it in an interview with Studs Terkel in 1963.[46] In the first beginning, he was Bobby Zimmerman in Duluth, Hibbing, and Minneapolis; in the second beginning, the real one, he was Bob Dylan in New York.

2

The Early Years in New York

Just forty years before Dylan arrived in New York, another brilliant and ambitious young writer arrived in New York from Minnesota. His name was F. Scott Fitzgerald, and he too understood that New York was a place where you could make your dreams come true if you were audacious enough and talented enough. Like Dylan, by the time he was 25, Fitzgerald had written something iconoclastic that received critical acclaim—his novel *This Side of Paradise*.[1] (The title may have suggested the title of Dylan's "Gates of Eden.")

Fitzgerald also understood that part of the makeover required to make your dreams come true might be a change of name. There is an eerie prescience in the back story of Jay Gatsby, the title character of Fitzgerald's now classic novel *The Great Gatsby*. In it, an ambitious, gifted boy is born into a Jewish family in the Midwest (Chicago in this case, not Hibbing). He realizes that in order to make it in America, he has to go to New York and seek acceptance in WASP society, so he changes his name (from Gatz to Gatsby—not as radical a change as the one from Zimmerman to Dylan). Once in New York, his disconnect from his father and his family forces him to tell lies about his past—different lies to different people. To be sure, Bob Dylan was no Jay Gatsby (Gatsby comes to a bad end, after all), but the similarities between them show how astutely Fitzgerald understood both the allure and the price of success in America—and how Fitzgerald's understanding was not confined to fiction. The enduring significance of Fitzgerald's insights is shown by the success in 1961, the year Dylan arrived in New York, of the story of Lula Mae Barnes from Texas, who moved to New York and changed her name to Holly Golightly, the principal character in Truman Capote's *Breakfast at Tiffany's*. (The book came out in 1958, and the film version came out in 1961.)

Dylan's description of his arrival in New York does not refer to *The Great Gatsby* or *Breakfast at Tiffany's*, since all his energy was directed toward the future. He writes in *Chronicles* that when he got to New York, "it was dead-on winter. The cold was brutal ... but I'd started out from the frostbitten North Country.... I could transcend the limitations."[2] Of course it is cold in

January in New York, but Dylan is not just talking about the weather here in the phrase "transcend the limitations." As he thinks back to the momentous day of his arrival in New York, he uses this crucial phrase because he understands, more or less consciously, that his whole career has been an ongoing process of transcending limitations. He transcended the limitations of folk music; then he transcended the limitations of rock and roll. Ultimately—and we would expect this from an artist who is not fully connected to the earth—his best work is about transcending the limitations of human existence itself.

So how did he survive the snow-packed streets of New York as a complete unknown from the North Country? Sounes says that "the reality of Bob's 'wild first half year' in New York is that he relied on the charity of kindhearted women."[3] Like Blanche Dubois, the heroine of Tennessee Williams's play *A Streetcar Named Desire*, he was able to rely on the kindness of strangers because he was a charming, beautiful boy, as the wonderful photographs in the book *Early Dylan* show.[4] The surviving tapes of the Newport Folk Festival from 1963 show the infectious grin that made women want to take care of him.

Once in New York, it took Dylan nine months to birth his career. At the end of his "first trimester," on April 20th, he played his first solo gig at Gerde's Folk City to good reviews. On October 24th—nine months to the day after he arrived in town—the legendary talent scout and agent John Hammond signed him to a contract with Columbia Records, which was at the time the most prestigious record label.

It surely helped him to survive the cold weather and loneliness knowing he was going to make it. His first girlfriend in New York, Suze Rotolo (who appears with him on the cover of *The Free Wheelin' Bob Dylan*,[5]) says that, after he signed with Columbia, he made a remarkable revelation. He told her, "This is the beginning of what I have always known. I am going to be big." She comments, "He said it calmly and knowingly, and it was true. No bragging, no look at me. Ain't I grand."[6] At least in part he was expressing here the cumulative effect of the markers of creativity in his early life. Still, there is something mysterious and ineffable in creativity, something that we cannot identify or explain. In any case, as someone once commented about Bing Crosby, he "fell upwards," making one right move after another to advance his career.

After Hammond signed Dylan, he passed Dylan along to Billy James, a marketing executive at Columbia, and Dylan records an exchange with James that expresses the imperative of originality that American individualism imposes on its great artists. James probably did not know anything about folk music, so he asked Dylan the same question that a receptionist had asked Elvis when he showed up to record at Sun Studios: "Who do you sound like?" Naturally, Dylan gave James the same answer that Elvis gave the receptionist: "Nobody."[7]

2. The Early Years in New York

As we know, there was nobody who could help him create an adult identity. When he finally met Woody Guthrie, the great folksinger was so ill that he could hardly talk. As important as Guthrie was to Dylan as an initial father figure/role model/artistic inspiration, the connection between them did not last. The New York to which Guthrie had led Dylan offered other candidates for father figures. One of these was a folksinger known as Ramblin' Jack Elliott, who briefly met Dylan's need for a role model. Dylan and Elliott went to New Jersey to see Woody Guthrie together.

> On the bus ride back into Manhattan, Bob told Elliott that he had listened to all his records. Elliott thought him a fascinating and engaging young man, "barely able to grow a beard at the time—he had a little peach fuzz—he hadn't even started to shave." Bob then began following Ramblin' Jack around, "like a puppy dog," which became tiresome to Elliott, who says he remembers trying to escape from him.
>
> When Elliott took a room at the Earle Hotel on Washington Square, Bob took a room a few doors down for a short time. Friends say Bob was copying Ramblin' Jack's performance style, adopting his mannerisms, even the way he held a guitar high up on his chest.[8]

Native Americans have a term that applies here; they say that certain spirits are "shapeshifters." (Folksinger Dave Van Ronk in *No Direction Home* calls Dylan a "shape changer.") Dylan was a shapeshifter if there ever was one. Suze Rotolo says of him at this time, "He was not linear; he was quirky and jumpy, receptive to what was around him."[9] Dylan has proven himself to be very "non-linear," i.e., endlessly inventive in changing the way he presents himself to the world. In effect, he was trying on Ramblin' Jack Elliott the way someone else might try on a shirt. But you do not wear the same shirt day after day for long, and pretty soon Dylan did not need Woody Guthrie or Ramblin' Jack Elliott as precursors any more.

For both social and personal reasons, Dylan needed to present himself to the world as a unique singer in the long American tradition of self-made men. However, we now have the evidence of *Chronicles*, in which Dylan reveals that in his early years in New York he had a lot of help in creating himself, as self-made men usually do. He educated himself by embarking on something as daring as his departure from Minnesota, which was a serious, long-term reading program.

Like many creative people, Bobby Zimmerman had found formal classes and homework assignments while in school stultifying. Dylan acknowledges in *Chronicles* that he was not a good student.[10] But once he was out of school, and settled in Greenwich Village, an environment where people took books seriously, and where there were bookstores on practically every corner, he set about educating himself. Or, as he puts it in *Chronicles*, "The place had an overpowering presence of literature and you couldn't help but lose your passion for dumbness."[11] Dylan lost his "passion for dumbness," his take on

American artists' need to maintain their cultural innocence, with an intensity that would have gotten him As in English and history back in Hibbing. (I am assuming here that he read the three works he mentions in his Nobel Prize talk while still in Hibbing, but we will probably never know for sure.) Since this is Bob Dylan we are considering, what he read matters. Between 1961 and 1965, Dylan read widely, and he thought deeply about what he read. Therefore, if we wish to decode Dylan, we must know what he read. As it turned out, his reading program had a decisive influence on the songs that he wrote during the early years in New York, the songs that we hear on the great albums *The Freewheelin' Bob Dylan* and *Another Side of Bob Dylan*.

In *Chronicles*, Dylan describes his stay in the apartment of a friend named Ray, who had a large library that spurred his enthusiasm for reading. "The books were something. They were really something."[12] He mentions reading Faulkner, Byron, Shelley, Longfellow, and Poe, for example. And then there were the Russians: Pushkin, Tolstoy, and Dostoyevsky, not to mention book after book on history and psychology.

However, he did not lose what he called his passion for dumbness right away. At first, he spoke disingenuously to interviewers, providing them with half-truths at best. Here is what he told one interviewer: "I don't read much. Usually I read what people put into my hands. But I do read Hemingway. He didn't really have to define what he was saying, he just said it. I can't do that yet, but that's what I want to do."[13]

Dylan's choice of Hemingway as one author he was willing to admit to reading bespeaks a significant personal and cultural affinity with important implications for his early songs. Like Hemingway, he had come from the North Country to seek his fame and fortune. Like Hemingway, he was interested in painting, and that interest influenced his prose style. Hemingway's adjective-free prose, which so attracted Dylan, came out of a desire to write prose that would produce an effect comparable to that of Cézanne's paintings. Although Dylan talks here about Hemingway's style, which was important to him, Hemingway also seems to have provided him with an image to which he returned again and again in his early songs—rain.

It rains throughout Hemingway's breakthrough 1929 novel about World War I, *A Farewell to Arms*. It rains in the famous final adjective-free sentence of that great novel: "After a while I went out and left the hospital and walked back to the hotel in the rain."[14] In context, that sentence has a devastating effect. Frederic Henry, the speaker, is walking back to the hotel in Switzerland from the hospital where his lover, Catherine Barkely, has died in childbirth. Henry does not need to express his grief. Because Hemingway understood the power of understatement, he left Henry's grief implied, and not stated. The effect is to draw us in, as the broad-brush strokes in the paintings of the Impressionists draw us in, to complete the image. In McLuhan's terms, Impressionist paintings are "cool," like television images. We feel his grief with a particular intensity because it is raining on him, and the rain has come to symbolize both the effect of his awful loss and the horrors that World War I visited on people.

As a generalized, environmental image, then, rain does not lend itself to simplistic ideological interpretations. Dylan apparently sensed this, for surely his "A Hard Rain's a-Gonna Fall" derives directly from the ending of *A Farewell to Arms*. The song suggests not so much a single explosion of the atomic bomb, which was on everybody's mind at the time, but also the murderous fallout from which we cannot escape, just as Frederic Henry cannot escape from his grief. When Dylan images nuclear fallout as rain, he makes it more familiar, and therefore more frightening. The Bomb was an especially frightening symbol of technological change—one that haunted people in the age of fallout shelters. This is why Dylan compares the effects of social change to the effects of hard rain in "The Times They Are a-Changin'."

Unlike Hemingway, Dylan does not make the rain the culmination of a narrative in "A Hard Rain's A-Gonna Fall," because there is no narrative at all—only a statement of a situation. (Bloom would call this Dylan's "swerve" from Hemingway.) Dylan begins seven lines in the second stanza with "I saw" and seven lines in the fourth stanza with "I met." The repetition of these verbs—the technical term is anaphora—which deny the possibility of a narrative, makes the tension build and build without resolution. Rain in Dylan's songs can thus have an aggressive quality. This is the case in the metaphorical use of rain in his ominous "Ballad of Hollis Brown." The rain motif in Dylan's songs culminates in the mesmerizing first line of "Just Like Tom Thumb's Blues," which refers to getting lost in the rain. That is to say, when you are lost in the rain in a foreign country where resurrection is denied to you, that is about as bad as it gets.

Hemingway once said that he liked to describe "what the weather was like," and Dylan's imagery of the rain is related to his imagery of rain as a symbol for social change, as in "Blowin' in the Wind." Like the rain, the wind often brings adversity and hard times, as in "Girl from the North Country." (Similarly, the rain "rattles heavily" in his poem "Walls of Red Wing.") This is why the absence of wind has a positive significance, and in Dylan's utopian poem, "When the Ship Comes In," we learn that "the winds will stop."

Another writer who had a great impact on the early songs was, of course, Hemingway's contemporary Woody Guthrie. I have in mind here not Woody Guthrie the author of the anthemic song "This Land Is Your Land," but Woody Guthrie the author of a wonderful memoir called *Bound for Glory*, which was first published in 1943. Dylan may have read *Bound for Glory* while still in Minnesota, or he may have read it during his reading binges in New York. We will never know. But it is impossible to imagine that he did not read it at some time or other.

Surprisingly enough, what Dylan learned from *Bound for Glory* was how to extend the emotional range of a song through humor. Repeatedly in the early songs, he sets up an absurd situation, only to undercut it with a deliberately inappropriate cliché. My favorite example comes from "Talkin' World War III Blues." After he dreams of a nuclear holocaust, he sings of lighting a cigarette on a parking meter. While we are still taking in the implications of such an extraordinary act, Dylan ends the stanza with the devastating line, "It was a normal day." And he uses a completely deadpan delivery for this line, knowing that any sarcastic or ironic inflection would detract from the effect. Like "A Hard Rain's a-Gonna Fall," "Talking World War III Blues" achieves its powerful effect by presenting the ordinariness of a situation that is both frightening and absurd—a situation to which Dylan offers us no solution.

Dylan probably acquired the knack for putting together such incongruities from *Bound for Glory*, and not so much from Guthrie's songs. From time to time in this remarkable book, Woody sets up expectations in two lines, and then undercuts them in a deadpan third line, very much as Dylan does in "I Shall Be Free." For instance, Guthrie says of a hypocritical man in Okeemah, "He had studied to be a preacher, read most of the books on the subject, and was bootlegging liquor in his eating place."[15] The same kind of humor effect occurs when Guthrie describes a job he had in a cheap hotel for transient workers: "It was my job to show folks to their rooms and show the rooms to the people, and try to convince them that they really was rooms."[16]

As Bryan K. Carman points out in his book *A Race of Singers*, Guthrie's life of myriad tragedies and personal hardships left him with a complex personality, and his legacy is equally complex: "This uncommon man was full of the contradictions that permeated the most ordinary lives."[17] Carman makes another comment that has great relevance for both Guthrie and Dylan: "His poems spoke of the need to distinguish himself from the mythic persona of Walt Whitman, yet time and again he presented himself as a 'prophet singer.'" This astute comment means that we cannot simply discuss the connection between Dylan and Guthrie; we must understand that Guthrie led Dylan back to Walt Whitman, someone who many American writers have had to come to terms with. Whitman was a precursor for Guthrie, and he became one for Dylan as well.

After interviewing Dylan in 2009, Douglas Brinkley wrote, "When tabulating literary influences, Dylan summons the name Walt Whitman, for *Leaves of Grass* continues to inspire him," and adds, "'I don't think the dream of Whitman has ever been fulfilled,' Dylan says."[18] Thus, we must give some attention to the awesome power of Walt Whitman and his relevance for American poetry in general and for Dylan in particular.

Whitman was not just a great poet; he was a uniquely great poet in that he had only one theme, which may be stated as follows: "I am America, and America is me." He is the greatest poet in Western culture who practiced only synecdoche, the use of the part for the whole. This passage from the second stanza of "As I Ebb'd with the Ocean of Life" shows this part-whole relationship quite clearly:

> As I wend to the shore I know not,
> As I list to the dirge, the voices of men and women wreck'd,
> As I inhale the impalpable breezes that set in upon me,
> As the ocean so mysterious rolls toward me closer, and Closer,
> I too but signify at the utmost a little wash'd-up drift,
> A few sand and dead leaves to gather,
> Gather, and merge myself as part of the sands and drift.[19]

Thus, there is no egotism, petty or otherwise, in Whitman's "Song of Myself," as the opening lines indicate:

> I celebrate myself, and sing myself,
> And what I assume you shall assume,
> For every atom belonging to me as good as belongs to you.[20]

If Whitman represented America, and America represented Whitman, then his work provides a precedent not just for the belief, first among folkies and then later among hippies, that Dylan represented the voice of his generation. Whitman's "I am America, and America is me" theme informs some key lines in Dylan's early songs. "With God on Our Side," for example, proclaims his anonymity. And the first three words of "I Shall Be Free No. 10" are "I'm just average"; moreover, the second line bonds him with "Everyman" when it says that I'm "the same as you." As this quote from Dylan indicates, Whitman remained a creative presence in his life when he had relegated Guthrie to the past.

What it comes to is that Dylan took what he needed from Guthrie and left the rest. We may take the relationship between Guthrie's "We Shall Be Free" and Dylan's "I Shall Be Free" as a case study in this process of assimilation. Guthrie's song is not a protest song, as the title might suggest. Instead, it is an odd combination of quirky lyrics and the promise of salvation. Guthrie sets the verses of the song in someone else's henhouse. He tried to steal a goose (it rhymes easily with "loose"); a preacher has a fight with a rooster, and so forth.

In "I Shall Be Free," Dylan retains the melody of Guthrie's version as well as Guthrie's phrasing and guitar style. While Dylan keeps the wacky sense of humor that plays on incongruities of various kinds and the **aabb** stanza form, he reworks the lyrics into a contemporary urban setting. In that song, President Kennedy calls him up; he says that Brigitte Bardot will make the country grow (another easy rhyme). He watches television and mocks a Brylcreem commercial.[21] He throws in the word "chitlins" (which he had surely never eaten), because it is in Guthrie's song. In a throwaway line about a "lady," Dylan introduces the forerunner of the lady in "Desolation Row," as well as the Sad-Eyed Lady of the Lowlands in the song of that same name.

In general, then, Guthrie's "We Shall Be Free" is a rural folk song performed by an older man, and Dylan's "I Shall Be Free" is a hip, urban song performed by a highly individualistic young man. (Dylan's change of the pronoun from "we" to "I" is indicative of his individualism.) Dylan sings the song at a faster tempo than Guthrie does, and plays and sings with great exuberance. As a matter of fact, Dylan is so full of himself that he can hardly sing for giggling.

Dylan combined Hemingway's stripped-down style with Guthrie's bursts of humor to create the songs that made him famous, the songs that most people still associate with him. "Blowin' in the Wind" is the most obvious one, of course. As Greil Marcus has said, the first line of Dylan's obituary will refer to "Blowin' in the Wind."[22]

The other masterpieces of protest are "The Times They Are a-Changin'" and "Masters of War." These songs created the lasting image of Dylan as a writer of protest songs, so we wish to understand how this happened.

To understand how it was possible for Dylan to become so famous so fast we must make a brief digression on the evolution of the popular song in America. In the heyday of Tin Pan Alley, in the 1930s and 1940s, great songwriters like George and Ira Gershwin and Cole Porter wrote songs that became "standards." A standard was a song such as Hoagy Carmichael's "Stardust." Such songs make up what we now call the Great American Songbook. These songs would be sung in a Broadway musical and/or a movie; many different singers would record these songs, and the sheet music would be sold so that people could play the songs on the piano in the parlor. A standard was a song that existed independently of the singer or singers.

In this respect, the important thing about the 1950s is that Elvis Presley, Chuck Berry, Little Richard, and the other rock stars of that great decade obsolesced the concept of the standard. In the 1950s, rock and roll, 45 rpm records, and Top 40 stations combined to create a situation in which the recording *was* the song; that is, "Hound Dog" is Elvis's version of "Hound Dog," and the song hardly exists separately from it. Sales of sheet music plummeted.

The point here is that folk music in the 1960s had virtually nothing to do with rock and roll. The audiences for these two styles remained quite distinct. As a result, in folk music, the concept of the standard still existed. Folk songs were, in principle, songs that everybody could sing in hootenannies, and thus lent themselves to performance by different singers, different instruments, and so forth. Like seeds in the springtime, folk songs could propagate rapidly. To cite the most obvious example, this is what happened to "Blowin' in the Wind." It rapidly became a standard that existed apart from Dylan's version of it. Thus, the singers Peter, Paul and Mary, as well as other groups, recorded it, and, in the process, they made famous the young prodigy who had written the song.

Then, too, the legacy of the McCarthy hearings in the 1950s and the persecution of groups such as the Weavers kept folk music apart from the general public's awareness of music, which was defined by AM radio Top 40 stations. Folk music fans knew that if they wanted to listen to Joan Baez and Bob Dylan, they had to buy their albums, because they could not expect to hear their music on the radio. The contrast between 33 1/3 rpm albums and 45 rpm singles had more to do with style than with revolutions per minute, and Dylan says as much in *Chronicles* when he comments that, "I had no song in my repertoire for commercial radio anyway."[23]

These considerations help to explain why "Blowin' in the Wind" defined folk music in the early 1960s. By the time of Dylan's first appearance at the Newport Folk Festival on July 28, 1963, he had taken over the folk movement. (It took him two and a half years.) With the easy confidence of a first-born with a younger sibling, he served as emcee at the closing concert, and called the Freedom Singers, Joan Baez (the lovebirds squeezed hands),[24] and Peter, Paul and Mary onto the stage. Although they were all older than Dylan, and were more experienced singers, they served as his backup singers for a rousing version of "Blowin' in the Wind." Everyone onstage knew it by heart, of course, as did everyone in the audience.

Dylan's image as the champion of the civil rights movement was not inaccurate—for a year or so, anyway. But, as images of great performers usually do, it over-simplified his genius. If we really wish to understand his early songs in depth, then we must realize that they express the two predominant attitudes of the civil rights movement—compassion and anger. Activists at the time felt compassion for the sufferings of the oppressed and anger toward those who were oppressing them. And these are two predominant attitudes of Dylan's early songs. When I wrote *Rock Eras*, I divided some of the songs from Dylan's acoustic period into anger songs and compassion songs.[25] I now believe that he wrote only two real anger songs in that period: "Masters of War" and "The Lonesome Death of Hattie Carroll." Although you might expect that any right-thinking folkie would write an anger song about the murder of civil rights worker Medgar Evers, Dylan's response to this terrible crime wasn't anger, but compassion: "Only a Pawn in Their Game."

In fact, Dylan got himself into trouble when he expressed compassion for Lee Harvey Oswald, the most hated man in American at the time, at a dinner on December 13, 1963. In the immediate aftermath of the assassination of President Kennedy, he went so far as to say that "I saw some of myself in him," and caused a predictable furor.[26]

It is obvious that "Girl of the North Country" and "Don't Think Twice, It's All Right" express care and compassion, but as I now listen to "Oxford Town" and "With God on Our Side," I find that they convey more sadness and dismay about the human condition than anger. If you listen to these songs, and then listen to "Blowin' in the Wind," it seems more like a song that asks a series of unanswerable questions about the absence of compassion in the world than a song that predicts a new day of justice and equality.

When Baez introduced Dylan at Newport in 1964, she said, "You know him, he's yours—Bob Dylan."[27] What Baez did not know, and what even Dylan did not know at the time, is that his first appearance at the Newport Folk Festival marked the peak of his folk music fervor. He soon began to turn away from it, and did so under the impact of one of the most important books he had ever read.

When Dylan returned to New York from Newport in the summer of 1963, he was no longer scrounging for his next meal. His income from record sales, concerts, and royalties had sufficiently stabilized so that he could rent an apartment of his own, a third-floor walkup at 161 West Fourth Street, and he proudly recounts in *Chronicles* that he even built some furniture for it.[28]

Dave Van Ronk visited Dylan in this apartment and saw something on one of Dylan's homemade bookshelves that has extraordinary implications for anyone who wishes to understand Dylan's evolution. Anthony Scaduto interviewed Van Ronk:

> Being a hayseed, that was part of his image, of what he considered his image at the time. Like, I once asked him, "Do you know the French Symbolists?" And he said, "Huh?" The stupidest "huh" you can imagine—and later, when he had a place of his own, I went up there, and on the book shelf was a volume of the French poets from Nerval to almost the present. I think it ended at Apollonaire, and it was all well-thumbed, with passages underlined and notes in the margins. The man wanted to be primitive, a natural kind of genius. He never talked about somebody like Rimbaud. But he knew Rimbaud, all right. You see that in the later songs.[29]

This exceptionally significant anecdote defines the historic moment when Dylan's private reality began to split away from his public image. In Dylan's stories about his life, he represented himself as a latter-day Huck Finn, an innocent in the big city— the hayseed part of his image. In *Chronicles*, he even refers to one of his hometown girlfriends as "my Becky Thatcher."[30] This was what he called his "passion for dumbness." Prodigiously gifted though he was, he *was* an innocent, and lacked the sophistication and general worldliness of the Beat poets and folksingers that he was spending time with. At first he made the most of his situation, telling people that he had spent time in exotic New Mexico, rather than prosaic Minnesota. Unlike Huck Finn, though, he did not "light out for the territory"; he did just the opposite—he "lit out" for the big city. But innocence did not suit his protean imagination for long, and his need to make up for lost time gave him at least some of the motivation to continue with his ambitious reading program.

And thanks to Van Ronk's anecdote we know that he expanded his literary interests, turning from great but accessible American authors like Hemingway to much lesser known and much more demanding authors like the French Symbolist poets Charles Baudelaire and Arthur Rimbaud. In fact, one could say that Baudelaire and Rimbaud are about as different from Hemingway and Guthrie as any pair of writers can be. Baudelaire and Rimbaud wrote deliberately difficult poetry for urban sophisticates, and their work remains challenging to this day.

As is usual with Dylan, we will never know for sure exactly when he discovered Baudelaire and Rimbaud, but the dramatic differences between "Blowin' in the Wind" and "Chimes of Freedom," which he sang at Newport in 1964, suggest that at some time in the summer or fall of 1963, Dylan bought the book Van Ronk is referring to: *An Anthology of French Poetry from Nerval to Valery in English Translation*. This anthology, which Angel Flores had edited, and which was first published in 1958, played a key role in making the poetry of the French Symbolists available in English. Dylan could have bought his copy at any of the numerous bookstores in Greenwich Village.

As Van Ronk sensed at the time, *An Anthology of French Poetry* played a key role in Dylan's evolution as a songwriter. By this time, Dylan had probably read some T. S. Eliot and some Allen Ginsburg. It must have come as a shock to find the inspiration for Eliot's and Ginsburg's work (and much of modern English poetry) in Baudelaire and Rimbaud. And we can find Dylan's sources for "Chimes of Freedom" in two of the most famous poems in the anthology, Baudelaire's "Correspondences" and Rimbaud's "The Vowels."

In "Correspondences," Baudelaire anticipates the visionary quality of "Chimes of Freedom" in the opening lines: "Nature is a temple from whose living columns/Commingling voices emerge at times."[31] What Baudelaire means by "correspondences" might well be rendered by "affinities," and Baudelaire presents affinities between the natural forest and the constructed temple, between trees and columns, and thus between the natural world and cultural artifacts.

The anticipation of "Chimes of Freedom" becomes even clearer in Baudelaire's second stanza, where Dylan read the following lines:

> Like long-drawn echoes for converging
> In harmonies darksome and profound
> Vast as the light and vast as light
> Colors, scents and sounds correspond.[32]

The striking phrase "harmonies darksome and profound" suggests synesthesia, the perception of one sense by another, as in "a delicious color" or "a red sound."

A poem in *An Anthology of French Poetry* that makes synesthesia explicit is "Vowels" by Arthur Rimbaud. This very unlikely subject for a poem begins with these lines: "A black, E white, I read, O green, O blue; /Someday I'll tell you your latest birth, oh vowels."[33] By matching—arbitrarily, to be sure—vowels with colors, Rimbaud matches sounds and color in unprecedented ways—ways that surely caught the eye of the young Dylan as he was discovering what he could do.

Thus, *An Anthology of French Poetry* contains poems that stand at the farthest possible remove from folk songs, not to mention the work of Hemingway and Guthrie. Unlike folk songs, these poems are explicitly, defiantly elitist; they flaunt their lack of coherence, not to mention social significance. Yet they appealed to Dylan in the early 1960s because Baudelaire, Rimbaud, and their compatriots were as besotted with words as he was. Like Dylan, they wanted to transcend the limitations of the culture that surrounded them, and they provided some models for doing that.

However, the French Symbolists cultivated a precious, hothouse quality in their work. For all their dazzling verbal virtuosity, Baudelaire and Rimbaud had limited appeal for an American artist who had responded to the guileless perfection of Hank Williams and the raw power of Elvis Presley. It is important to understand that this is a not a matter of the triumph of American popular culture over European elitist culture, which would be the easy and obvious interpretation of the situation; rather, it is a curious example of the fertile juxtaposition of poems and songs in Dylan's exceptionally receptive sensibility. As Van Ronk says, the French Symbolists had a lasting effect on Dylan's songs, although rarely does that effect appear as clearly as it does in "Chimes of Freedom," which opened up exciting possibilities in the songs that were to follow.

"Chimes of Freedom" and other songs of the era, such as "I Shall Be Free No. 10" (not to mention "Like a Rolling Stone"), gave Dylan the confidence to give up his carefully cultivated image as a "hayseed," to use Van Ronk's term, and to come out as a sophisticate. At a 1965 press conference in San Francisco someone asked Dylan, "What poets do you dig?" And he answered casually, "Rimbaud, I guess."[34]

At this crucial moment let us pause to consider what had happened, and how we can define Dylan as an artist. When he got to New York, he experienced all around him cultural oppositions of various kinds. As we know, there was the opposition of rock and roll on one hand and folk music on the other. In technological terms, this amounted to an opposition of the 45 rpm singles that disc jockeys played on Top 40 stations that people listened to on their car radios as opposed to the 33 1/3 rpm albums that people listened to on their stereos at home. And then his reading program led him into another opposition, the opposition of the plain-spoken eloquence of American writers like Hemingway and Guthrie as opposed to the obscure brilliance of French writers like Baudelaire and Rimbaud. In the great year of 1965 he resolved these oppositions in his song "Like a Rolling Stone" and the other masterpieces in his album *Highway 61 Revisited*. In general terms, what this means is that we can best understand Dylan the innovator as Dylan the synthesizer of disparate cultural traditions.

Dylan's quasi-mystical sensibility propelled him away from the plains of the civil rights movement, with its good-hearted people and "singable" songs, where chimes always ring and never flash, to the mountaintops of experience. The essential attitude that defined the civil rights movement was its refusal to discriminate on the basis of race. It is as though Dylan took this attitude and estheticized it by applying it to sense perception. He refused to discriminate on the basis of sense perception—one sense could be substituted for another, and thus chimes could flash. For the next several years, Dylan followed this new attitude wherever it wanted to lead him.

He took this new attitude and new style onto the stage at the Newport Folk Festival in 1964. By this time everyone had lived through the assassination of President Kennedy and the beginnings of Beatlemania. Dylan sang "Chimes of Freedom," which came out on his album *Another Side of Bob Dylan*, and surely some of the folkies got restless as they listened to this complex song. Whatever "Chimes of Freedom" is, it is empathically not a folk song, or something that anybody could sing at a hootenanny. It marks an essential change in his work. "Chimes of Freedom" confirms the key statement that Dylan makes to Scorsese in *No Direction Home*: "I went through Guthrie."

"Chimes of Freedom" is the first Dylan song whose long, rolling lines and rich, evocative images achieve a majestic quality; it both anticipates and makes possible the masterpieces of his electric period. When Dylan sings the song, he pauses after "of," like this: "chimes of ... freedom flashing." This phrasing emphasizes the alliteration and also what was new in the song, which is the synesthesia that he had learned from Baudelaire and Rimbaud. Chimes do not literally flash—light does that. (Chimes may ring and resound, for example, but they do not flash.) It is worth lingering on this use of synesthesia because Dylan had never used it before, and was never to use it again. This anomaly cries out for explanation.

Synesthesia is related to synthesis, and "Chimes of Freedom" is the first song that demonstrates what makes Dylan so special—his exceptional ability to synthesize different works and different styles. Thus, we may understand "Chimes of Freedom" as a synthesis of various radically different works. The one that Dylan's audience at Newport 1964 would have known is "If I Had a

Hammer" by Lee Hays and Pete Seeger.[35] They originally copyrighted that song in 1958, and it had become a standard on the folk circuit by the time Dylan got to New York. Peter, Paul and Mary covered it in 1962, and—this was a rarity for a folk song—it made the Top 10. Other folkies recorded it as well. The stanza form of "Chimes" resembles that of "Hammer." Both songs are written in 8-line stanzas and have no separate chorus. In both songs, the last line is the same in each verse.

"If I Had a Hammer" refers to a hammer, of course, but what interests us here is the beginning of the second verse, which has to do with ringing a bell. In this context, it is worth noting that Dylan devotes a whole paragraph in *Chronicles* to his fondness for bells.[36]

The last stanza of "If I Had a Hammer" refers to "the bell of freedom," which may have suggested to Dylan the word "tolling," which occurs seven times in "Chimes"—more than any other word in the song. Dylan lists the groups of people for whom the bell is tolling, and that phrase evokes the second immediate source for the song, John Donne's "Meditation XVII" (1624). Although Donne's metaphorical conceits give a density to his poetic style that makes him very different from Whitman, both these great poets affirm their belief in the unity of humanity. In this Meditation, Donne writes, "Any man's death diminishes me, because I am involved in *Mankind*. And, therefore, never send to know for whom the bell tolls. It tolls for *thee*."[37] Before going any further, let us note how close in spirit Dylan is to Donne in compassion songs such as "Only a Hobo."

Dylan may well have come to Donne's "Meditation" through Hemingway's 1940 novel *For Whom the Bell Tolls*. Hemingway's protagonist, Robert Jordan, fights in a Freedom Brigade in the Spanish Civil War, a conflict with suggestive analogies to the civil rights movement of the 1960s.[38] In the novel Jordan expresses just what Dylan must have been feeling—a growing discomfort with rigidity, no matter what ideology it advocated.

A key difference between "If I Had a Hammer" and "Chimes of Freedom" may be summed up in the difference between two phrases. The last line of "If I Had a Hammer" in each verse reaches out to the whole land. Pete Seeger's songs, like those of Woody Guthrie and Hank Williams before him, are stuck inside the visible, tactile world, whereas Dylan's chimes extend their compassion to everyone in the universe. "Chimes of Freedom" adumbrates the theme of transcendence that will inform some of Dylan's masterpieces, so it is appropriate that its reach so greatly exceeds that of "If I Had a Hammer."

Who perceives the chimes of freedom flashing? "We" do. The singer is accompanied by a person or persons unknown and unidentified. I suspect that the "we" harks to the affirmation of community that is repeated in the next to last line of each verse in "If I Had a Hammer." The "we" also anticipates the observers "Lady and I" in the song "Desolation Row."

And what is the situation of this "we"? Whoever these people are, they go by a church where there has been a wedding, and a summer thunderstorm breaks out. (For once for Dylan, rain represents the turbulence of possibilities rather than something threatening.) They duck into a doorway, a transitional space and thus a very significant one for Dylan.[39] While they stand there, the sound of the wedding bells merges with the sound of thunder. A wedding is a union of two people, and thus suggests the union of the wedding bells and the thunder. For someone in a state of mystical transport, the next step would be to say that the sensory perceptions of sight and sound themselves merge, that it was not just the lightning that was flashing—it was also the chimes that were flashing.

The reconciliation of the opposites of sight and sound into a unity of experience is consistent with marriage as the merger of a man and a woman into the unit of a couple. Similarly, once Dylan's creativity took the form of a reconciliation of the opposites of folk music and French Symbolist poetry, he was on his way. His markers of creativity had enabled him to take advantage of the stimulating environment of New York to create extraordinary synergistic energy.

There is one other significant book that Dylan read during his first three years in New York—a book that had a decisive effect on his career and his songs. It was published in 1964, and would have been much discussed among the painters, poets, and intellectuals that he was spending time with, and it changed the way he thought about himself and his art. Just as Ariadne left threads that help Theseus to find his way through the labyrinth in Greek mythology, so Dylan left us some clues that guide us through the labyrinths of his songs.

Dylan read, or read some of, or read about, or listened to discussions about (take your pick) Marshall McLuhan's *Understanding Media*, a seminal book on media theory that was published to much acclaim and controversy in New York in 1964. Nowadays McLuhan is known for two catchphrases, "The medium is the message" and "the global village," and his book has so many references to events and people of the late 1950s and early 1960s that some people may find it hard reading. Nevertheless, people who study communications technology still refer to it as "ground zero" of media studies.

McLuhan argued in *Understanding Media* that technology does not simply exist "out there," and that it does not just create ever more efficient ways to get things done. McLuhan said, rather, that through technology we extend our organs and senses, thereby creating complex, deeply personal interrelationships with media whose consequences we ignore at our peril. Hence, the subtitle of the book, *The Extensions of Man*.

One of McLuhan's most dramatic propositions, and one that surely got Dylan's attention, is his reversal of the old romantic image of the alienated artist. Unlike most previous critics—and poets such as Allen Ginsberg—who had lamented the alienation of the artist from the world of technology and business, McLuhan asserted that:

> In the history of human culture there is no example of a conscious adjustment of the various factors of personal and social life to new extensions [i.e., to new media] except in the puny and peripheral efforts of artists. The artist picks up the message of cultural and technological challenge decades before the transforming impact occurs.[40]

Or, in the words of British writer Wyndham Lewis, whom McLuhan liked to quote, "The artist is continually engaged in writing a history of the future because he is the only one who understands the nature of the present."[41] If there was one thing that people kept saying about Dylan, it was that he understood "the nature of the present." When Peter Yarrow introduced Dylan at the 1964 Newport Folk Festival, for example, he said that "Dylan has his finger on the pulse of his generation."

And what was the nature of the present, according to McLuhan? He believed that the world was undergoing a profound change as a result of electric technology that was starting to replace literacy. He said "the ultimate conflict between sight and sound, between written and oral kinds of perception and organization, is upon us."[42] For McLuhan, the sounds of radios, telephones, record players, and the like were changing our perceptions. He conceptualized this change as the replacement of the eye, the organ that we used for reading, by the ear, the organ that we use for hearing. McLuhan says of "Western man" that "his own electric technology now begins to translate the visual or eye man back into the tribal and oral pattern with its seamless web of kinship and interdependence."[43] Moreover, in a sentence that must have pleased Dylan, he says "radio and gramophone gave us back the poet's voice as an important dimension of the poetic experience."[44] Finally, very much in the spirit of the 1960s, McLuhan provocatively treated high culture and popular culture as equally valid and equally interesting in passages such as this: "The advent of electric media released art from this strait jacket [of literacy] at once, creating the world of Paul Klee, Picasso, Braque, Eisenstein, the Marx Brothers, and James Joyce."[45]

If we consider the evidence of what Dylan wrote in 1964–5 with McLuhan in mind, there are only two possibilities. The first is that Dylan included McLuhan, who was the talk of the town in 1964 and whom he could hardly have avoided, in his reading program, which was much more extensive and serious than we ever suspected. The other possibility is that Dylan's songs from the mid-1960s constitute a startling empirical confirmation of McLuhan's theories. The first hypothesis seems much more likely and much more reasonable. How else than by reference to McLuhan's opposition of the eye and the ear are we to make any sense at all of Dylan's comments on the eye and the mouth in the liner notes to his album *Highway 61 Revisited*? Dylan writes, "I cannot say this word eye anymore.... When I speak this word eye, it is as if I am speaking of somebody's eye that I faintly remember.... There is no eye—there is only a series of mouths—long live the mouths."[46]

In the liner notes for *Bringing It All Back Home*, Dylan also personalizes what McLuhan wrote. In them he juxtaposes high culture and popular culture more in the spirit of McLuhan than of Pop Art in order to set us up for a deadpan putdown: "i would not want to be bach, mozart, tolstoy, joe hill, gertrude stein or james dean/they are all dead."[47] (Dylan wrote this during his e. e. cummings phase, when he adopted that poet's refusal to use capital letters.)

If Dylan took seriously McLuhan's announcement that the electric age had arrived, and that the artist was the only one who understood the nature of the present, then he had a rationale for going electric, especially since Chuck Berry created his rock and roll classics like "Maybelline" on the electric guitar. McLuhan gave Dylan some timely encouragement to embark on his role as synthesizer of high culture and popular culture. After all, nothing said popular culture like the electric guitar.

Two songs from 1964–65 seem especially McLuhanesque: "My Back Pages," on the album *Another Side of Bob Dylan*, and "Ballad of a Thin Man," on *Highway 61 Revisited*. Let us consider them in chronological order.

"My Back Pages" comes as close to denouncing the civil rights movement, and indeed all social causes, as anything Dylan ever wrote, so it is appropriate that it is on *Another Side of Bob Dylan*. He wrote it in the eight-line stanza method that he was commonly using then; the last two lines serve, in effect, as the chorus. In the song, he offers a chronological paradox; he says that he is younger than he was because of the rejuvenating effects of electric technology, which has reconciled the oppositions that had caused him constant agitation, as in the first two lines of the second stanza. These oppositions were making him old before his time, and the title "My Back Pages" tells us that Dylan associated such oppositions with literacy, as McLuhan did.

"My Back Pages" derives from Dylan's reading in another way, as well. The song shows us how he came to terms with the legacy of Allen Ginsberg and the Beat poets, much of whose work consists of a verbal flailing about, and which proclaimed their sensitivity and alienation from the bland conformity of the 1950s at considerable length. Dylan used the freedom to create surrealistic images for a higher purpose. In each eight-line stanza, the first six lines contain bizarre images whose purpose is to show the chaos that results from the dichotomies that literacy creates. The soothing refrain suggests that the new orality created by the electric age has resolved those dichotomies. The refrain also implies that he has overcome the legacy of the Beat poets, who had fascinated him in the past.

In "Ballad of a Thin Man,"[48] the thin man's body is an analogue to the pencil, the very symbol of literacy that he carries even when he does something as casual as walk into a room. What is the defining feature of the thin man's life? He is "very well read." Dylan, as the artist with his finger on the pulse of the present when the oral, integrative technology of electricity was replacing the visual, fragmented technology of print, jeers at the thin man, who is literally and metaphorically out of touch with what is happening. In general, the tone of "Ballad of a Thin Man" resembles that of "Masters of War," one of his two earlier anger songs. Still, this is representative of Dylan, and his anger is not unmixed with compassion, and he tells the thin man to wear earphones. That is to say, he should be made to experience the healing effects of sound, which will begin to balance the visual orientation of literate sensibility.

"Ballad of a Thin Man" leads directly to "Like a Rolling Stone," the song that Dylan played on the electric guitar at Newport in 1965, thereby shocking the folkies at Newport. For all its importance—and it deserves Greil Marcus's terrific book about it[49]—the song has defied interpretation because people have not understood Dylan's assimilative creativity.

The twilight of the gods—or at least of the folk god Bob Dylan—came on the evening of July 23, 1965, when he played with The Hawks, the group with whom he had just recorded "Like a Rolling Stone."[50] In the tapes of that landmark event, one can hear the boos while they are still tuning up their electric instruments. When you watch the version that Scorsese shows in the documentary *No Direction Home*, you realize that you are watching cultural change close-up and personal; it is messy, chaotic, and unpleasant. Even kind, good-hearted Pete Seeger tried to pull out the cords because he could not understand the words. Something was happening there, and he did not know what it was, so it drove him a little crazy.[51]

The aftershocks of that concert, and of "Like a Rolling Stone," reverberated throughout the 1960s and beyond. No single performance had caused such shock and dismay for more than half a century—since May 29, 1913, to be precise. It was on that date that Serge Diaghilev's Ballets Russes performed Igor Stravinsky's ballet *The Rite of Spring* and caused an unprecedented furor. Modris Eksteins examines the numerous wildly contradictory accounts of that evening in his book *Rites of Spring*, and concludes:

> To have been in the audience that evening was to have participated not simply at another exhibition but in the very creation of modern art, in that the response of the audience was and is as important to the meaning of this art as the intentions of those who produced it. Art has transcended reason, didacticism, and a moral purpose: art has become provocation and event.[52]

Although the differences between a song and a ballet, between Bob Dylan and Igor Stravinsky, are so obvious that they do not need to be stated, the

2. The Early Years in New York

historical and cultural analogies between the two performances are provocative and important.

In both cases, the audiences expected pleasant, predictable music, and what they got seemed to them raw, dissonant, and deeply upsetting. The folkies in Newport were dressed very differently from the society audience in Paris, but their boos and outrage when their (justifiable, to them) expectations were denied and even mocked, are comparable. And when Dylan and The Hawks went on tour in England with "Like a Rolling Stone," the audiences became apoplectic. Marcus says:

> There were banners unfurled and signs raised. There were cheers and applause, curses and cheers for the curses. In Sheffield, a bomb threat was phoned in to the hall. People in the crowd tried to shout each other down. There was unison slow handclapping to throw the musicians off their time, or to create a noise too big for even their own noise to overcome.[53]

And it was not just in England. Throughout 1965 and 1966, audiences showered Dylan with palpable hatred worldwide.

So why did he do something that turned doting audiences into hateful audiences? This is a more specific version of one of the key questions that agitated people in the mid-1960s: Why did Dylan go electric? Joseph Hass, of *The Chicago Daily News*, asked Dylan this question on November 27, 1965, and Dylan managed to avoid giving a direct answer by citing the economics of the music business: "It cost bread to make enough money to buy an electric guitar, and then you had to make more money to have enough people to play the music. You need two or three to create some conglomeration of sound."[54]

In "Like a Rolling Stone," Dylan stridently, aggressively announces his new-found maturity, and defies people to ignore him. This ironic, challenging song has multiple meanings and draws on multiple sources. For the first time, we must bring some knowledge of movies, popular music, and literature to a Dylan song in order to interpret it properly. No wonder it has remained an enigma for so long.

To start with, we may ask if the singer is jeering at Miss Lonely. The song is so intense and Dylan sings it at such a fast tempo that it is tricky to establish the tone. Still, autobiographical references do have some significance, if only to give an initial sense of the song. Dylan knew all too well what it was like to come to New York as a complete unknown, with no direction home, and he knew what it was like to be scrounging for his next meal. He had a lot in common with Miss Lonely, as he had acknowledged in 1963 that he had a lot in common with Lee Harvey Oswald. Hence, the singer feels compassion for her. Fortunately, the song is much too complex to allow us to say, "Oh, it's Dylan," because Dylan is *both* the singer *and* Miss Lonely.

We know, more or less, who Dylan is, but who is Miss Lonely? The name "Miss Lonely" offers a clue that leads us to yet another book, *Miss Lonely-*

hearts. This novel was written in 1933 by Nathaniel West, who was born as Nathan Weinstein, and who therefore shared Dylan's ambiguous Jewish-American identity. (Dylan probably read *Miss Lonelyhearts* in the edition that came out in 1957.) If the singer in "Like a Rolling Stone" is both a man and Miss Lonely, then that gender ambiguity has a precedent in the opening sentence of West's novel: "Miss Lonelyhearts ... sat at his desk and stared at a piece of white cardboard."[55] The grammatical oddity of this sentence is explained by the fact that Miss Lonelyhearts is a man who writes what Sherlock Holmes would have called an "agony column" for a newspaper that is unnamed, just as Miss Lonelyhearts himself is never named. It is his profession as a writer to provide compassion to those who pour out their hearts to him in long letters—and this feature may well be what made the book significant for Dylan, who felt so much compassion for so many at the time. *Miss Lonelyhearts* has no plot, because West strings together the weird chapters of his novel very much as Dylan strings together the weird verses of his songs. Neither writer felt constrained by the demands of plot and story.

More than any other work of American literature—certainly more than anything written by the Beats—*Miss Lonelyhearts* anticipates not just Dylan's compassion, but also his surrealistic take on American vernacular culture. To take just one example, Miss Lonelyhearts's editor, the weirdly named Shrike, makes the following announcement: "God alone is our escape. The church is our only hope, the First Church of Christ Dentist, where He is worshiped as Preventer of Decay."[56] God as the Preventer of Decay is so like Dylan, and *Miss Lonelyhearts* was written almost 30 years before Dylan got to New York!

To return to "Like a Rolling Stone," the first line, "Once upon a time," has great thematic importance, as first lines in Dylan's songs often do. Anything that begins "Once upon a time" is a fairy tale, which is what "Like a Rolling Stone" is. It is an ironic, multi-leveled version of a fairy tale, to be sure, but a fairy tale nevertheless. It is not just any fairy tale, either; it is *the* essential American fairy tale—a story of democratization. This fairy tale is one in which everybody lives happily ever after, because everybody is democratized (i.e., included in the end). To quote Dave Van Ronk in the documentary *No Direction Home*, "If there is an American collective unconscious, he was channeling it." If the "American collective unconscious" has a home, it is the Dream Factory—Hollywood. We find some useful analogies for "Like a Rolling Stone" not in songs, but in movies.

The point is clearer in larger narrative works such as *Shrek* (2001), which could not have influenced "Like a Rolling Stone," but which I cite to show how common the situation of the song is, and has been. At the end of this charming movie, all the animals/creatures dance and sing together because the evil prince, who represents elitism, has been defeated, and Shrek includes the animals, although he had previously excluded them. I mention *Shrek* because the Dream Factory excels in putting out such fairy tales of democratization, and some understanding of gender roles in them will help to create a helpful context for understanding Dylan's ironic version of this much-told tale.

In American popular culture as a whole, the woman often has some combination of money and high culture; the man often represents the common people. Thus, when the man and the woman fall in love, the man in effect democratizes the woman. Cartoons such as the Disney animation feature film *The Lady and the Tramp* (1955), which Bobby Zimmerman probably saw when he was still stuck in Hibbing, are well suited for telling the fairy tale of democratization that incorporates these conventionalized gender roles. The story in that movie is that Lady, a pampered cocker spaniel who lives in a ritzy part of town, runs away from home when two cats move in and meets a mongrel dog, Tramp. A great deal of the plot concerns what happens when Tramp teaches her how to live on the street.

The street, both in the movie and in Dylan's song, serves as the prime site and symbol of democracy, where people of all classes mingle and are on the move, as America historically has been on the move. In teaching Lady to live on the street with ordinary dogs, Tramp, in effect, democratizes her. We Americans love fairy tales about democratization such as this, and this story line has such enduring appeal that Disney reworked it in the movie *Beverly Hills Chihuahua* (2008).

This enduring plotline in American movies begins in 1934 with *It Happened One Night*, which, in one way or another, has served as the model for practically every romantic comedy since then. It stars Clark Gable, who, as a reporter, represents democracy, of course. Paulette Goddard, a spoiled heiress, represents elitism. The comic bits usually involve Clark Gable teaching her how to live on the street. Naturally, they find true love at the end. This plotline, in which the man represents democracy and the woman represents elitism, allows for numerous variations, both comic and dramatic. It also appears in two great, but radically different, movies from 1951: *A Streetcar Named Desire* and *The African Queen*.

The American organization of gender roles in this way serves to organize "Like a Rolling Stone." We may suppose that Dylan, consciously or unconsciously (we will never know which), drew on these movie plot lines when he was writing it. What Dylan does is consistent with what Shrike in West's novel says about Miss Lonelyhearts, referring to him as "a comforter of the poor in spirit."[57] Dylan challenges Miss Lonely in the song to learn to live on the street, not just because in American culture democratization must be presented as progress, but also because he urges/exhorts Miss Lonely to claim her feelings and to create something that she does not have: an authentic life. What could be more American than presenting democratization as the American dream of an authentic life? Miss Lonely does not have an authentic life any more than Paulette Goddard's character Ellen does in the beginning of *It Happened One Night*. In that movie, Ellen runs away—she dives overboard from her father's yacht, actually—and we must assume that Dylan's Miss Lonely has run away, too. She senses the lack of authenticity in her life, and thus the purpose of the song is to help her achieve that authenticity. At the private school Miss Lonely attended, she stayed drunk and told lies about her life to cover up what she had done. She needed "alibis," which tellingly rhymes with "lies." For all the aggressive tone of that first crashing drum beat and the complexity of its lyrics, "Like A Rolling Stone" is a compassion song, and the singer functions as a spiritual guide. With regard to Dylan's evolution, it represents a softer, kinder version of "Ballad of a Thin Man."

When one feels compassion, one's feelings go outward to another person. And the autobiographical clues in the song ("like a complete unknown") also point outward. Gender roles, as they were presented in the popular culture of the 1950s, help us to understand that, among many other things, "Like a Rolling Stone" is a cleverly coded response to "Hound Dog," and thus to Dylan's most threatening precursor, Elvis.

To understand the connection between "Hound Dog" and "Like a Rolling Stone," let us consider what they have in common. What do we know about the woman to whom Elvis sings? She claimed that she was "high class," but she lied, he wails, his grammar flaunting his working-class (i.e., democratic) credentials. In both "Hound Dog" and "Like a Rolling Stone" the male singer addresses a woman who has higher social status, but who does not know how to cope. If Elvis is disappointed in the woman, Dylan tells Miss Lonely that she does not know how to scrounge for her next meal.

If "Like a Rolling Stone" is in part a reply to "Hound Dog," it has dazzling audacity, because it asserts that Dylan can rework the same material Elvis owned, and match him at his own game—if not beat him. This hidden encounter with Elvis may account for the urgency of Dylan's tone. No wonder the song is so strident; it took everything that Dylan had to write and perform it. No rock star takes on Elvis lightly—and Dylan certainly did not. But his genius rose to the occasion; it gave him his highest-charting song. Artistically, "Like a Rolling Stone" freed Dylan to write his even more audacious songs, "Desolation Row" and "Visions of Johanna."

One more movie has relevance to "Like a Rolling Stone," but only if we understand that the opposition between uptown and downtown that defined the bohemian quality of Greenwich Village was not absolute. Even in Greenwich Village coffeehouses, people read *The New York Times*, and when they read the Arts and Entertainment section in the early 1960s, they could not have missed articles about the play that was a blockbuster hit on Broadway, and later one of the most successful musicals ever made—*My Fair Lady*. The

Broadway version had opened in 1956 and set records for the longest run of any musical. The movie version appeared in 1964, the year of Beatlemania, and at the Oscar ceremony, just before Dylan recorded "Like a Rolling Stone," it received Oscars for Best Picture, Best Director (George Cukor), and Best Actor (Rex Harrison). It received four other nominations. The original cast album, which also came out in 1956, enjoyed such enormous success that even Dylan probably heard it.

My Fair Lady is a British version of the Cinderella story in which aristocratic Professor Higgins teaches a working-class girl, Eliza Doolittle, how to speak properly so that she can pass for an elegant lady. It has had lasting appeal and has inspired subsequent movies such as *Pretty Woman* (1990) and *Maid in Manhattan* (2002). Also, it shows another aspect of the relationship between democratization and gender roles. In America, stories about social mobility for women are comedies, whereas stories about social mobility for men, especially white men, such as *The Great Gatsby* and *The Godfather*, are tragedies. White men, who are supposed to embody democracy, lose their souls when they experience upward mobility.

"Show Me," a song from the musical *My Fair Lady* that Liza sings to Freddie (on the street, significantly), has great relevance for "Like a Rolling Stone." Liza's frustration with both Freddie and Professor Higgins is as much stylistic as sexual. She rants that men use a genteel style that drains all the feeling out of words. Freddie's solo, "On the Street Where You Live," which precedes "Show Me," amply demonstrates this problem. Although Professor Higgins took her in and gave her upward mobility by changing the way she talked, she now realizes that it is not enough.

"Like a Rolling Stone" reverses the situation of "Show Me," because Miss Lonely, rather than coming *in* from the street, as Liza does both at the beginning and at the end of *My Fair Lady*, goes *out* to the street. As Liza understood when she first came to Professor Higgins for elocution lessons, a change of place involves a change of speech habits and social status as well. Liza comes in from the street and loses her working-class speech patterns—a plot that works only because it is set in England.

Dylan, on the other hand, intuitively understood how democratization works in America, so he urges Miss Lonely to face the changes that she must make in order to live with integrity. A key aspect of these changes, naturally, is the change in language. Dylan's line about language is surely Miss Lovely's shocked response to street profanity, and it points up a deliberate contrast between *My Fair Lady* and "Like a Rolling Stone." In the context of the musical, a comment about language would refer to Professor Higgins's oh-so-elegant speech, to which Liza aspires. In Dylan's song it refers to street profanity, to which Miss Lonely must become accustomed in order to live a fuller life.

A little over four years had passed since Dylan arrived in New York on that cold winter day in 1961, and it is fair to say that no major American artist changed so much and assimilated so much of what New York had to offer in such a short period of time. He had begun his career by merging the folk musical idiom with literary sources, and it is indicative of his rapid maturation that musical, literary, and movie sources all come together in "Like a Rolling Stone." The songs "Blowin' in the Wind," "Chimes of Freedom," and "Like a Rolling Stone" mark three key moments in Dylan's early evolution: folk songs, the decisive turn away from folk songs, and the electric renunciation of the folk ethic. Of these three, "Chimes of Freedom," with its echoes of the French Symbolists, anticipated the next momentous stage of his evolution, the integration of the American popular culture with European high culture.

3

Affinities with Franz Kafka, T.S. Eliot and Pablo Picasso

In what sense was Dylan a man of his time? As is usual with him, no simple answer seems possible. He writes in *Chronicles* that when he started thinking about writing songs, he did not think that his work would be popular.[1] But Dylan soon took his finger off the pulse of his generation, and turned against it. In *Chronicles*, he made the most shocking statement of his life when he wrote that in the middle and late 1960s, what he "was fantasizing about was a nine-to-five existence, a house on a tree-lined block with a white picket fence, pink roses in the backyard."[2] Pink roses in the backyard, indeed!

Even when we make due allowance for Dylan's tendency to put people on, this statement bespeaks a disconnect with his generation's experience in the 1960s. He also had a disconnect with his father, and with the small-town life that his father represented. That brings us to his grandfather, Zigman Zimmerman, born in 1875 in Odessa, Russia, a port on the Black Sea.

Zigman Zimmerman matters here because his generation was the generation of the heroic poets and painters of High Modernism, whose assault on nineteenth-century complacency in Europe anticipated, and to some extent informed, Dylan's assault on the complacency of America in the 1960s. To understand Dylan in the depth that he deserves, to decode his great songs of the mid–1960s, we must understand that he has significant affinities with three great modernist artists, all born within a decade of Zigman Zimmerman—a prose writer, a poet, and a painter. In order of increasing importance (and lifespan), they are Franz Kafka (1883–1924), T.S. Eliot (1883–1965), and Pablo Picasso (1881–1973).

Franz Kafka

We can learn more about Dylan's cultural heritage as a Jew by studying his affinities with Kafka than by studying his brief infatuation with Judaism in the 1970s. As part of the group of audacious Jews who created what we know as "modernity," Kafka took dreams and nightmares as the stuff of literature. Rather in the spirit of Rimbaud, who had advocated the "derangement of all the senses," Kafka took an absurd premise and developed it into a consistent narrative. This is why his impact on modern literature, and on Dylan, was greater than Rimbaud's. Hence, the first sentence of his short story "The Metamorphosis" (1915) is arguably the most important single sentence in all of twentieth-century literature: "As Gregor Samsa awoke one morning from uneasy dreams he found himself transformed in his bed into a gigantic vermin."[3] Notice that Kafka gives no context or explanation for this nightmarish metamorphosis; he simply states that it happened, and the rest of the story works out the implications of the metamorphosis. By merging the categories of literature and nightmare, fantasy, and narrative in this way, Kafka had an enormously liberating effect on writers, who could create any surrealistic situations and characters that they wanted to and blithely ignore the predictable objection, "But it's not realistic."

Whether directly or indirectly, Dylan benefited enormously from Kafka's heritage to twentieth-century writers, which often came out as black humor. Dylan's songs like "Motorpsycho Nightmare" and "Bob Dylan's 115th Dream" put a humorous spin on Kafkaesque situations, very much in the spirit of, and probably under the impact of, Stanley Kubrick's movie *Dr. Strangelove* (1964).

T.S. Eliot

With characteristic understatement that hides what he wants to hide, Dylan writes in *Chronicles*, "I liked T.S. Eliot. He was worth reading."[4] We will probably never know for sure just what Dylan read by Eliot, whether it was his poetry, his criticism, or both. Still, what attracts our attention to this revelation in *Chronicles* is that Dylan admits to "liking" a figure from high culture, especially one who differed from him in so many ways. Eliot was a studious WASP (white Anglo-Saxon protestant) from a wealthy St. Louis family, and Dylan is ... well, Dylan. Despite these obvious differences, Dylan shares attitudes with Eliot that are of vital importance and have to do with what it means to be a poet and with the poet's attitude toward the past.

Dylan famously refers in "Desolation Row" to Eliot as someone who was fighting with Ezra Pound. That putdown of Eliot as an elitist provides another thread from our songwriting Ariadne; among other things, it offers evidence that Eliot's accomplishments made Dylan the ephebe at least a little uncomfortable.

Although Dylan protests too much about it, he says again and again in *Chronicles* that he dislikes being a celebrity—or disliked being a celebrity in

3. Affinities with Franz Kafka, T.S. Eliot and Pablo Picasso 53

the 1960s, anyway. Eliot's essay "Tradition and the Individual Talent" shows that Eliot identified the isolating effect that Dylan disliked then about American celebrity culture.

> We dwell with satisfaction upon the poet's difference from his predecessors, especially his immediate predecessors; we endeavour to find something that can be isolated in order to be enjoyed.[5]

Eliot does not just object to what we would call celebrity worship; he offers, and insists on, actually, the possibility of interpreting relationships and interrelationships among poets and poems that coalesce into "an ideal order ... which is modified by the introduction of the new (the really new) work."[6]

In "Tradition and the Individual Talent," Eliot says that "the poet's mind is in fact a receptacle for seizing and storing up numberless feelings, phrases, images, which remain there until all the particles which can unite to form a new compound are present together."[7] In his essay "The Metaphysical Poets," Eliot puts it like this, densely and polysyllabically: "A degree of heterogeneity of material compelled into unity by the operation of the poet's mind is omnipresent in poetry."[8] Compare this principle to something that Dylan once told John Cohen and Happy Traum in the *Sing Out!* interview in November 1968. In response to the eternally recurring question of how he got ideas for his songs, he for once gave as honest an answer as he could:

> It's like this painter who lives around here—he paints an area of twenty miles, he paints bright story pictures. He might take a barn from twenty miles away, and hook it up with a brook right next door, then with a car ten miles away, and with the sky on a certain day, and the light on the trees from another certain day. A person passing by will be painted alongside someone ten miles away. And in the end he'll have this composite picture of something which you can't say exists in his mind. It's not that he started off willfully painting this picture from all his experiences.... That's more or less what I do.[9]

Whether he knew it or not—and I believe that he did know it—Dylan is paraphrasing here Eliot's reference to the poet's mind as a catalyst for "a degree of heterogeneous material." Although neither Eliot nor Dylan uses the painters' term "collage," an artistic work that combines heterogeneous elements from different sources, they both clearly think of a poet as a collage-maker. The artist is thus a synthesizer who gathers a variety of elements from different sources and creates a kind of unity among them. And this new unity constitutes the kind of artistic innovation that has appeared again and again in modern art.

If the poet synthesizes various elements into a whole, where do these elements come from? While some of them come from the present, it is apparent that both Dylan and Eliot, as different as they were, nonetheless shared a respect bordering on reverence for the past. It was as important to Eliot as it is to Dylan not to think of the past as separate from the present, something remote and distant. Both artists had an acute awareness of what one might call the living presence of the past.

Dylan says in *Chronicles* that when he went to the New York Public Library, he did so in order to read about the Civil War. For all the world, like a graduate student working on a dissertation, he "started reading articles in newspapers on microfilm from 1855 to about 1865 to see what daily life was like."[10] Dylan then writes three dense, impassioned pages about the Civil War in the present tense. The present tense gives us an essential clue; since Dylan was Dylan, the past came alive for him:

> The age that I was living in didn't resemble this age, but yet it did in some mysterious and *traditional* way. Not just a little bit, but a lot.... Back there, America was put on the cross, died and was resurrected. There was nothing synthetic about it. The godawful truth of that would be the all-encompassing template behind everything that I would write[11] (emphasis added).

Dylan's odd use of the word "traditional" here provides a thread that leads directly to Eliot. In "Tradition and the Individual Talent," Eliot gives the following well-known characteristic of tradition:

> Tradition ... involves ... the historical sense ... and the historical sense involves a perception, not only of the pastness of the past, but of its presence.... This historical sense, which is a sense of the timeless as well as of the temporal and of the timeless and of the temporal together, is what makes a writer traditional. And it is at the same time what makes a writer most acutely conscious of his place in time, of his contemporaneity.[12]

If Dylan did read "Tradition and the Individual Talent"—and, to repeat, I believe that he did—he did not just read Eliot and decide to become a traditional poet. Still, it seems likely, though, that he found a confirmation in Eliot for his eccentric sensibility, a precedent that helped him define himself to himself.

Eliot spoke of "the historical sense," a sense "of the timeless as well as of the temporal and of the timeless and of the temporal together." Here is how Dylan describes his historical sense in the early 1960s—and by implication today as well:

> The madly complicated modern world was something I took little interest in.... What was swinging, topical, and up to date for me was stuff like the Titanic sinking, the Galveston Flood, John Henry driving steel, John Hardy shooting a man on the West Virginia line.... This was the news that I considered, followed, and kept tabs on.[13]

Although Eliot took little interest, to use Dylan's phrase, in the *Titanic* sinking (which was actually news during Eliot's life) and the other events that Dylan mentions, he would have understood the sentiment and recognized Dylan's acute historical sense. Another way to describe the historical sense is that those who have it cannot distinguish between the past and the present. Hence Dylan "kept tabs on" the events from what others called the past.

These quotations show that Dylan did, and does, have a historical sense just in Eliot's sense of the phrase. They show that for him the past is just as real and just as immediate as the present. They make it very likely that he encountered the idea in Eliot's writing, which put into words something that he had vaguely sensed for a long time. I suspect that this is often the way influence works.

It is worth pausing here to notice how radical—how conceptually radical—the historical sense is in America. The Pilgrims who founded America came here to get away from the past, and, ever since, we Americans in one way or another have been telling each other that we "put the past behind us." The belief that we can, and should, put the past behind us informs a great deal about America, and surely gave Eliot a motivation to leave America for more traditional England. For Eliot, who remained unmoved by his own vernacular culture, America was a place of cultural marginality.

Oddly enough, even New York became increasingly a place of cultural marginality for Dylan as he matured, and people urged him to "get with it," "to live in the moment," and so forth. His estrangement from the "madly complicated modern world" of the present prompted him to leave New York for a more traditional city (Nashville) to do the most important thing in his life—record music.

What is more relevant for us is that since Eliot had something of the philosophy graduate student and professor in him, he articulated some of the key principles that inform Dylan's sensibility in ways that Dylan never could. In any case, it helps immensely in interpreting Dylan's songs to keep in mind that he had an acute, indeed agonizing, historical sense.

For an artist, history means tradition in the form of the great artists from the past. And if Dylan feels no real distinction between the past and the present, then his precursors press upon him until he comes to terms with them. In extreme cases, and great artists usually present us with extreme cases, artists feel no real distinction between their work and that of others. It all merges into a single continuum. Other people, who lack the historical sense and an awareness of the immediacy of tradition (and this includes most people who write about popular music), believe that when artists open their work to others by incorporating their images and themes, they are merely imitating. Like Eliot, Dylan did not believe this, and felt free to write against the work of his predecessors/precursors in a variety of ways. He had, and has, an intensely assimilative sensibility. What does this mean? And what does it mean to "write against" the work of one's predecessors?

The problematic issue in works that are written against other works is that the listeners, or readers as the case may be, have to know the original in order to contrast it with the new work and get the point. That is to say, people have to bring prior knowledge of the original to the new work in order to appreciate it. This requirement excludes many people, of course, which is why intertextuality occurs less frequently in popular culture than in high culture. Nevertheless, there are some works that we can reasonably expect everybody, more or less, to know, and one such work is the song "White Christmas." The fact that most people know "White Christmas," because it is played endlessly every Christmas season, gives a special poignancy to "Blue Christmas," a song that Billy Hayes and Jay Johnson wrote for Elvis. "Blue Christmas" uses intertextuality. It assumes that listeners know the Irvin Berlin/Bing Crosby classic. We can say, then, that "Blue Christmas" is written against "White Christmas," and becomes a more poignant song because of the contrast.

When ephebes pass from merely imitating their precursors to writing against their work in such a way that the new work forces upon us a different perception of the earlier work, then ephebes are beginning to work through their anxiety of influence. The juxtaposition of the old work and the new work then takes on something of the quality of the cutting contests that Louis Armstrong participated in while in New Orleans. It is a male contest for supremacy carried out through art.

More generally, though, writing against someone else's work means something like what Greenblatt says about Shakespeare, who was supposedly caught while poaching deer. "Throughout Shakespeare's career as a playwright he was a brilliant poacher—deftly entering into territory marked out by others, taking for himself what he wanted, and walking away with his prize under the keeper's nose."[14] When Dylan was not studying or going to classes at the University of Minnesota, he literally poached: he stole some records.[15] At the time he was young, unformed, and probably a little desperate. Still, the incident symbolizes something essential about his creative genius. Because he constantly juxtaposes his work with that of others, we gain greatly in understanding when we apply Eliot's ideas about tradition to his work.

If we examine the significance of tradition in the various arts, we realize that painters have usually had more historical sense than writers, if only because so many painters spent days and sometimes weeks sitting in drafty museums copying masterpieces. (This is no doubt one source of the attraction that painting holds for Dylan.) In this sense, Eliot was urging writers to become more like painters.

Before proceeding to the very large subject of Dylan and the visual arts, we need to deal with one other matter, namely the specific origin of intertextuality in Dylan's songs. What is at issue is the difference in the understanding of creativity that is implicit in folk culture and in high culture. Genuine folk art is usually anonymous, and its practitioners such as potters and weavers share motifs and images as a matter of course. As Todd Harvey has shown in detail in *The Formative Bob Dylan*, this is what Dylan did when he began writing songs. Thus, Dylan's "A Hard Rain's a-Gonna Fall" uses some images from the folk song "Lord Randall." The point is that Dylan continued to use themes and images from other works in his electric period as well. Then, however, he was using material from high culture, where the cultural assumption is that each work is different and unique. And he was no longer poaching. He was using quotations as an aesthetic strategy. He was audaciously opening his own work to that of various precursors and thus deliberately inviting comparisons between his work and theirs. He was using his work as a comment on theirs.

As we know, this practice is called "writing against the previous work." To write against an earlier work is to evoke it in order to subvert the work or—more generally—the cultural ambience from which it came. Edouard Manet's painting "Le Dejeuner sur l'Herbe" (1863) offers an instructive precedent for Dylan's use of sources. This painting, which shows two clothed men having lunch on the grass in the company of a nude woman shocked proper Parisians both because of its subject matter and also because it had deliberate analogies with "A Pastoral Concert" (1508), which is usually attributed to the Venetian painters Titian and Giorgione. This painting hung in the Louvre, so that Parisians would have known it well, and Manet audaciously invited them to compare it to his painting, and to think of them together. It is a prime example of what Eliot meant when he said that the really new work rearranges the ideal order of things. After "Le Dejeuner sur l'Herbe" it was no longer possible to think of "A Pastoral Concert" in the same way.

Manet was painting against Titian and/or Giorgione when he created "Le Dejeuner sur l'Herbe," which thus offers one of the earliest examples of what we have come to call "edgy" work. Edgy work is often off-putting and disturbing, and no one has ever created more edgy, off-putting, and disturbing great work than the artist with whom Dylan has profound, far-reaching affinities—Pablo Picasso.

Pablo Picasso

Dylan writes in *Chronicles*: "Picasso had fractured the art world and cracked it wide open. I wanted to be like that."[16] Although Dylan was fascinated with Woody Guthrie and even Ramblin' Jack Elliott for a while, he was just trying them on. Here for once we have the sincere voice of the mature Dylan looking back over his life and opening up to us for a moment by saying "I wanted to be like that." Let us pause to note the exceptional importance of this revelation. Dylan has never admitted to wanting to be like anybody else but Picasso. But then he did not have to want to be like Picasso, because he already *was* like Picasso. If Dylan read *Picasso's Picassos*, published the year he came to New York, he could also have found a preview of his life in David Duncan's characterization of Picasso as "a friend who has shared all others' innermost secrets and has been the pivot for many of their life, while himself always shielding dreams in the limitless preserves of a mind where no one else may tread."[17]

Dylan may have modeled himself on Picasso to some extent, but it is more than that. A series of analogies in their lives and work goes way beyond anything that Dylan could have planned, and suggests far-reaching elective affinities—affinities that suggest that we can productively think of each artists' work in terms of the other's. Before considering these affinities, though, it will be helpful to place Dylan's enthusiasm for Picasso in the context in which it arose—the New York art world of the 1960s.

Fortunately for Dylan, his first girlfriend in New York, Suze Rotolo, was Italian, and interested in art. She writes in in her thoughtful, revealing memoir *A Freewheelin' Time* that she introduced her prodigy of a boyfriend, who was still fresh from the provinces, to art, and especially to Picasso: "At the Museum of Modern Art, I took him to see Picasso's 'Guernica,' and other much-loved paintings...."[18] Subsequently, she refers to "leafing through" the 1962 Picasso book.[19] She has in mind *Picasso: An American Tribute* (edited by John Richardson). This was the catalog for a large, cooperative Picasso show divided among no less than nine different galleries. It ran from April 24 to May 19, 1962, and dominated the New York art world during Dylan's second spring in the city.

Picasso: An American Tribute seems to have affected Dylan profoundly, because it may well have inspired two of the most provocative lines in two of his greatest songs. It contains "The Fruit Dish," a major work of Synthetic Cubism from 1912. If ever there was a work in which "infinity goes up on trial" (as in "Visions of Johanna"), this is it. That was indeed the point of Cubism, that it renounced the infinite perspective that had dominated Western art since the Renaissance. Very much in the spirit of the modernist revolt against the Renaissance and all that it implies, Dylan gives Mona Lisa "the highway blues" in "Visions of Johanna."[20]

However, Dylan's fullest identification with Picasso, in which he merges their creative endeavors, comes in the song "Desolation Row," in the reference to rearranging faces. This line refers to Picasso's habit of rearranging the faces of the women whom he painted in the 1930s. *Picasso: An American Tribute* includes "The Flower Seller" (1937), who has both eyes on one side of her head, and there is a straight line from her forehead to the end of her nose. Picasso also rearranges the faces of his models in other paintings reproduced in the book, such as "Girl with Rooster" (1938) and "Dora Maar" (1939).

3. Affinities with Franz Kafka, T. S. Eliot and Pablo Picasso

Dylan also identified with circus performers in the 1960s, telling one interviewer, "I'm an acrobat."[21] More specifically, during his press conference on December 3, 1965, when he answered "Rimbaud, I guess," to the question, "What poets do you dig?," he continued, "W. C. Fields, the family, you know, the trapeze family in the circus…."[22] Not just any trapeze family, but "the trapeze family in the circus." He is referring here to Picasso's famous painting "The Saltimbanques Family" (1905).

Dylan could have seen this haunting painting in the National Gallery in Washington, or—more likely—he saw one of the many reproductions in books or in poster format. It depicts a family in circus outfits; a man, a fat clown, three children, and a mysterious woman who sits to the side. Earlier painters who had depicted jugglers and clowns showed them in the context of the circus; this is not true of Picasso. His circus family seems to be in the middle of a desert, with no signs of habitation anywhere. In the first line of the third stanza of "Like a Rolling Stone" Dylan uses such recurring images of Picasso's Rose Period as jugglers and clowns to represent the world of color and movement that Miss Lonely missed out on.

More generally, *Picasso: An American Tribute* belonged to a group of Picasso books that were published in New York in the late 1950s and early 1960s. These books include other Picasso books by David Douglas Duncan: *The Private World of Pablo Picasso* and *Picasso's Picassos*. Two major Picasso books that came out in 1962 were Anthony Blunt's *Picasso: The Formative Years: A Study of His Sources* and Rudolf Arnheim's book about Suze Rotolo's favorite painting, *Picasso's "Guernica": The Genesis of a Painting*. And in 1964, Hans Jaffe published his *Pablo Picasso* and Fernande Olivier published her memoir, *Picasso and His Friends*. Clearly, anybody who was interested in art had plenty of Picasso paintings to look at in New York's galleries and museums, and plenty of opportunities to read about him.

These exhibits and books enhanced Picasso's already great reputation even more in the New York art world, and a statement by Sally Ganz about her late husband, Victor Ganz, who was a major collector at the time, indicates as much. "He thought that most of contemporary art derived in one way or another from Picasso, that Picasso was a sort of father figure for most of the artists of the time."[23] As readers of Harold Bloom, we know to substitute "precursor" for "father figure" in this statement.

As a matter of fact, Picasso was the great precursor for most postwar painters, like Jasper Johns, who "accepted Picasso as the premier painter of the time, and based his understanding of painting on Picasso's pictures."[24] Roy Lichtenstein, for example, was so intimidated by Picasso that he was paralyzed by him. When Lichtenstein was in Paris after the war, he went to the building in which Picasso's studio was located, but could not bring himself to enter it.[25] (Very much the same thing happened with Dylan and Elvis. In

2009 Dylan admitted to Douglas Brinkley, "I didn't meet Elvis because I didn't want to meet Elvis."[26])

Dylan and Lichtenstein figured out a typically American swerve from European high culture that enabled them to deal with Picasso; they did the same thing more or less at the same time. They both thought that it would be possible to democratize Picasso by making his work a part of everyday life. In August of 1965, Dylan told Nora Ephron and Susan Edmiston, "Just think how many people would feel really great if they could see a Picasso in their daily diner."[27] In 1967, Lichtenstein told an interviewer from *Artforum* that "a Picasso has become a kind of popular object—one has the feeling that there should be a reproduction of a Picasso in every home."[28] Lichtenstein's and Dylan's strikingly similar comments both express a felt need at the time to assimilate Picasso into an American context, but they may also have a common source in Tom Wesselman's "Still Life #30," from 1963. It shows a kitchen table with groceries, a painted window with a plastic flower, a real refrigerator door, replicas of 7-UP bottles—and on the wall there is a reproduction of Picasso's 1927 painting, "Seated Woman."[29] Still earlier than Wesselman's assimilation of Picasso into an American private space is the use of Picasso's "Three Musicians" on the wall of the apartment in the movie *The Apartment* (1960), which starred Jack Lemon and Shirley McLaine. The Jack Lemon character does not mention or even look at the painting, and no one in the film has any interest in art, so this may have been simply a whim on the part of the art director. Still, I cite it here as a sign of the times.

The similarities between Dylan and Lichtenstein deserve more detailed commentary than I can give them here. It must suffice to mention that these two Jewish artists, who probably lived within a few blocks of each other in Greenwich Village in the early 1960s, both profited greatly from their study of Picasso. In doing so, they joined the long tradition in which American artists benefited from exposure to European art. However, Dylan and Lichtenstein both responded to Picasso and the European high art tradition that he represented by synthesizing them with a democratic style taken from what was then called "mass culture." Thus, Dylan took up the electric guitar to accompany his innovative lyrics, which smacked of the French Symbolists, and Lichtenstein adopted the visual style of comic books for reworking Picasso's images. For example, Lichtenstein's painting "Femme au chapeau" (1962) applies the flat tones of a comic book style to Picasso's "Woman in Gray" (1942).[30]

And, to use one of his phrases, Dylan "kept tabs" on the art world at the time, as he acknowledges in *Chronicles*.[31] Dylan's reference in "It's Alright Ma, I'm Only Bleeding" to debates about the reality of the world comes directly from the art world of the 1960s in which artists like Tom Wesselman, Jim Dine, and Robert Rauschenberg were introducing everyday objects into their paintings.

Dylan's songs have various affinities with the Pop Art of the 1960s. Pop Art also affected the titles of Dylan's songs, most obviously in "I Shall Be Free, No. 10." This use of a number in a title is taken from the artists' practice of indicating a painting's position in a series of paintings on a particular theme, as in Tom Wesselman's "Great American Nude, No. 10" from 1961. In the *Blonde on Blonde* album, Dylan acquired a habit of using nonsensical adverbs in song titles, such as "Queen Jane Approximately," a habit that probably comes from similar nonsensical titles that the Surrealists gave to their works, such as Marcel Duchamp's "The Bride Stripped Bare by Her Bachelors, Even." Finally, the odd title of *Blonde on Blonde* seems to be Dylan's wordplay on the painting of Ad Reinhardt, who specialized in black on black paintings at the time. Reinhardt's "Abstract Painting, Black" from 1960–61 is an example. Reinhardt had a show called "Paintings, Black, 1953–65" at the Betty Parsons Gallery, as well as a major show at the Jewish Museum in 1966–67.

Amid this swirl of activity around Picasso and modern art, at a time when Dylan was especially receptive to artistic trends, the most important book about art that he ever read appeared. It was the fifth of the key books that he read during his first years in New York, and it came into his hands from a most trustworthy source, Suze Rotolo. In 1964 she went to Perugia, Italy, to study art, and here is her account of something that happened while she was there:

> While in Italy I read Françoise Gilot's memoir *Life with Picasso*. I expected to learn about Picasso, an artist I love, but instead the book turned into something different. It made me think about Bob. I forgot all about Picasso. I felt I was reading a book of revelations, lessons, warnings. Even though Picasso was a lot older man than Bob and had experienced a lot more, their personalities were so similar that it was astounding.[32]

Rotolo witnessed the creation of Bob Dylan the superstar as no one else, not even Joan Baez, had. We recall it was to her that he confided, after he signed with Columbia, that he had always known that he was "going to be big." If she found the similarities in the personalities of Picasso and the charismatic young artist she was in love with "astounding," then it would be impossible to imagine that she did not write to him and urge him to read the book for himself. In all probability, this is what happened. To use a phrase from Dylan again, this book is surely one that was "really something."

To understand *Life with Picasso*, and its meaning for Dylan, we need to know a little about Françoise Gilot, the woman who wrote it. She was born in 1921, and met Picasso in 1942 during the German occupation of Paris. She was 21, and he was 61. Her relationship with Picasso lasted for nine years, from 1944 to 1953. She bore him two children, Claude and Paloma, the famous designer. Perhaps because she was also a painter, Picasso spoke more openly to her about his work than to anyone else, so *Life with Picasso* offers unique insights into the thought processes of a genius.

Let us imagine what it might have been like for the young Dylan, with his Columbia contract in hand, sensing that he was on the verge of greatness, to sit in his third-floor room at 161 W. Fourth Street and read this remarkable book. What he found in it led him to think about Picasso, but not as a threatening precursor. Dylan's own paintings show no effects of Picasso's work at all.[33] Picasso worked in a different medium, after all, so he served as something like a mentor or a role model. Dylan's father was incapable of mentoring him, and Dylan never had and was incapable of having the kind of close friendship with a fellow artist that Picasso had with Matisse. Instead, Picasso was an imaginary friend, mentor, and role model. In some ways, Picasso was the only close male companion that Dylan ever had.

Consider this passage, for example. One day, Picasso was explaining to Gilot how he worked with still life paintings, and said something that must have jumped off the page at Dylan: "Painting is poetry and is always written in verse with plastic rhymes, never in prose."[34] It must have come as a revelation to Dylan that Picasso identified painting with poetry. In fact, Picasso had an interest in and respect for poetry that is highly unusual for a painter. He had a close friendship with the poet Paul Eluard, and the Yale Art Gallery had an exhibit, "Picasso and the Allure of Language," in 2009, which explored his relationships with writers and the ways in which language affected his work.

Dylan found in Picasso both a justification to try his poet's hand at painting, and to take seriously the interrelationships between words and images. He may well have been thinking of Picasso when, during the *Playboy* interview, he told Nat Hentoff that "contrary to what some scary people think, I don't play with a band now for any kind of propaganda-type or commercial-type reasons. It's just that my songs are pictures and the band makes the sound of the pictures."[35]

And how did Picasso understand the function of painting? He told Gilot that, when he discovered the African statues in the Trocadero Museum, he realized that "painting isn't an aesthetic operation; it's a form of magic designed as a mediator between this strange, hostile world and us, a way of seizing power by giving form to our terrors as well as to our desires. When I came to that realization, I knew that I had found my way."[36] Thus, Picasso thought of painting as more than painting, as a force. With Picasso in mind, we can think of "Desolation Row" as a form of musical magic that creates a place under threat by hostile real estate agents, a place that gives form to our terrors, and also offers refuge from them.

Gilot was astonished to find that Picasso could and would paint for three or four hours at a time, and she asked him if he got tired. "'No,' he said. 'That's why painters live so long. While I work I leave my body outside the door, the way Moslems take off their shoes before entering the mosque.'"[37] That is to say, when Picasso painted, he was not just applying paint to canvas; when he was creating, he had what we could now call an out-of-body experience.

And we have some evidence that Dylan also wrote his songs in a way that he did not and could not control. We learn in *And a Voice to Sing With* that Joan Baez watched him write, sensing that he had gone to a place where she could not follow him. She addresses him directly as she recalls the time when they were living together in Carmel, "You stood at the big kitchen windows with your typewriter perched on top of a waist-high adobe structure and faced the hills."[38] And although Dylan does not refer to any out-of-body experiences when he was creating, he does acknowledge that when he was performing, he was not just plucking guitar strings. He says, "It was like parts of my psyche were being communicated to *by angels*"[39] (emphasis added).

As usual with Dylan, it is the anomalies that create important markers. Nowhere else in *Chronicles* does Dylan refer to angels, so we can take him seriously here. The exceptional, deliberate obfuscation of this passage indicates that he creates something like a NO TRESPASSING sign. He is willing to tell us that there is something vital here, but he is not willing to tell us any more about it.

However, if we read this passage with Picasso's statements about painting in mind, we can conclude that for Dylan, as for Picasso, the creative act operated in a way that closely resembles the psychic practice of channeling. Dylan cannot control creativity any more than Picasso ever could, and both of them could create because they were connected to something beyond themselves. Obviously, then, there is, and was, no point in asking them about the meaning of what they did.

Both Gilot and Baez express profound empathy for the great men whom they loved, and who hurt them so badly. They both realize that although the men's gifts isolate them, everybody around them wants a part of them. Gilot muses about Picasso that "he was the most solitary of men within that inner world that shut him off from the army of admirers and sycophants that surrounded him."[40] Baez blends sympathy and honesty when she addresses Dylan:

> Sometimes I think that you pulled away from all reality on that English tour of spring 1965. You were mantled with praise, sought after by hysterical fans, appealed to by liberals, intellectuals, politicians, the press, and genuinely adored by fools like me, and I don't think you ever really recuperated.[41]

Great achievements bring fame, and fame has its own challenges, as Picasso knew, and as Dylan was about to find out. Picasso helped prepare him for those challenges, insofar as anybody could.

One of the challenges of fame is dealing with clueless interviewers who do not, and cannot, understand the mysteries of creativity, and who mostly want sensational pull quotes that will sell magazines and newspapers. When Bobby Zimmerman was still a toddler, Picasso said something that informs

Dylan's attitude toward interviewers in the 1960s and 1970s, and explains his bizarre non-answers to nonsensical questions. Picasso once told someone, "You must not always believe what I say. Questions tempt you to tell lies, particularly when there is no answer."[42] Notice the last phrase: "Particularly when there is no answer." Although it is true that Picasso and Dylan sometimes wanted to cover their creative tracks for reasons of their own, it is also true that they were as baffled by the creative process as anybody else. And when they realized that interviewers did not want to hear this ultimate truth about something that was so precious to them, they felt free to make things up. And that is what they did. Dylan certainly did. It is enough to flip through the pages of *Bob Dylan: The Essential Interviews* to confirm that.

When Rotolo writes that she sensed "revelations, lessons, warnings" in *Life with Picasso*, she probably has two passages in mind, both of which deal with that great man's attitudes toward women. Gilot records that Picasso once told her, "For me, there are only two kinds of women—goddesses and doormats."[43] Like Gilot, both Rotolo and Baez had the gut-wrenching experience of being moved from the first category to the second. The second passage contains a warning to Gilot that came from her friend Genevieve. "'You're headed for a catastrophe,' she said. I told her she was probably right but I felt it was the kind of catastrophe I didn't want to avoid."[44] Rotolo had this warning, at least, although she chose not to heed it, as Gilot had not; Baez had no warning at all.

The preceding discussion has made it clear that Dylan and Picasso have a remarkable series of affinities. Moreover, it is very likely that when Dylan read *Life with Picasso* it clarified his intuitive sense for the form that his life would take. The affinities between Dylan and Picasso have such density that only a series of detailed templates can do justice to them. The following list shows just how detailed these affinities are:

1. *A genius is born in circumstances that favor creativity.*

Pablo Ruíz y Picasso was born an only child on October 25, 1881, in Malaga, Spain. His father, an art teacher, lost his job, and moved the family first to Coruña in the year of his birth, and then to Barcelona in 1885.

Robert Allen Zimmerman was born on May 24, 1941, in Duluth, Minnesota. He is a Jew, a first-born, and born in an area of cultural marginality.

2. *He has the kind of problematic relationship with his father that often fosters creativity.*

Dylan's father and Picasso's father both lost their jobs, and forced their families to move at a time when this made a deep impression on their sensitive sons. Picasso's father was an art teacher, so the son had a special interest in surpassing his father. Picasso claimed that his father asked him to finish a drawing of a pigeon by doing the feet; he said that he did this so well that his father gave up painting. John Richardson, Picasso's biographer, comments that "Pablo's love for his father evidently had a patricidal tinge to it."[45]

Dylan's father was stricken with polio in 1946 and lost his job. Moreover, there is something odd and unresolved in Dylan's relationship with his father, and we will probably never know what it was. We recall that he says something in *Chronicles* that he cannot possibly believe: "My father was the best man in the world and probably worth a hundred of me, but he didn't understand me."[46] One does not have to be a psychologist to sense that Dylan is overcompensating, and thus hiding something hostile in that absurd phrase "the best man in the world."

3. *He feels the call of his art at an early age.*

Picasso's first surviving drawing was done in 1890, when he was nine. And he continued drawing and painting for the rest of his life, of course. He had his first serious exhibition in Barcelona at the age of 18.[47]

Bobby Zimmerman was a hit when he sang at a family party in 1946 at the age of five. People (other than his parents) said that he would be famous. When he sang "Rock and Roll is Here to Stay" in the Hibbing high school auditorium on February 6, 1958, the principal turned off the microphone,[48] thus anticipating what Pete Seeger would want to do that memorable night only seven years later at Newport in 1965.

When Bobby Zimmerman enrolled at the University of Minnesota in 1959, but did not go to class, he became interested in folk music for the first time and realized what his future would be. He made some very early recordings in the fall of 1960 and told his dumbfounded girlfriend at the time that the Library of Congress would be interested in them.[49] "I needed to play for people and all the time," Dylan says in *Chronicles*.[50] He needed to play for people as Picasso needed to create art; it was all either of them ever cared about, or ever wanted to do.

4. *He leaves a provincial capital for the big city when he is about 19 years old.*

Picasso arrived in Paris in October of 1900, just before his nineteenth birthday. He had done as much as he could in Barcelona. Dylan left Minneapolis, and arrived in New York on January 24, 1961, four months before his twentieth birthday.

5. *After a false start or two, he finds early success.*

Although Picasso remained poor in the early years in Paris, a dealer offered him a contract soon after his arrival.[51] Dylan signed a contract with Columbia Records nine months after arriving in New York.

6. *His early work has originality, but remains within the bounds of accepted conventions. Earlier works by established artists are points of departure.*

Picasso's first major work in Paris was "Moulin de la Galette" (1900), and Picasso's biographer says that in it Picasso "challenged" Renoir and Toulouse-Lautrec, who had painted the same scene. His Blue Period began around the middle of 1901 and lasted a little over three years. As he gained confidence, his colors warmed and his work entered the Rose Period, which lasted roughly from 1904 to 1906.

Dylan's early songs in New York, such as the anthemic "Blowin' in the Wind," sounded like the songs that the folkies were used to, such as Guthrie's "This Land Is Your Land," but with richer imagery.

7. *At about the age of 25 he creates a major Work that defines a cultural era.*

Picasso's twenty-fifth birthday was on October 19, 1906, and by late summer of 1907, he realized that he had done as much as he could on "Les Demoiselles d'Avignon."

Dylan recorded "Like a Rolling Stone" on June 25, 1965, about a month after his twenty-fourth birthday on May 24, 1965.

8. *The Work has the effect of an exorcism.*

Richardson says that Picasso's "'Demoiselles' was an exorcism of more than private demons; it was also an exorcism of traditional concepts of 'ideal beauty.'"[52] In "Like a Rolling Stone" the singer calls on Miss Lonely to leave her false life in a private school and to begin an authentic (i.e., democratic) life symbolized by the street.

9. *He creates the Work at least in part as a way of working out his anxiety of influence and completing the Work leaves the artist shaken, and leads to rejection by admirers.*

Picasso was painting against El Greco's "Apocalyptic Vision" (1608–14).[53] Picasso's dealer Daniel-Henry Kahnweiler described Picasso's state after finishing "Les Demoiselles," saying that to say "a short period of exhaustion followed [the 'Demoiselles'] is an understatement. Picasso suffered from a terrible spiritual isolation. There was nobody with whom he could share the exaltation and anguish of being way ahead of his time."[54] Richardson writes:

> Work on the "Demoiselles" condemned the twenty-five-year-old Picasso to a life of seclusion. Although friends sympathized with his aspirations, none of them was capable of understanding the pictorial form that these aspirations took. When he allowed Salmon, Apollinaire and Jacob to see the painting, they were baffled and took refuge in embarrassed silence, or the faintest of praise.[55]

Reactions such as these from sophisticated Parisians who were Picasso's closest friends help explain why "Les Demoiselles" wasn't exhibited in public until 1916.

Dylan was singing against Elvis's "Hound Dog." In 1999, a British fan recalled seeing Dylan at the stage door after he sang "Like a Rolling Stone" on stage: "He looked as if he'd been in a car crash—somebody totally shocked."[56] When Dylan performed "Like a Rolling Stone" at Newport in 1965, it drove Peter Seeger to hysteria. When he and The Hawks took the song on tour that year, his former fans in the audience did not greet it with silence or the faintest of praise. They greeted it with boos and jeers and cries of "Judas."

10. *The Work represents a synthesis of a well-known classic in his field and African art.*

Picasso once told the photographer Brassaï that Cézanne "was [his] one and only master."[57] Picasso was overwhelmed by Cézanne's "Large Bathers" at the Salon d'Automne in 1906, and that masterpiece gave him the immediate impetus to begin "Les Demoiselles." Yet it is the angular, subhuman faces of the women in "Les Demoiselles" that make it so edgy and challenging, even today. These faces derive from the faces of the African statues that Picasso first saw in the Trocadero Museum, and then bought to keep in his studio.

What Cézanne was to Picasso, Elvis was to Dylan. "Les Demoiselles" amounted to a response, a very complex response to be sure, to the "Large Bathers," just as "Like a Rolling Stone" amounted to a response to "Hound Dog." We recall that Baez says that when she met him, Dylan and his friends said that he was going to be "bigger than Elvis Presley."[58] By 1965, the rivalry that gave rise to Dylan's need to overcome Elvis had been germinating for ten years. Like Picasso, Dylan hid his tracks very well. But the tracks are there if you know where to seek them.

Although Elvis never experienced any perceptible anxiety of influence, he did pay tribute to Muddy Waters, whose electric blues songs, like "Got My Mojo Working," provided a source for Elvis, Chuck Berry, and many other late rock stars.

11. *He can maintain a viable career despite wide-spread rejection of the Work because of market segmentation.*

In the book *Making Modernism: Picasso and the Creation of the Market for Twentieth-Century Art*, Michael Fitzgerald shows the far-reaching artistic importance of what he calls "the aesthetic and financial confluence of the avant-garde and the mainstream that had begun by the First World War."[59] Fitzgerald's larger point is that the Parisian art market before World War I had various segments. A large part of it preferred the kind of slick salon painting that Picasso detested, of course. But innovative, even disturbing, modern art was subsidized in the early twentieth century by members of the *haute bourgeoisie* as far apart in location as Sergey Shchukin in Moscow and Eusebi Guell in Barcelona.

The comparable market segmentation for American popular music in the 1960s occurred as a matter of demographics, not income. To understand this segmentation, we can consider two groups—people born at the beginning of the baby boom, in 1947–8, and those born in the middle of it, in 1953–54. The first group was 20 in 1966–7; it had experienced the ecstasy of "Beatlemania," and then matured as the Beatles matured. The second group was 14 in 1968, and this meant that it entered adolescence at a time of profoundly disorienting social change. Unsure of themselves, as 14-year-olds notoriously are, and even more unsure of the world around them, they wanted music that acknowledged the times, like Sonny and Cher's "The Beat Goes On" and The Monkees' "Pleasant Valley Sunday," but which did not frighten or disorient them. To borrow a term from Malcolm Gladwell, "Like a Rolling Stone" marked the tipping point between these two groups.

At just over six minutes, "Like a Rolling Stone" was long—shockingly long for its time. It is a big song, as "Les Demoiselles" is a big painting. The song caused consternation in Columbia's marketing department, and although Columbia did release it as a single and got some AM airtime, it really belonged on an album, like the rest of Dylan's work in the mid- and late 1960s. The larger point is that those baby boomers born in 1946–7 made the transition with Dylan to the greater length and greater freedom to innovate that 33 1/3 rpm albums (the usual format for classical music at the time) allowed. The baby boomers born in 1953–4 did not make this transition, and formed the audience for Motown groups, for example. At a time when college kids wanted ecstasy, Motown offered them entertainment—great entertainment, to be sure, but entertainment nevertheless. At a time when the world was threatening to go out of control, the college-aged youth who constituted the primary audience for rock and roll wanted music and performers that also threatened to go out of control—to "test the limits of reality," as Jim Morrison once put it. "Like a Rolling Stone" created a line of demarcation between these two groups, as "Les Demoiselles d'Avignon" did in its time.

12. *A shrewd Jewish businessman guides his career.*

Picasso signed a representation agreement with Daniel-Henry Kahnweiler in 1912, and "except for a rift of ten years or so (during and after World War I) their association, which brought them so much glory and fortune, would last until Picasso's death."[60]

Dylan's relationship with Albert Grossman ended badly, with legal charges and counter-charges, in 1981. Still, "the business relationship between Bob and Albert Grossman is a key element in Bob's career. Some believe that, without Grossman, Bob would never have become an international star. 'Whatever was wrong with Albert, he believed in Bob, he really did,' says [Dave] Van Ronk."[61] By signing with Albert, and then marrying Sara, Dylan created a situation in which his closest professional and social relationships were with the kinds of people he was most familiar with—Jews.

13. *Creating the Work makes it possible for him to create during the next several years a series of works that revolutionize both his field and modern culture in general.*

Understanding the comparable historical significance of "Les Demoiselles" and "Like a Rolling Stone" also makes it possible to understand the

3. Affinities with Franz Kafka, T. S. Eliot and Pablo Picasso 69

overall configuration of their creators' careers. In the early years of Picasso's stay in Paris, usually called his Blue and Rose periods, Picasso used the colors and images of Post-Impressionism to create paintings that showed the alienation of modern life, often using circus performers as his subjects.

If we omit Dylan's first album as having mostly historical interest today, his first phase in New York, which corresponds to Picasso's Blue and Rose periods, consists of his first two major albums, *The Free Wheelin' Bob Dylan* (1963) and *The Times They Are a-Changin'* (1964). On these albums, Dylan performs the songs more or less in the style of other folksingers of the time.

After Picasso synthesized harsh angularity and non-representational colors in "Les Demoiselles," he could not return to his earlier style. Although no one saw "Les Demoiselles" in public until 1916, the effects of it showed up in Picasso's work that people did see, and that Kahnweiler did buy. The style that he and Braque created in 1908–10 has of course come to be called Cubism because it tends to present objects as geometric forms, although objects that defy three-dimensional space. Because he was so concerned with form, Picasso suppressed color in these paintings, using a limited palette of grays and browns, as in "Man with Mandolin" (1911).

Dylan's album *Highway 61 Revisited* corresponds well enough to this phrase of Picasso's cubism. It begins with "Like a Rolling Stone," which shocked people all over the world, and includes the title song, "Highway 61 Revisited." Both songs make connections between the past and the present.

Once he had assimilated the experiments with form, Picasso moved on to what is now called Synthetic Cubism, in which color makes a dramatic reappearance. It is often said that "Still Life with Chair-Caning" (1911–12) began this new phase. This painting brings in color and texture in an odd way by including oilcloth painted to look like chair caning. Picasso pasted it onto the canvas to create a startling effect.

Although "Desolation Row" appears on *Highway 61 Revisited*, it corresponds to Synthetic Cubism in its use of outside materials. By including famous people such as Einstein and Casanova in the song, Dylan also brings in their historical associations as well.

14. *He has a relationship with a woman who is also an artist in his field and later rejects her in a humiliating way.*

Françoise Gilot, another painter, was to Picasso as Joan Baez, another singer, was to Dylan. After Picasso turned 70 in 1951, he became obsessed with death and old age. He turned on Gilot, and said things to her like, "You're a monster, the lowest form of human life. You see how your mere presence is enough to make me ill? If I see any more of you I'll die."[62] After she moved out of La Galloise, the house that she had shared with Picasso, he removed all her books, paintings, and personal objects. She never saw them again.

Dylan invited Baez to come with him on the tour of England in 1965, and then tormented her by refusing to ask her to sing with him. Baez closes her chapter about him with the following anecdote:

> Having bought him a dark blue Vyella shirt, with great trepidation, I went unannounced and uninvited to knock at his door. It was answered by Sara, whom I'd never seen before and who had been flown in to look after Bob. Everyone had carefully avoided telling me that she was there. She took the package from me with a patient and quizzical look on her lovely face, blinked her massive black eyes, thanked me softly, and shut the door.[63]

It takes a generous spirit indeed to characterize one's victorious rival as someone "who had been flown in to look after Bob."

15. *His rejection of the woman is related to a stylistic change in his work.*

Picasso often marked a new phase in his art by taking up with a new woman. The interrelationships between his women and his work offer too much complexity for detailed consideration here, so it must suffice to mention one quotation. He once commented to Gilot, "If you knew how Marie-Therese suffered when I began making portraits of Dora Maar...."[64]

In 1962–3, Baez was both Dylan's lover and his mentor, very much as Rotolo had been. (She and Rotolo overlapped for a certain period.) Baez brought him along on her tours, and introduced him on stage. In the movies and photographs taken at the 1963 Newport Folk Festival, she glows with happiness when she is with him.[65] For her, this relationship combined the two great passions of her life, folk music and political activism, and it must have seemed like a dream come true. However, in ways that neither of them could have understood at the time, their relationship was linked to the acoustic guitars that they both played, and when Dylan changed from the acoustic guitar to the electric guitar, it signaled the permanent end of their connection as lovers and the temporary end of their collaboration as singers.[66]

16. *The woman writes a book that contains important revelations about the way he creates and thinks.*

Gilot's *Life with Picasso* anticipates Baez's *And a Voice to Sing With*.

17. *After creating an astonishing series of innovative works that establish an enduring reputation, he returns to a classical style as a way of assimilating what he has done.*

No artists can innovate indefinitely, not even Pablo Picasso and Bob Dylan. Eventually even innovation becomes a goal in itself, and does not serve the artist well. After Cubism and Synthetic Cubism, Picasso returned to a representational style in his Classical Period, usually considered to fall between 1917 and 1923. As is usual with Picasso, this change of style was associated with a new woman. In this case, it was Olga Khokhlova, his Russian-born first wife. To look at his Art Deco–like portrait of her done in 1917, you would never know that the same artist had painted "Les Demoiselles."

The Dylan album that corresponds to Picasso's portrait of Olga is *Nashville Skyline*. Stylistically, it amounts to a return to his folk period in that he plays acoustic guitar and avoids the rowdy style of, say, "Rainy Day Women #12 & 35." He also avoids the intertextuality of "Desolation Row" in the very accessible songs on the album. It is no wonder that the sweet, sexy "Lay Lady Lay" from *Nashville Skyline* is the song most people think of in connection with Dylan after "Blowin' in the Wind."

To recapitulate, this chapter has examined Dylan's connections with, and use of, European High Modernism in the persons of three of its most important representatives. It is now possible to understand his artistic genealogy as consisting of two general elements. On one hand, it is obvious that he responded to and benefited from the American popular culture that he grew up with in Hibbing; more than anyone else, that meant Hank Williams and Elvis Presley. Their work constituted more than a way station in his evolution, as Woody Guthrie's songs did. It entered his consciousness and stayed there, informing his songs in a variety of ways.

The revelations of *Chronicles*, as well as the discussions of this chapter make it apparent that during the time he spent in New York in the 1960s, he gradually combined American popular culture with European high culture. If American popular culture means primarily music, one of the performing arts, then European high culture meant primarily literature and painting, two presentational arts. Artists write and paint in private, and they present the results in public. As Dylan became ever more famous, he increasingly needed privacy and seclusion, and painting in particular took on ever greater appeal for him.

Here, then, is Bob Dylan's artistic genealogy. From European literature, it is Franz Kafka and T.S. Eliot; from American popular culture, it is Hank Williams and Elvis Presley; and from European painting, it is Marc Chagall and Pablo Picasso. This genealogy features intriguing sets of cultural relationships, and their meaning deserves some discussion here.

The most basic of these relationships is the one between the past and the present, and we know how Dylan had, and has, what Eliot called a "historical sense," a sensibility that connects the past and the present in a seamless whole. As a result, the works of dead artists are just as alive and relevant and contemporary as those of living artists.

And then there is the relationship between America and Europe, which Americans usually perceive as the relationship between high culture and popular culture. Dylan values the private arts of writing and painting, which represent for him European high culture. In assimilating high culture, Dylan was rebelling against Main Street, in Hibbing and elsewhere, just as much as taking up the electric guitar was rebelling against the folkies. In both cases his creative intuition kept reaching out until it found limitations. And since Dylan is who he is, his genius kept driving him to transcend those limitations.

Just as his protean sensibility accepted both the past and the present as equally relevant, it also accepted high culture and popular culture as equally meaningful. For him, American popular culture meant the performing arts—music and movies, of course. Moreover, the preceding discussions have shown that he relied, consciously or subconsciously, on the narrative structure of Hollywood movies for an understanding of the way gender roles were affected by the relationship between democracy and elitism.

The previous chapters show that in the most general sense Dylan was, and is, a synthesizer. He synthesized folk music and rock and roll; high culture and popular culture; European culture and American culture. Much of the negative reaction to his work has therefore come from people who want to maintain the autonomy of the particular culture. For Dylan, synthesis and creativity are interchangeable, as they were for Picasso and Eliot.

These conclusions make it possible to find other artists who have significant affinities with Dylan. Duke Ellington is also a major composer and a Medal of Freedom winner, who also had a record of sustained creativity at the highest level for a very long time. He synthesized high culture and American popular culture and was acutely sensitive to the achievements of European and world culture. His career resembles Dylan's, although his style does not. Take away Ellington's band and give him a guitar instead of a piano, and you have somebody very much like Dylan.

Section II: Songs and Songwriting

4

Songs of Transcendence
Highway 61 Revisited *and* Blonde on Blonde

Dylan says in a passage from *Chronicles* that he headed for New York from "the frostbitten North Country, a little corner of the earth where the dark frozen woods and icy roads didn't faze me. I could transcend the limitations."[1] He says that he could transcend the limitations of geography because he was a "visionary." Significantly, he uses the same verb when describing what first attracted him to folk music: "Folk songs transcended the immediate culture."[2] By using "transcend" in these two highly significant contexts, Dylan as Ariadne gives us a key insight into his masterpieces of the 1960s. This chapter will show that his visionary imagination produced a trilogy of songs united by the theme of transcendence: "Mr. Tambourine Man," "Desolation Row," and "Visions of Johanna." These songs have a remarkably consistent pattern when we think of them as thesis, antithesis, and synthesis. It is only a moderate exaggeration to say that everything that he wrote before those three songs led up to them, and that everything that he wrote after them followed them in one way or another. This generalization includes "Sad-Eyed Lady of the Lowlands," which came to him with great urgency as a kind of coda to this trilogy. Table 1 shows the chronology of the relevant songs, and it helps us to understand the potential thematic commonalities when we realize that these songs were recorded within a period of about 20 months.

Table 1. Chronology of Songs

Title of Song	Album of First Release	Date of Recording
"Chimes of Freedom"	*Another Side of Bob Dylan*	June 8, 1965
"My Back Pages"	*Another Side of Bob Dylan*	June 9, 1964
"Bob Dylan's 115th Dream"	*Bringing It All Back Home*	January 13, 1965
"Mr. Tambourine Man"	*Bringing It All Back Home*	June 9, 1964
"Gates of Eden"	*Bringing It All Back Home*	January 15, 1965
"It's Alright Ma, I'm Only Bleeding"	*Bringing It All Back Home*	January 15, 1965
"Like a Rolling Stone"	*Highway 61 Revisited*	June 15, 1965
"Desolation Row"	*Highway 61 Revisited*	July 29, 1965
"Ballad of a Thin Man"	*Highway 61 Revisited*	August 2, 1965
"Just Like Tom Thumb's Blues"	*Highway 61 Revisited*	August 2, 1965
"Visions of Johanna"	*Blonde on Blonde*	November 10, 1965
"Sad-Eyed Lady of the Lowlands"	*Blonde on Blonde*	February 15, 1966

The recording dates are from Heylin's *Revolution in the Air: The Songs of Bob Dylan.*

Before discussing "Mr. Tambourine Man," the first song in the trilogy, we need to take up again the issue of the impact of Marshall McLuhan's *Understanding Media* on Dylan. If Dylan announced change in "The Times They Are a-Changin'," in *Understanding Media* McLuhan asserted, "Rapidly, we approach the final phase of the extensions of man—the technological simulation of consciousness...."[3] What mattered for Dylan is that McLuhan defined the order that was changing differently from the way social activists of the 1960s defined it. For McLuhan, it was the old visual, literate one-thing-at-a-time order that was giving way to what he called an "electrically configured" world. He goes on to say that "it is a world not of wheels but of circuits, not of fragments but of integral patterns."[4] We note here, as in other places, a suggestive similarity between McLuhan's phraseology and Dylan's songs. Any Dylan fan who reads that sentence will immediately think of Dylan's song "This Wheel's on Fire," and with good reason.

McLuhan believed that print culture (and all that it implied) was giving way to a new oral culture created by electricity. This made sense to Dylan's emerging artistic self-definition. His engagement with European modernism in the work of Kafka, Eliot, and Picasso was pulling him further and further away from Woody Guthrie, Pete Seeger, and Joan Baez, and the here-and-now aesthetic that they represented. It matters, too, that McLuhan was a devout Catholic; he was all the more devout for being a convert. To use a phrase from the 1960s, McLuhan advocated a liberation theology, because the subtext of his work is the liberation of spirituality from literacy, which, without quite saying it, he associated with Protestantism. He does say, "The mark of our time is its revulsion against imposed patterns.... There is a deep faith to be found in this new attitude—a faith that concerns the ultimate harmony of all being. Such is the faith in which this book has been written."[5]

This passage surely found resonance with Dylan as he was discovering the relationship between creativity and spirituality.

For a Christian such as McLuhan, faith leads to salvation. For Dylan, typically, the situation is a little more complicated. No matter what creed Dylan has taken up, be it social activism in the 1960s or Judaism and then Christianity in the 1970s, sooner or later his restless psyche wants to transcend the limitations of the creed in question. That pattern suggests that he cannot remain satisfied for long with any particular set of beliefs, since he has a spiritual restlessness that will be satisfied only with transcendence itself.

Naturally, this is not what Dylan thought he was doing in 1962 and 1963, or even in 1966. He did not set out to write a cycle of songs about transcendence any more than Picasso had set out to invent Cubism in Paris some 60 years earlier. Creativity is rarely, if ever, a matter of conscious intention. It would seem that creativity has a mind of its own, so to speak. We can now make sense of what he did because we have had lots of time to think about it. We know what came before Dylan, and what came after him, and that knowledge makes the patterns of creativity clearer and more identifiable. And these patterns allow us to decode his mysterious songs.

We begin with "Mr. Tambourine Man," and its McLuhanesque qualities. Describing the psychic state of literate people, McLuhan writes, "With our central nervous system strategically numbed, the tasks of conscious awareness and order are transferred to the physical life of man...."[6] In the second stanza of "Mr. Tambourine Man," when the singer is ready to begin his evolution away from literacy and all that it implies, he acknowledges that his "senses have been stripped."

However, joy comes to him—joy as sound, very much in the spirit of McLuhan. You might hear "laughter," he tells us. And the tambourine? It creates rhythm, but no melody. McLuhan writes, "Melody is the *melos modos*, 'the road round,' a continuous, connected, and repetitive structure that is not used in the 'cool' art of the Orient."[7] The rhythm of percussion, the back beat that Chuck Berry promised us we could not lose, is what defined rock and roll, distinguishing it from the sweet melodies of the songs that were popular in the 1940s and 1950s. Hence, there is the appeal of the tambourine man as the muse who proclaims and symbolizes liberation from the restrictions of the past, be they geographic, social, or conceptual.

We can now best proceed not by asking about the meaning of "Mr. Tambourine Man," but about to what genre "Mr. Tambourine Man" belongs. The same question will prove essential in interpreting "Desolation Row," "Visions of Johanna," and "Sad-Eyed Lady of the Lowlands," as well. Answering this question immerses us into the evolutionary stream of American and European poetry, and eases the interpretive task by providing other works to which the song can be compared.

Fortunately, Bloom provides a key, as he often does. As McLuhan led us into "Mr. Tambourine Man" in the context of the 1960s, Bloom leads us to the relevant precedent for the song in the work of Walt Whitman. Bloom says that "the American crisis-poem was stationed by Whitman at the shifting point where beach and sea meet. American poets have followed him there in order to compose what James Wright termed 'the shore-ode.'"[8] Bloom continues, "The shore-ode may be considered the American equivalent of the English crisis-ode…. The crisis concerns the poet's ability to write the next poem"[9]—or the next song, as the case may be.

Whitman's shore-ode is "Out of the Cradle Endlessly Rocking," and there is no more powerful poem in American literature. The pulsing energy of its lines practically pushes them off the page:

> Out of the cradle endlessly rocking,
> Out of the mocking-bird's throat, the musical shuttle,
> Out of the Ninth-month midnight,
> Over the sterile sands and the fields beyond, where the
> child leaving his bed wander'd alone, bareheaded,
> barefoot,
> Down from the shower'd halo,
> Up from the mystic play of shadows twining and
> twisting as if they were alive….[10]

You can get a sense for the deep connection between "Out of the Cradle Endlessly Rocking" and "Mr. Tambourine Man" by trying an experiment. If you read the opening lines of Whitman's poem out loud, and then listen to Dylan sing his song, you will hear that the poem and the song share the same urgent rhythm.

To understand the relationship between Whitman and Dylan in greater depth, it helps to remember that the part/whole relationship that defined Whitman's work gave Whitman all the material that he needed. He is unique in Western poetry in that he hardly ever uses metaphors, and when he did use them, he resorted to well-known ones such as the ocean of life in the preceding poem, and the cradle as the symbol of birth. But, in a sense, the artist must be reborn every time he begins a new work, because relying on what he has done in the past is a form of creative death. The boy in Whitman's poem springs forth from the metaphorical cradle to be reborn on the beach, which is, after all, the point of the shore-ode and the joy that it expresses. The beach, the site of Dylan's dance of liberation in the last stanza of "Mr. Tambourine Man," is a transitional space between land and water.

This transitional space is the natural equivalent of the manmade space of the doorway, where "we" stand in Dylan's "Chimes of Freedom," and which marks the transitional space between ordinary experience and mystical transport. Transitional spaces provide an appropriate analogy for Dylan's role as a mediator between European high culture and American popular culture. (Thus, Dylan stands in a doorway looking out into the street on the cover of *Street Legal*.) There is then a key link between the songs "Tambourine Man" and "Chimes of Freedom." Writing "Chimes of Freedom," the prime indicator of his transition away from folk songs toward his mature work, made it possible for him to write "Mr. Tambourine Man." In turn, writing "Mr. Tambourine Man" made it possible of him to write the other two songs of the trilogy.

Still, he has not yet made it to the exalted yet threatened space of "Desolation Row." We may even sense some uncertainty in his belief in himself when he asks the tambourine man to play a song. He had never before asked anyone to play a song for him. The idea of the tambourine man may have come from Whitman's "messenger":

> The messenger there arous'd, the sweet hell within
> The unknown want, the destiny of me.[11]

These lines probably also served as Dylan's source for "The Wicked Messenger."

Since this is a shore-ode and thus a crisis poem, it concerns the poet's ability to write the next poem, as Bloom said, and in particular the next major poem in his trilogy, which is very major indeed: "Desolation Row." In part, the crisis came because he felt caught between two diametrically opposed poets, Whitman and Rimbaud. If Whitman's long, surging lines proclaimed his identification with all of America (uniquely for his time, Whitman was without racial or sexual bias), Rimbaud's tight hexameters were consistent with his own isolation and self-involvement. If Whitman used only the most common metaphors, and used even those rarely, Rimbaud's every line abounds with metaphors and comparisons—the more outrageous the better.

The last line of the first stanza of "Mr. Tambourine Man" contains a key to a sterile street. Thus, we have the opposition of the man-made street at the beginning and the natural beach at the end. The street is the linear space that people most commonly experience and McLuhan associates with literacy. He says, "The principles of continuity, uniformity, and repeatability derived from print technology have, in England and America, long permeated every phase of communal life. In those areas, a child learns literacy from traffic and street...."[12]

In cultural terms, if the street is "ancient," it must refer to Europe, because America has no ancient streets. The phrase thus hints at Baudelaire, the prime poet of Paris and thus of the European urban environment. Significantly, this street is empty, and thus will not support dreaming. This representation of Baudelaire and the French Symbolists as sterile, as a dead-end street, to use the obvious metaphor, is Dylan's way of proclaiming that he has transcended them. Although their imagery gave him exciting possibilities that folksongs lacked, he eventually sensed that their intense (and very

French) self-involvement denied the possibilities for transcendence that he sought.¹³ What he sought, and eventually found, was a middle way between the extremes represented by Whitman on one hand and Baudelaire on the other—a way that would combine Whitman's ability to reach beyond himself with Baudelaire's intricate imagery.

To return to the windy beach, it is here in this symbolic transitional space that Whitman begins to merge with McLuhan. In Dylan's "My Back Pages," he proclaimed the rejuvenation that the release from literacy brings. Rather than simply proclaiming rejuvenation and leaving it at that, in "Mr. Tambourine Man" he makes a more definitive statement because he itemizes what he is leaving behind: the street in the first stanza, his stripped senses in the second stanza, and protest songs in the third stanza. Only after leaving behind all this baggage from the past, which no longer serves him, can he, in the fourth and final stanza, celebrate his liberation and dance.

Whitman imaged just such a poetic rebirth in these lines from "Out of the Cradle Endlessly Rocking":

> Over the sterile sands and the fields beyond, when the
> child leaving his bed wandered alone,
> bareheaded, barefoot....¹⁴

Since the child, an American Adam, has no cultural memories to leave behind, and since Whitman writes in the third person here, the "sterile sands" amount to an equivalent of "the ancient empty street." In both cases the poet wishes to leave sterility behind.

Before leaving "Mr. Tambourine Man," it is worth pausing for a moment to notice a significant precedent for the song by a poet whom Dylan may never have read, but whom he more closely resembles than any other twentieth-century poet—Wallace Stevens. Stevens, who was a successful insurance executive, lived a life radically different from Dylan's. As a great poet—arguably the last great American poet before Dylan—he wrote dense, enigmatic poetry replete with references to Picasso and other artists.

In particular, Stevens's "The Idea of Order at Key West," which Bloom identifies as Stevens's key shore-ode, closely anticipates "Mr. Tambourine Man." The telling difference is that Stevens includes as a muse (a source of inspiration equivalent to Mr. Tambourine Man) a woman, an unnamed "she." The poem is a powerful affirmation of the autonomy of creation.

> She was the single artificer of the world
> In which she sang. And when she sang, the sea,
> Whatever self it had, became the self
> That was her song, for she was the maker. Then we,
> As we beheld her striding there alone,
> Knew that there never was a world for her
> Except the one she sang and, singing, made.¹⁵

4. Songs of Transcendence

This female "artificer of the world," in Stevens's felicitous phrase, stands for poets who create worlds by singing about them, which is what Dylan did in "Desolation Row" and "Visions of Johanna." The artificer of the world, the progenitrix of it, anticipates Dylan's mysterious female characters who represent what I will call the eternal feminine.

Dylan does not dance, or even move, in "Desolation Row," which is a longer and more complex song than "Mr. Tambourine Man." Appropriately for the middle song in a trilogy, it is also the longest. Although it has multiple sources and multiple levels, and one has to listen to the song again and again to tease out its larger meaning, it has its origins in Dylan's own work—in "Gates of Eden." The relationship between "Gates of Eden" and "Desolation Row" offers a classic example of the way one work by an artist can lead to a later, larger work.

In "Gates of Eden" Dylan begins to stretch the wings that his angels had lent him. He combines in this remarkable song the startling imagery of the French Symbolists with the oppositions between the sacred and the profane that will take fully realized form in "Desolation Row." It was, as we used to say, mind-blowing when Dylan used surrealistic images in this fast-paced song.

The disorienting imagery coheres, however, as it develops the opposition between what is inside the gates of Eden and what is outside it. Inside the gates of Eden and only there, is laughter. Inside the gates of Eden people do not discuss a subject of intense interest to avant-garde painters in the 1960s—what is real and what is not. Presumably this is because the peace that "passeth" understanding prevails there. People there are free from sin and the strife that the legal system implies.

The exceptionally powerful sixth stanza of "Gates of Eden" begins with a reference to the "motorcycle black Madonna." This first use of a symbolic woman, perhaps an analogous figure to Stevens's "artificer of the world," combines opposites in a way that anticipates some key images of "Desolation Row" and "Visions of Johanna." With the image of the gray flannel dwarf, Dylan refers, as he often does, to movies of the 1950s. In this case, it is *The Man in the Gray Flannel Suit* (1956), which starred Gregory Peck as an executive who must make moral choices as he ascends the corporate ladder. The dwarf, whose height indicates his moral stature, is related to the title character of Dylan's "The Ballad of a Thin Man."

In "Gates of Eden," Dylan found the opposition between the sacred and the profane that the symbiosis of his creative drive and his developing spirituality required. He will succeed in integrating the imagery and the opposition in the conceptually more ambitious "Desolation Row."

And in "Desolation Row" Dylan has the longest poetic reach of his career, so to speak. If in "Mr. Tambourine Man" he came to terms with Whitman and

Baudelaire, in "Desolation Row" he both comes to terms with, and simultaneously enlists the aid of, T. S. Eliot and Dante Alighieri (1265–1321). Dylan refers to Dante in "Tangled Up in Blue," which he wrote in 1974, not by name but as "an Italian poet from the thirteenth century." There are no references to other poets or artists in this song, or in any other of his songs from this period. An anomaly such as this impassioned reference to Dante, which disrupts the flow of the song, indicates something vitally important. We may suppose that he was referring to Dante's role in showing him how to be a visionary poet while also writing a personal poem.

Dante is, in fact, the principal character of the *Divine Comedy* (1308–1321), his key work and one of the greatest works in world poetry, which tells the story of his journey through hell, purgatory, and paradise in the first person. He has two guides during his journey—the Roman poet Virgil and a woman named Beatrice. We know a good deal about the historical Beatrice, who was Beatrice Portinari (1266–1290). Legend has it that Dante and she first met when Dante was nine and she was eight. Although Beatrice was murdered at the age of 24, Dante continued to love and venerate her. It is worth noting these particulars because Dante's use of Beatrice will prove instructive in analyzing "Desolation Row," "Visions of Johanna," and "Sad-Eyed Lady of the Lowlands."

An updated yet nameless version of Beatrice—Lady—resides at the center of "Desolation Row." (That is Dylan's capitalization, incidentally.) Lady has no name or attributes, but she surely derives from Beatrice, Dante's companion. Dylan's breakthrough into spirituality manifests itself through what Goethe called the eternal feminine. Thinking about Dante's journey through heaven and hell, and about Beatrice's crucial role as guide and muse, Goethe ended his *Faust* with a now-famous sentence: "Das ewig weibliche zieht uns hinan." ("The eternal feminine draws us onward.") The eternal feminine certainly draws Dylan on throughout "Desolation Row," through "Visions of Johanna," and comes to rest as the poet adores her from afar in "Sad-Eyed Lady of the Lowlands."

Like most features of Dylan's songs, the presentation of women evolved rapidly. I noted earlier that in the song "Girl of the North Country," he expresses not just regret, that staple of American love songs, but also compassion, a much less frequently encountered emotion. He asks his listener to make sure that she has a coat. Oddly enough, though, the turning point toward the eternal feminine was "It Ain't Me, Babe." If "Girl of the North County" is unusual, "It Ain't Me, Babe" was unique when Dylan wrote it and remains unique to this day. For the first time, an American popular song written by a man whimsically but forcefully rejects women's expectations about men, which are often as unrealistic as men's expectations about women.

The logical development of this attitude appears in Romeo, the only person on Desolation Row who is going to be expelled. At first glance, the expulsion of Romeo seems odd, since one might think that he resembles Casanova. Romeo, however, constitutes yet another anomaly in Dylan's canon. Romeo is the only character who refers to an actual song: "You Belong to Me," which deserves some separate commentary.

"You Belong to Me" is credited to three writers: Pee Wee King, Chilton Price, and Redd Stewart. The first, and biggest, hit version of "You Belong to Me," and the one that Bobby Zimmerman probably heard in Hibbing, was by Patti Page that came out in 1952. The song enjoyed such popularity as a codification of 1950s' gender roles that Jo Stafford and Dean Martin covered it as well. "You Belong to Me" crossed stylistic boundaries, however. Bobby Zimmerman might have also heard the rock version by Gene Vincent and the Blue Caps, in Hibbing in 1958. In New York in 1962 Bob Dylan might have heard a later version by The Duprees.

The history of this song, whose title contains a summary of gender roles in America during the 1950s, helps to explain why Romeo is being expelled from Desolation Row. And in turn Romeo's expulsion helps us to understand what sets Desolation Row apart from the world that surrounds it.

The many recordings of "You Belong to Me" made it an inviting target for Dylan as the author of "It Ain't Me, Babe." The idea that a man can belong to a woman, and vice versa (the song had hit versions by both male and female singers) is not acceptable for the higher consciousness of those who dwell on Desolation Row, so Romeo must leave. He must take with him his song and all that it implies.

Dylan does not just discard the idealized feminine ideals of the 1950s or stand them on their head as Mick Jagger did in his subversive lyrics for the great Rolling Stones songs of the 1960s. Rather, Dylan endows them with a spiritual essence, and, like Dante, enlists their help as the eternal feminine. The eternal feminine appears modestly in "Desolation Row" in the couple, "Lady and I." They represent something like a balance of the male and female principles, although they remain abstract, since we learn nothing about them.

As if to make up for this, Dylan gives us Cinderella, whom he associates with Bette Davis. Bobby Zimmerman could have seen the original Disney *Cinderella* (1950) in Hibbing, and then again when it was re-released in 1957. Cinderella represents another of Dylan's experiments in taking movies and fairy tales dear to the hearts of Americans and adapting them for his own purposes, as he did in "Like a Rolling Stone."

It takes a little detective work to show why Cinderella has the body language of Bette Davis. The last movie in which Davis starred that Dylan might have seen before he wrote "Desolation Row" was *Hush, Hush, Sweet Charlotte* (1964). That gives us a place to start. In that movie, Davis plays an insane murderer, and thus a polar opposite to Cinderella. When Cinderella, by the combinatory logic of Dylan's imagination, imitates Davis by taking on her body language, she represents something like a synthesis of positive and negative female roles. As such, she lives on Desolation Row. She sweeps up not ashes, as in the Disney version, but the debris left after an act of violence. Whatever it was, it was presumably perpetrated by the agents and the superhuman crew, an act that seems all the more disturbing because Dylan leaves it unexplained and unnamed. In restoring order to her world, she heals it, as the angelic representatives of the eternal feminine often do.

We find another version of the eternal feminine in the fourth stanza—Ophelia. This is the last image dealing with gender roles. Although she is frigid and romanticizes death (there may be a causal connection here), she does see a rainbow, and her awareness of it brings her close to Desolation Row. She has what we might call the potential for balance. The women have realized their potential to serve as the eternal feminine to varying degrees, as the men also have varying degrees of higher consciousness.

And now we take up the significance of T. S. Eliot's "The Waste Land" (1922), that challenging, defiantly elitist masterpiece of high modernism, for "Desolation Row." Eliot wrote this collage of cinematic fragments in free verse, with occasional rhymes. It has quotations from, among others, Baudelaire and Dante (in the original languages, of course). Fortunately for posterity, Eliot as the critic explained what Eliot as the poet had done in a series of footnotes.

For all their obvious differences of style and temperament, Eliot and Dante have something in common as poets: they both created places. Dante created the Inferno, the Purgatorio, and the Paradiso in his *Divine Comedy*. (Incidentally, that progression corresponds quite nicely to the progression of "Mr. Tambourine Man," "Desolation Row," and "Visions of Johanna.") If the *Divine Comedy* ends in a utopia, a perfect place, then "The Waste Land" is a dystopia, a place that is the opposite of a utopia, at least at the beginning. Eliot revered Dante, so "The Waste Land" represents, among other things, Eliot's swerve from him. Dante's and Eliot's places both created stimulating, useful precedents for Dylan in creating "Desolation Row."

"Desolation Row," whose name probably derives from John Steinbeck's 1945 novel *Cannery Row*, is Dylan's only major song with an imaginary place name in the title. We ask: What kind of place is Desolation Row? The answer is that it is an orderly place, like the places that Dante visits. In his great poem, Dante settles some personal accounts with the people of Florence who exiled him, but mostly he follows medieval theology, which created an elaborate order of punishments for sinners. Hell, for example, has seven circles, beginning with one for virtuous pagans and unbaptized children, and going down to the last one, for suicides and others who committed terrible crimes.

4. Songs of Transcendence

Whereas Dante's metaphysical places are all-inclusive, Desolation Row is not, because it continues the opposition of inside and outside that Dylan began in "Gates of Eden." Some people are inside it, and some people are outside it. It will soon become apparent, however, that Dylan places people in the moral geography of Desolation Row as carefully and thoughtfully as Dante does, and for analogous reasons. At the moment, however, we wish to understand how there can be an inside and outside, and Dylan gives us a hint in the cultural reference to the hunchback of Notre Dame in line six of the third stanza.

Bobby Zimmerman probably saw the movie version of *The Hunchback of Notre Dame* in Hibbing when it came out in 1956. It starred Anthony Quinn in the title role and Gina Lollabrigida as Esmeralda, and it may well hold a key to "Desolation Row." Those who know the story of Victor Hugo's novel will recall that the hunchback takes refuge inside the cathedral in accordance with medieval practice, but he is betrayed by Frollo. From this incident, we can conclude that Desolation Row, like Notre Dame, is a place of refuge that attracts people capable of love and compassion. It thus represents life and fertility, which explains why people do two things there associated with life and fertility—they either make love or expect rain.

A literary theorist would say that "Desolation Row" is "over-determined," which is another way of saying that it has multiple sources. In addition to Dante's cosmic places and the Notre Dame Cathedral, another magical place may have been swirling around in Dylan's subconscious at the time, and that is Camelot. The musical *Camelot*, written by Alan Jay Lerner and Frederick Loewe, opened in New York in 1960, and closed in 1963. It was playing when Dylan arrived in New York, and was still playing as he started to make a name for himself. The cast album was America's top-selling album for 60 weeks; Dylan could hardly have avoided knowing about it. Like Camelot, Desolation Row is a place of harmony; and, like Camelot, Desolation Row is threatened by people who come in from the outside and disrupt its harmony.

Like Notre Dame and Camelot, Desolation Row is under siege, and it is dangerous to go there. Dylan makes this point with the precarious situation of Casanova, a reference to the great Italian lover and memoirist Giacomo Girolamo Casanova de Seingalt (1725-1798). Casanova represents the first of the two key activities of Desolation Row—making love. However, he has been caught by the forces represented by "agents" (real estate agents?) and the "superhuman crew" (comic book monsters?).

As the most intertextual of Dylan's songs, "Desolation Row" has a definite elitist quality, and thus it is his only song in which democratizers turn vicious. And that is what the agents and the superhuman crews are—democratizers. Or, to use the term supposedly coined by King Charles I when faced with democratizing upstarts during the English Civil War, they are Levelers, because they want to bring everyone else down to their level. It arouses their anger when they meet someone who knows more than they do, so they bring out the heart-attack machines. In the case of Casanova, it is not so much that he knows more than they do; rather, he represents feeling, and that threatens them as much as knowledge.

We can now take up in greater detail "The Waste Land," and Dylan's swerve from the early part of it. Again and again, Eliot creates images of his dystopia as a place of dryness and sterility in famous lines such as these:

> A heap of broken images, where the sun beats,
> And the dead tree gives no shelter, the cricket no relief,
> And the dry stone no sound of water.[16]

This list concludes with one of the most powerful images, not just in "The Waste Land," but also in modern poetry: "I will show you fear in a handful of dust."

As Eliot contemplated war-ravaged Europe in the early 1920s, he saw alienation and anxiety about the world. Writing in the aftermath of the assassination of President Kennedy, and perhaps anticipating that more assassinations were to come, Dylan responded deeply to the fratricidal violence that had so agitated him when reading about the Civil War at the New York Public Library. Hence, he puts Cain and Abel near Desolation Row.

It is now possible to state the fundamental difference between "The Waste Land" and "Desolation Row." Eliot's poem progresses from the sterility of the West to the transcendence of Eastern spirituality. He quotes—in Sanskrit—from the Upanishads, a Hindu text, and in fact ends his poem with "shantih, shantih, shantih," using the Sanskrit word for peace. Dylan noted this movement of "The Waste Land," and used it in his most explicit song of transcendence, "I Shall Be Released."

In "Desolation Row" itself, however, we find no evolution or progression. As in the *Divine Comedy*, Dylan's characters do not progress spiritually or in any other way. The difference between Desolation Row and the undefined space outside it amounts to an opposition between fertility and violence—life and death, roughly. Characters that embody these characteristics are placed in accordance with their consciousness. Hence, we have characters inside Desolation Row like Cinderella/Bette Davis, who balance gender roles. Romeo is inside, but about to be expelled; Casanova is on the outside, but belongs inside.

Dylan may have gotten the idea of balancing personalities and gender roles from various aspects of "The Waste Land." Both aspects of Eliot's creative personality appear in "The Waste Land." For example, the critic Eliot suggested in a footnote that the poet and the critic were two aspects of a single self. The principal symbolic character in "The Waste Land," who unites the two selves, is Tiresias:

4. Songs of Transcendence

> I Tiresias, old man with wrinkled dugs
> Perceived the scene, and foretold the rest—
> I too awaited the expected guest.[17]

In a key footnote, Eliot the critic tells us that:

> Tiresias, although a mere spectator and not indeed a "character," is yet the most important personage in the poem, uniting all the rest. Just as the one-eyed merchant, seller of currants, melts into the Phoenician Sailor, and the latter is not wholly distinct from Ferdinand Prince of Naples, so all the women are one woman, and the two sexes meet in Tiresias.[18]

Who is Tiresias, that he bears such a heavy symbolic load? In classical mythology, he was a blind prophet of Thebes who was transformed into a woman for seven years. Picasso and his fellow modernists were interested in the symbolic possibilities of such a man/woman. Picasso's friend and poet Guillaume Apollinaire wrote a play called "The Breasts of Tiresias."

A man/woman would have been too weird for Dylan's American audience. (Another way of saying that would be that it did not suit his thematic purposes.) However, he did take from "The Waste Land" the idea that symbolic characters could combine within themselves two aspects of a single self, for example, Cinderella/Bette Davis, of course.

The closest equivalents to Tiresias in "Desolation Row" are the only two permanent residents (in addition to "Lady and I"): the "Good Samaritan" and Einstein. As the Christian embodiment of compassion, the "Good Samaritan" occupies symbolic pride of place and helps us to understand the symbolic positioning of the other characters as well.

Einstein, and only Einstein, gets a full stanza to himself. Although in the 1950s his name became a synonym for "genius," in "Desolation Row" he has additional meaning. For one thing, he is the only Jewish character. For another, he may have been the founder of Desolation Row, because "long ago" he was famous for playing an electric violin. Einstein's first paper was "On the Electro-Dynamics of Moving Bodies," and the understanding of electric bonds within the atom is essential to many aspects of modern physics. Expecting rain like other residents of Desolation Row, he sniffs drainpipes. He recites the alphabet to make obvious the absurdity of the literate sensibility in which one thing comes after another. McLuhan wrote in *Understanding Media*, "The printed book had encouraged artists to reduce all forms of expression as much as possible to the single descriptive and narrative plan of the printed word. The advent of electric media released art from this straitjacket at once...."[19] And of course Dylan's Einstein is an artist; he plays not just any instrument, but the traditional Jewish instrument, the violin. It is not unreasonable to suppose that the musical *Fiddler on the Roof*, which opened in 1964, and which was a smashing success (it ran for over 3,000 performances), suggested to Dylan the idea of making Einstein a violinist.

Thus, we can understand why the one direct borrowing from "The Waste Land" in "Desolation Row" is a symbolic character, "the fortune-telling lady," who moves from outside to inside. This is Eliot's version:

> Madame Sosostris, famous clairvoyante,
> Had a bad cold, nevertheless
> Is known to be the wisest woman in Europe....[20]

She has in her tarot deck the symbolic balanced characters such as the Phoenician sailor that Eliot mentioned in his footnote.

Speaking of balance, and the need for it, we may guess that it is precisely because "Desolation Row" owes the most to Eliot that Dylan includes Eliot, along with Ezra Pound, as elitists (in the captain's tower). In his most demanding song, he sensed the need to play off his own elitism with a democratizing reference to the poet to whom he owed the most.

"Visions of Johanna," the third and final song in Dylan's trilogy of songs about transcendence, is one of the most puzzling and enigmatic songs in the history of American songwriting. We can begin to understand it by noticing that in the sequence of thesis ("Mr. Tambourine Man"), antithesis ("Desolation Row"), and synthesis ("Visions of Johanna"), "Visions of Johanna" has key differences from "Desolation Row." Unlike "Desolation Row," "Visions of Johanna" has no intertextuality (with the exception of the name Johanna itself, of course). If "Desolation Row" positions people according to their ability to show love and compassion, that is to say, according to their consciousness, the point of "Visions of Johanna" is to take consciousness quite literally to the next level, and thus to transcend both place and, ultimately, consciousness itself.

The main character in the song, though, is the singer, who is paired with Johanna, or, strictly speaking, with visions of Johanna. (Johanna herself is not physically present, which is, after all, the point of the song.) The idea of the poet/singer who is led onward by visions of the eternal feminine derives from Dante's love/obsession with Beatrice, of course, with an assist from Goethe. And the name Johanna suggests "Jehovah," the ancient Hebrew word for God. Thus, Johanna/Jehovah brings together the masculine and the feminine in a way that was probably suggested by Tiresias in "The Waste Land."

Nevertheless, in "Visions of Johanna," Dylan leaves behind the complexities and intertextuality of Eliot's High Modernism, as he had left behind the dense imagery of the French Symbolists in "Mr. Tambourine Man." To conclude his trilogy, he brings it all (i.e., European Modernism) back home (as the title of Dylan's album *Bringing It All Back Home* implies) and positions his song as part of the evolution of American popular songs.

Before we discuss such arcane matters as higher consciousness and its relation to language, we can usefully begin by relating "Visions of Johanna" to the tradition from which it comes, and thus to its genre. Dylan as Ariadne comes to our help here. Just as in "Like a Rolling Stone," the phrase "once upon a time" tells us that what is to follow is a fairy tale, so in the same way the word "night," to which Dylan gives a heavy accent in the first line of "Visions of Johanna," tells us that this is a night song.

We can understand what a night song is by noting the situation of the singer in "Visions of Johanna." It is late at night, and he cannot get to sleep. He is listening to the radio and distracted by the sound of the heat pipes. But really, his problem is that his visions of Johanna will give him no rest. When we describe his situation in this way, we realize that it corresponds to the situation of so many male singers in the history of American song. In many American songs of the 1940s and 1950s, it is late at night, and the man cannot sleep for a variety of reasons. Perhaps his woman has left him; perhaps she betrayed him; perhaps he betrayed her. Sometimes she is simply not there. In any case, he cannot sleep for thinking about her. The night song had so much emotional potential that it transcended musical styles and attracted some of America's greatest singers and songwriters, as Table 2 shows.

Table 2. Night Songs

Singer	Song Titles	Dates of Release
Muddy Waters	"Rollin' and Tumblin'"	1950 (earliest recorded version is "Minglewood Blues"by Gus Gannon's Jug Stompers, 1927)
Ernest Tubb	"Walking the Floor Over You"	1941
Bobby Edwards	"You're the Reason I Can't Sleep at Night"	1961
Frank Sinatra	"Dancing on the Ceiling"	1930 (by Rodgers and Hart)
Frank Sinatra	"In the Still of the Night"	1937 (by Tommy Dorsey)
Frank Sinatra	"I Couldn't Sleep a Wink Last Night"	1943
Frank Sinatra	"In the Wee Small Hours of the Morning"	1955 (Title song of Sinatra's album *In the Wee Small Hours of the Morning*)

The table makes it apparent that the appeal of the night song ranges from Ernest Tubb to Muddy Waters to Frank Sinatra, so it spans the gamut of vocal styles in mid–twentieth-century American popular music. Although no other night song states the situation as explicitly as Bobby Edwards's "You're the Reason I Can't Sleep at Night," all of these songs create a situation in which the man is so agitated that he cannot sleep. In Muddy Waters's great version of an old blues tune, he is rolling and tumbling in bed at night. (Dylan covered "Rollin' and Tumblin'" on his *Modern Times* album.) In Ernest Tubb's version the man cannot stay in bed, so he walks the floor.

Frank Sinatra summed up the evolution of the night song, and brought it to perfection, in his 1955 album, *In the Wee Small Hours of the Morning*, which featured both the title song and Cole Porter's "In the Still of the Night."[21] He also included "Dancing on the Ceiling," which Rodgers and Hart wrote in 1930. In that song, the man lies in bed and imagines that the girl he loves is dancing overhead on the ceiling.[22] The thematic unity of the songs on *In the Wee Small Hours of the Morning* has led people to call it the first concept album.[23] In 1956, Sinatra followed up *In the Wee Small Hours of the Morning* with *Only the Lonely*, a very similar album. Bobby Zimmerman probably listened carefully to both these albums in Hibbing. We know that he listened to *Only the Lonely* because it featured "Ebb Tide." Dylan says in *Chronicles* that Sinatra's version of that song affected him deeply.[24]

If Sinatra's standard repertoire of songs about loneliness affected Bobby Zimmerman so deeply, what was a young songwriter to do when he felt the call to write a night song? By bringing the night song to perfection, Sinatra left nothing for subsequent singers and songwriters to do with it. Great singer though Sinatra was, he could not have done this without the help of historical circumstances, and they gave Dylan a way out of his artistic dilemma.

The night song, in which a man aches with loneliness, arose in an era of gender roles that put strict limits on what the sexes could say to each other. And when the sexes could talk to each other, often at night, they had limited access to telephones if they were in different cities—long distance calls were expensive. That era was passing in 1955, the year of both *In the Wee Small Hours of the Morning* and "Hound Dog." The night song had diminishing social resonance and power to evoke feelings, so Dylan took what seems in retrospect a logical step. He took the longing caused by ineradicable memories of the symbolic woman, and made a metaphysical dilemma out of it.

That is to say, Dylan created a swerve and did so through his usual practice of synthesis. It was commonplace for male singers and songwriters to refer to their beloveds as angels, and these songs ranged from "Angel Eyes" by Sinatra to "Angels in the Sky" by The Crewcuts in 1955 to "Teen Angel," which was a big hit from Mark Dinning in 1959. Dylan carried out in "Visions of Johanna" what Bloom calls a tessera, or completion by antithesis. In effect, he completed the night songs by making the man be kept up at night not by thoughts of his beloved, a real woman, but by a symbolic woman, the eternal feminine. The ultimate source for this eternal feminine is Dante's Beatrice, of course. In "Visions of Johanna" he brings together some ideas and images from high culture in a song that ultimately derives from popular culture. And that is only appropriate, since the first word in the song, deliberately placed, is "ain't," which rescues the song from any possibility of pretentiousness.

We may also say that "Visions of Johanna" antithetically completes "Desolation Row." Whereas consciousness determines the characters' position inside or outside of Desolation Row, that position itself is at best a refuge from hostile forces. In "Visions of Johanna" the conflict between those who are inside and those who are outside is internalized and ultimately resolved. In the process, consciousness itself is dissolved.

The evolution of the eternal feminine also allows us to connect "Visions of Johanna" not just with earlier popular songs, but also with "Desolation Row." In effect, Dylan doubles the eternal feminine in "Visions of Johanna." He shows two stages of development of the eternal feminine, rather than as he had done with Ophelia and Cinderella/Bette Davis in "Desolation Row." Thus, Louise and her lover represent another version of "Lady and I" from "Desolation Row."

Louise and her (unnamed) lover replicate the two key activities of the inhabitants of Desolation Row, who symbolize fertility. That is why Louise and her lover are so entwined, and also why Louise shows you "a handful of rain." (Dylan may have gotten the idea for this provocative phrase from the title *A Hatful of Rain*, a 1957 movie about drug addiction starring Eva Marie Saint.) Louise also serves as the vehicle for a denial of sight. In a post-literate society, you cannot look at much because the very act of looking, of concentrating one's senses in the eyes, is no longer appropriate in a world moving toward the unification of the senses. What Louise's cryptic statement implies is a key to the song, and is stated in the first word of the title, the opposition between outer looking and inner visions.

"Visions of Johanna" is about transcendence, and the transcendence of, among others, Dylan's precursors (as defined by Bloom). We may find instructive analogies—analogies that enrich our understanding—but no more anxiety of influence. In "Visions of Johanna," he has worked through all his discernible anxieties of influence, and although later he continued to write against earlier songs, he did so without "anxiety."

With this in mind, we can say of "Visions of Johanna" what Bloom says of Whitman's "Song of Myself": "But his majestic poem, like all his wholly realized works, is centered only on his isolate self, and on 'Emersonian' seeing, which is not far from shamanistic practice, and has little to do with observation of externals."[25] We will return to this phrase "little to do with observation of externals" in a moment, but first note the analogies with "Visions of Johanna" in section 25 of Whitman's "Song of Myself":

> We also ascend dazzling and tremendous as the sun,
> We found our own O my soul in the calm and cool of the day-break.
> My voice goes after what my eyes cannot reach,
> With the twirl of my tongue I encompass worlds and volumes of worlds.[26]

Dylan does not use Whitman's analogy between the rising of the sun and the ascent of the soul, but the sense of uncaused transcendence without an ultimate goal is comparable.

The negation of sight that Louise asserts has as its equivalent something like a progressive negation of the observation of externals, to use Bloom's phrase, as the song progresses. Hence, there is the emphasis on the physical environment at the beginning of the song. The singer is in a loft (i.e., somewhere in downtown New York). He listens to a country music station on the radio[27] and hears the heat pipes cough.

The second stanza extends the space to an empty lot, and even there the women (presumably hookers) negate sight in a game of blindman's bluff.[28] This negation of sight brings us back to Louise, and for the first time it becomes apparent that Louise serves as a foil for Johanna. Her association with sex and rain make her something of an earth goddess, and in "Visions of Johanna" that is a limitation. Whereas Louise is tied to the earth, Johanna represents the eternal feminine as transcendent. Louise reminds the singer of Johanna's physical absence and, thus by implication, of her spiritual presence.

The third stanza abruptly shifts to autobiography, as does the reference to the "complete unknown" does in "Like a Rolling Stone." The "little boy lost" is still caught up in romance, and is thus still tied to the here and now, whereas the singer cannot explain his visions.

The fourth stanza represents an antithesis to the third, a swerve from autobiography to art history, which is to say to Picasso and the denial of perspective in his Cubist paintings. Yet this swerve itself continues the theme of the negation of sight, in particular the infinite space of Renaissance and post–Renaissance painting that is symbolized by the Mona Lisa, the ultimate painted image of the eternal feminine. Here, women are dissociated from sight, and also from their bodies.

The next to the last line of "Visions of Johanna" brings us abruptly back to our animal selves, however, with a reference to a mule. The Rolling Stones thought that this line was so bizarre that they gave it expression on the cover of their 1970 album *Get Yer Ya-Ya's Out*, which does indeed show jewels and binoculars hanging from the head of a mule. Jewels are stones whose flash and glitter appeal to the eyes, and binoculars are devices that extend the eye. In "Visions of Johanna" vision trumps sight every time, so visions of Johanna make anything that appeals to physical sight a cruel joke because it denies transcendent (i.e., non-visual) reality.

The final stanza of "Visions of Johanna" negates specifically Christian transcendence, since the Madonna has not appeared. However, what Hamlet calls this "too, too solid flesh" begins to dissolve, to give way to a higher order in which all debts are paid, and thus no ties to the earth remain. Finally, ultimately, the singer proclaims in triumph, "my conscience explodes," and the key word "conscience" has two meanings here. First, it means conscience as a repository of the duality of the Western world, which divides acts into good acts and evil acts. To go beyond what Nietzsche called "good and evil" is to transcend earthly morality and mortality. Beyond that, though, "conscience" has something of the French quality of "consciousness." If the flesh corrodes and the consciousness explodes, all that is left is pure spirit—the visions of Johanna and nothing else. Once transcendence has been achieved, the song must stop because transcendence involves the transcendence of words themselves, which are always tied to specific physical circumstances, such as those detailed in the first stanza of the song. This is a key point for Dylan's future evolution as a songwriter, and we will return to it.

Although it is too much to say that Dylan borrows from Dante here, it is worth noting the similarities and distinctions between the ending of "Visions of Johanna" and the ending of the *Paradiso*. In the final canto, canto XXXII, St. Bernard offers a prayer to Mary that includes these lines:

> Lady, thou art so near God's reckonings
> that who seeks grace and does not first seek thee
> would have his wish fly upward without wings.[29]

We may suspect that Dante's/St. Bernard's emphasis on Mary as the key to transcendence explains why the Madonna in "Visions of Johanna" has not appeared. This is how Dylan swerves from Dante. What the last line of "Visions of Johanna" implies is what Dante then goes on to state:

> What then I saw is more than tongue can say.
> Our human speech is dark before the vision.
> The ravished memory swoons and falls away.[30]

But Dante does not stop here, as Dylan does. Having said that his vision transcends speech, he goes on for several more pages to describe what he did see.

We can better appreciate the climactic/orgasmic conclusion of "Visions of Johanna"—"my conscience explodes"—by comparing it to Elizabeth Gilbert's genuine, although brief, experience of transcendence. In her book *Eat Pray Love*, she acknowledges the frustration that readers have when writers tell them that transcendence is indescribable or simply give readers a cryptic phrase, as Dylan does. While living in an ashram in India, Gilbert was sitting in a meeting room, and had a genuine, if brief, experience of transcendence.[31] Gilbert's conscience and consciousness exploded because they could not contain her infinitude. Significantly, in her experience, transcendence had no significant characteristics. Her physical circumstances fell away, very much as the physical world falls away in "Visions of Johanna." Any attempt to describe transcendent states, even by so gifted a writer as Gilbert, results in a demonstration of the inadequacy of language, which results in something like the paradoxes of kaons, the riddles that Zen masters use to help their students achieve higher states of consciousness. What remained for Gilbert was the vision, as the visions of Johanna—and only Johanna—remain in the song.

Something else that remained for Dylan the artist was the engagement with Dante—not exactly an anxiety of influence, because Dylan was himself a strong poet by this time. (Anybody who could write this trilogy of songs about transcendence was a strong poet.) Rather, Dylan's (probably subconscious) sense that he could do more with Dante's poetry merged with his personal situation at the time, and resulted in "Sad-Eyed Lady of the Lowlands."

As Clinton Heylin said in *Revolution in the Air*, Sara Dylan is the likely immediate subject of "Sad-Eyed Lady of the Lowlands."[32] However, if "Sad-Eyed Lady of the Lowlands" is not only, or uniquely, about Sara, the serious interpreter of Dylan's songs wishes to ask what else one can say about the song. For example, one could ask such questions as: Why does the Sad-Eyed Lady have a "mercury mouth" and why does the singer have "warehouse eyes"? The biographical interpretation gives us no answers for these and other possible questions that one might raise about the song.

For once, though, we know something about the circumstances of the composition of the song, and they give us clues, but no more than that, for an interpretation of it. Heylin says that Dylan "may have come up with that magnetic chorus at their Chelsea hotel love nest, but the bulk of the song was written in Tennessee from February 15 [1966] through the wee hours of the next morning."[33] So "Sad-Eyed Lady of the Lowlands" is quite literally a night song, written in the wee small hours of the morning, as Dylan sat in the studio.

As a night song, and an exaltation of the eternal feminine, it is thus linked to "Visions of Johanna." Given the way Dylan wrote it at a fever pitch, we may say that Dylan had some Dante left over. One thinks here of Dylan's reference in an interview to "being communicated to by angels." Dante had excited him so much that he sensed that he could do more with his great Italian predecessor, who was sufficiently distant in time and place that Dylan seems not to have had any anxiety of influence from him.[34]

And how do these considerations help us to do what really matters—namely, to interpret the song? They help us to define our expectations about the song, just as defining "Visions of Johanna" as a night song defined its place in the evolution of American song writing. Given the presence of Dante in Dylan's creative unconscious at the time, we may define "Sad-Eyed Lady of the Lowlands" as a poem of courtly love.

As the term courtly love indicates, poems of courtly love were created at courts—specifically at the courts of what is now southern France in the Middle Ages. During the Crusades, husbands were often absent for long peri-

4. Songs of Transcendence

ods, so troubadours could express their devotion to married women without incurring their husbands' jealousy. Although this kind of thing is understandably hard to document, courtly love was first a verbal, and then ultimately a spiritual, exercise with little or no contact between the parties.

Courtly love songs fit very nicely into Dylan's ongoing engagement with the eternal feminine. The title and the idea for "Sad-Eyed Lady of the Lowlands" probably come from *La Vita Nuova (The New Life)*, the poetic exercise about courtly love which Dante wrote in 1295. Among other things, it is concerned with the death of his beloved Beatrice. Dante imagines that he sees mourning women, and writes:

> O you who bear a look of resignation,
> moving with eyes downcast to show your grief,
> where are you coming from?[35]

Probably because of the inspiration from Dante and the tradition of courtly love, "Sad-Eyed Lady of the Lowlands" is Dylan's only song with a Catholic ambience. The Lady herself is Spanish; she has a "hollow face," so the implication is that she is one of the statues of the Madonna that are carried in processions on holy days in Catholic countries.

But this is not the thirteenth century, and Dylan is not a Catholic, so he places in her arms not the Christ child that we expect, but "the child of a hoodlum." In doing so he combines the sacred and the profane in a single image of the eternal feminine. Here, we once again notice Dylan, the synthesizer of opposites, at work.

The overall situation of "Sad-Eyed Lady of the Lowlands" has something of the qualities of both "Desolation Row" and "Visions of Johanna." As in "Desolation Row" there is an inside and an outside. The Lady is inside, of course, and the singer is at her gate—presumably the gate to a monastery. And then there is "them"—people without attributes. We know only one such group—"the Kings of Tyrus."

When Dylan refers to the Bible, it is usually to the Old Testament, and that is the case here. (The training for his Bar Mitzvah had a lasting effect.) In Jeremiah 25, the prophet causes various nations to drink "the wine cup of this fury," and prominent among them are "all the kings of Tyrus" (Jeremiah 25:22). If the Sad-Eyed Lady represents the sacred, and she surely does, then the kings of Tyrus and all of "them" represent the profane. The singer is between them, neither in nor out; he is in another version of the transitional, or liminal, spaces that recur in Dylan's songs. This situation goes back to the singer on the beach in "Mr. Tambourine Man" and still further back to the "we" in the doorway in "Chimes of Freedom." Such transitional spaces provide expressive images for his role as a synthesizer of opposites, as a mediator between high and low culture. He is in expectation of enlightenment, so to speak, and repeatedly asks the Lady whether he should come in or leave. His attributes indicate his ambiguous status; his "warehouse eyes" refer to the inferior status of physical sight as opposed to spiritual vision that we are familiar with from "Visions of Johanna." In the spirit of McLuhan's opposition of sight and sound, he has "Arabian drums," so he too combines opposites.

Although I will discuss the stanza form of "Sad-Eyed Lady of the Lowlands" in detail in another chapter, here I wish to note that it is written in unusually complex 13-line stanzas. The fourth and eighth lines of each of the five stanzas pose a rhetorical question, and in four of these stanzas the questions rhyme. These lines in these stanzas ask, "Who among them…." For example, the questions end as "…bury you?," "carry you?," "outguess you?," and "impress you?" or "employ you?" and "destroy you?" (The constraints of this exceptionally demanding stanza form forced Dylan to use an approximate rhyme or no rhyme at all.)

The repetition of these oppositions in "Sad-Eyed Lady of the Lowlands" emphasizes the distinction between the sacred and the profane. It is as though the song hangs suspended between these two poles. What this suspension, or stasis, means for Dylan's evolution is that after he finished the album *Blonde on Blonde*, he was in the position of Kansas City in the famous song from *Oklahoma!* He had gone about as far as he could go. He needed to assimilate his achievements, and that assimilation took the form of two radically different albums—*John Wesley Harding* and *Nashville Skyline*.

5

Songs of Assimilation
John Wesley Harding *and* Nashville Skyline

The parables and allegories of the short songs on the album *John Wesley Harding* came as a shock to many people after the long, challenging masterpieces of *Blonde on Blonde*. The sexy, accessible songs on the album *Nashville Skyline* came as a shock after the serious songs on *John Wesley Harding*, which were neither sexy nor easily accessible. No American artist had ever defied the principles of show-business marketing by releasing three such radically different albums in quick succession like this, and their diversity of styles during the apocalyptic years of the late 1960s left people reeling.

The passage of time certainly makes it easier to grasp the overall coherence of an artist's work. To make the obvious analogy, Picasso's evolution makes much more sense now than it did in the 1920s. Similarly, Dylan's evolution makes more sense now than it did in the 1960s. We can now identify themes and patterns and analogies that seemed obscure (at best) at the time. One such analogy is the one between Dylan and Wallace Stevens, an analogy that deserves separate and careful consideration if we are ever to understand twentieth-century American culture as a whole.

A poem by Stevens deserves mention, because it startlingly anticipates Dylan's evolution. Stevens's "The American Sublime" immediately follows his shore-ode, "The Idea of Order at Key West," and the final stanza of "The American Sublime" is:

> The spirit and space,
> The empty spirit
> In vacant space.
> What does one drink?
> What does one eat?[1]

This is a classic Stevens ploy—he invites/challenges us to make a connection between seemingly disjointed, disconnected lines.

These lines interest us because they condense Dylan's evolution in the late 1960s. The empty spirit/the vacant lot (the one where the hookers play blind man's bluff) in the second stanza of "Visions of Johanna" is what is left after transcendence. The phrase "the empty spirit" makes more sense when we recall that achieving emptiness in Buddhist terms is another way of saying "achieving enlightenment." Various Buddhist spiritual practices have as their goal the emptying out of the psyche so that the psyche can merge with the universe—so that it can become the void, as Elizabeth Gilbert put it.

To continue with Buddhism for a moment, Buddhist teacher Jack Kornfield wrote a book called *After the Ecstasy, the Laundry* about dealing with what you do after you experience higher states of consciousness. Just as Gilbert soon came down to earth, Dylan in his last two albums of the 1960s came down to earth as well. After an experience of transcendence, one returns to the body, which still has its needs. The genteel Stevens limits himself to the body's needs for food and drink. In "I'll be Your Baby Tonight," Dylan refers to a bottle, but emphasizes sex, that ever-popular staple of 1960s rock and roll. Still, Kornfield's phrase "after the ecstasy, the laundry" catches the dynamic in both Dylan's and Stevens's work.

Dylan had to be silent about transcendence because it goes beyond words, but being silent permanently was not a viable option for a great songwriter at the height of his powers. It is only a slight exaggeration to say that many of his later songs represent an assimilation of the implied period of transcendence that follows the explosion of conscience/consciousness at the end of "Visions of Johanna."

This assimilation involved the broadening of experience that informs *John Wesley Harding*, and it begins with the photograph on the album's cover. (As Dylan noted in *Chronicles*, album art mattered in the 1960s.) On previous albums Dylan had appeared either alone or with a woman—with Suze Rotolo on *The Freewheelin' Bob Dylan* and with Sally Grossman on the famous cover of *Highway 61 Revisited*. On the cover of *John Wesley Harding*, he appears for the first time with three other men—two South Asian musicians brought to Woodstock and a local man.

By the time of *John Wesley Harding*, he could no longer credibly say that his name meant "nothin'," as he had in "With God on Our Side." On the contrary, his name had taken on legendary proportions, and he had to acknowledge that fact in his songs, or lose all credibility. As a result, the Whitmanesque element of unity with the common folk in the great cause of American democracy disappeared from them. He could no longer speak *for* the people; he was Bob Dylan, and he had to speak *to* the people, whether he liked it or not. Like Moses, and like Dr. King, he had been to the mountaintop in "Visions of Johanna." Now he began to accept the consequences of that experience. The results of this new relationship with his audience appear in the parables and allegories that fill the album *John Wesley Harding*.

Only one song on *John Wesley Harding* uses significant intertextuality, and it is "I Dreamed I Saw St. Augustine," which completes the cycle of mystic visions begun in "Chimes of Freedom." It requires intertextuality because it is Dylan's way of saying an emphatic goodbye to his past as a socially active folkie. In "I Dreamed I Saw St. Augustine," he found a way to connect where he had been in the past with where he was in the present. "I Dreamed I Saw St. Augustine" is written against the old union standard, "I Dreamed I Saw Joe Hill," a song to which Dylan devotes two entire pages in *Chronicles*.[2] A few words about the real Joe Hill will help to clarify the meaning of the song.

Joe Hill (1879–1915) was a slightly mysterious man—a vagabond, union organizer, and poet. His organizing activities aroused the hostility of the powers that be, and he was found guilty of murder on very flimsy evidence by a Salt Lake City court. Although dignitaries such as Woodrow Wilson pled for clemency, he was executed.

The song "I Dreamed I Saw Joe Hill" takes the life of its hero and mythologizes it. In effect, it turns him into a secular Christ figure. Hill was shot, and his body died, but the spirit that he gave to the union cause lived on. It transcended the here and now. No wonder Dylan wanted to rework the song; it gave him a chance to make an artistic connection between social activism and spirituality. Given the choice, he chose spirituality.[3]

But why does Dylan substitute St. Augustine, of all people, for Joe Hill? The answer goes back to a key source for Dylan in the 1960s, Eliot's "The Waste Land," which was written at about the same time as "I Dreamed I Saw Joe Hill." In one of the several puzzling passages in "The Waste Land" we read:

> To Carthage then I came
> Burning burning burning
> O Lord Thou pluckest me out
> O Lord Thou pluckest
> Burning.

Fortunately for us, Eliot the critic explained these lines, which follow a passage from the Buddha's Fire Sermon: "The collocation of these two representatives of eastern and western asceticism, as the culmination of this part of the poem, is not an accident."[4] If Joe Hill seems out of place in the company of the Buddha and St. Augustine, let us remember what they have in common. All three lived lives of self-denial, and believed unshakably in the causes they represented. In each case, the man achieved certain immortality because his cause lived on after his death, and his life inspired subsequent generations to follow in his footsteps. Even if Joe Hill and St. Augustine are not exactly interchangeable, they have just enough in common so that Dylan's substitution makes cultural sense.

In the song "I Dreamed I Saw St. Augustine," St. Augustine tells Joe Hill that the age of martyrs, like the age of miracles, has passed. Only the last stanza reveals that the dream is a nightmare, and that the singer believes that he participated in his murder. Startling though it is, the conclusion of the song derives from Dylan's sense of kinship with the outcast. It was this sense of compassion that had attracted him to the civil rights movement in the first place, and caused a scandal in 1963 when he said that he felt a certain affinity with Lee Harvey Oswald. The larger point is the participation of the singer in the sins of the world, just as he shares the anxiety of his listeners in "I'll Keep It with Mine."

In the song "John Wesley Harding" Dylan gives the title character a symbolic name. As various people have noticed, the name's initials JWH are another version of "Yahweh," the personal name of God in the Hebrew Bible, as Johanna is another version of "Jehovah." In the passage that the King James Bible renders as "I am the Lord the God" (Exodus 20:2), the original says, "I am Yahweh your God." Bobby Zimmerman's bar mitzvah training appears yet again.

John Wesley Harding comes across as something like a Western Robin Hood, not exactly a lawman like the Gary Cooper character in *High Noon* (1952), but "a friend to the poor," a lawgiver, like the God of the Old Testament. He has some of the qualities of both. As someone who is strong yet compassionate, he begins a series of songs that might be called songs of artistic self-definition.

Dylan continues the Old Testament frame of reference for self-definition in "The Wicked Messenger," who came from "Eli," a variant of the name of God as spoken in Arabic, Hebrew, and Aramaic. If John Wesley Harding is stronger than those whom he helps, the wicked messenger is set apart from those to whom he speaks. The soles of his feet burn, marking the way he does not really belong on the earth. In another Old Testament reference, the seas part, marking his Moses-like role. But this is not Israel. This is America, so people want only good news and happy endings, which Dylan cannot provide.

"Drifter's Escape" rings in yet another change on the opposition of the sacred and the profane. In this case it is a matter of human law, as opposed to what is by implication divine law. As the drifter is found guilty, a bolt of lightning strikes the courthouse, enabling him to escape. There is no specific Old Testament source for this incident, so we turn for once to the New Testament, which has a precedent for lightning as a sign of God's will. In Matthew 24:27 we read, "For as the lightning cometh out of the east, and shineth even unto the west; so shall also the coming of the Son of man be."

"The Ballad of Frankie Lee and Judas Priest," one of the longest songs Dylan has ever written—eleven 8-line stanzas—explicitly draws on the implicit authority of the title song to state a moral about the importance of helping your neighbor. Dylan abandons that authority, and the separateness that it implies, in "Dear Landlord." This moving song, which Dylan sings with exceptional force and passion, amounts to a plea for reconciliation not between the metaphysical categories of the sacred and the profane, but reconciliation as an end to the estrangement between the businessman and the artist that is implicit in "Desolation Row"—the estrangement that Bobby Zimmerman had experienced back in Hibbing. After all, they share a common humanity.

Dylan brings it all back home in the song "I Pity the Poor Immigrant." Since almost all Americans are immigrants—people or descendants of those who came to America either voluntarily or involuntarily—he makes of it a compassionate meditation on the deceptive promises of American life. Although "I Pity the Poor Immigrant," which surely has some relevance to Dylan's immigrant grandfather Zigman Zimmerman, is shorter and denser than "The Ballad of Frankie Lee and Judas Priest," both songs share a concern with life and its temptations in a way that is free of metaphysics. The immigrant is poor in the double sense of "unfortunate"—lacking in money and in happiness, as well. The immigrant is suspended—stuck—between home and his new country, between his laughter and his death, and between laughter and violence. That is to say, he is caught between the promise of the American dream and the reality of his life. This is such a great theme in American culture that the song seems like a version of *The Great Gatsby*, by F. Scott Fitzgerald, stripped of its plot. It also anticipates the future. (Bruce Springsteen took the tension between the promise of the American dream and the reality of people's lives as one of his great themes, and Dylan's "I Pity the Poor Immigrant" has exceptional relevance for Springsteen's career.)

Dylan's ongoing concern with the relationship between the sacred and the profane sometimes amounts to a distinction between God's emissary and the common folk, and that distinction appears in "I'll Keep It with Mine," on the album *Blonde on Blonde*, a song that is related to Dylan's subsequent ambiguous benediction to his fans, "Forever Young." What is the "it" that the singer will keep? It is something that gives him a kinship with them; "you" have it, and so does the singer. The song makes the most sense if we assume that "it" stands for something problematic, like "anxiety."

The singer's listeners believe that they can give him (i.e., project onto him) their anxiety, and he will take it away. They believe that he will solve all their problems and give them all the answers. In fact, though, he is all too human, and has his own anxiety—even if it is only the anxiety about taking on other people's anxiety. Anxiety, the song implies, is part of the human condition; everybody has some. The singer is saying that he will keep their anxiety with his own anxiety as an act of generosity and kindness.

What is implied in this acceptance, though, is the singer's bargain with his audience. In exchange for taking on their anxiety, he gets to tell them the truth. He does so by presenting an allegory that anticipates the several allegories on *John Wesley Harding*. Dylan the songwriter thinks back to his days as a folkie, when songs about railroad conductors such as the legendary Casey Jones, enjoyed great popularity. Except that the conductor has become an allegorical figure who is "stuck," and this is a key word for Dylan. When you are stuck, as in "Stuck Inside of Mobile with the Memphis Blues Again," you cannot move, grow, or change. (Being stuck and unable to overcome the precursor is the ephebe's greatest fear, of course.) Since the conductor is stuck on the line, he will be at the same place at the same time tomorrow. Like the train that he drives, he has a mechanical, predictable quality, and thus he stands for the people who predictably want the singer to assuage their anxiety for them. He agrees to take on their anxiety, if not resolve it, in his capacity as a wicked messenger who tells people things that they do not want to hear.

If *John Wesley Harding* is one long prayer, the album *Nashville Skyline* is one long seduction. The songs are more grounded in the here and now than anything that Dylan had ever written. This crucial fact explains the popularity of "Lay Lady Lay," of course. It is probably the most popular song Dylan has ever recorded, especially among women. After all, what could be more grounded than making love?

Dylan's new emphasis on sex and sexuality in *Nashville Skyline* does not mean that he is not up to his old tricks. He had to do something, after all, and it may not be too much to suggest here that *Nashville Skyline* offers an example of the way strong poets become their own precursors. This being so, at some point they need to create a swerve from their own work, and swerve Dylan did. *Nashville Skyline* sounds like nothing he had recorded before, and like very little that he has recorded since then. As the title indicates, it sounds like Nashville the heartland, not New York the big city. When you think about it, you realize that New York, representing big-city sophistication, and Nashville, representing heartland authenticity, constitute the two poles of his synthesizer's sensibility.

However, Dylan was still using intertextuality, although in a new and playful way that was in keeping with the mellower music that he was writing. Then it was not so much that the songs used intertextuality, but rather that Dylan does something like what jazz musicians call riffing on old standards. When we know what those old standards (old in the history of rock and roll, anyway) were, the knowledge that we bring to the new songs enriches their meaning.

Dylan was still writing night songs, only they were not night songs like "Visions of Johanna." Instead, they were night songs in the hedonistic spirit of the Rolling Stones's 1967 hit, "Let's Spend the Night Together." (Actually, we can consider the whole album *Nashville Skyline* as a response not to the specifics of the Rolling Stones song, which was considered shocking at the time, but to its hedonistic spirit.) Still in these songs, Dylan synthesized singers and styles as the Stones never did. In "Tonight I'll Be Staying Here with You," he refers by name to the song "The Night Time Is the Right Time," which had been a breakout hit for Ray Charles in 1958. And, there is a reference to casting a spell, which suggests "Witchcraft," one of Sinatra's standards, a song that he included on *Sinatra: A Man and His Music*, a retrospective album that won a Grammy for Album of the Year in 1967. Dylan had probably heard it just before he wrote "Tonight I'll Be Staying Here with You."

And then there is "I'll Be Your Baby Tonight," whose charm and simplicity belie the fact that it belongs to a mostly forgotten subgenre of songs from the early 1960s—answer songs. By 1961, rock and roll had acquired a certain self-awareness that allowed for intertextuality, and sometimes a hit song whose title was a command or a question would be answered by another song. Answer songs rode on the coattails, as it were, of the popularity of the first song. Thus, Jeanne Black's "He'll Have to Stay" responded to Jim Reeves's "He'll Have to Go." Marilyn Michaels answered Ray Peterson's "Tell Laura I Love Her" with "Tell Tommy I Miss Him," and Damita Jo answered the Drifters's "Save the Last Dance for Me" with (predictably) "I'll Save the Last Dance for You." Even Elvis received the honor, if that is the right word, of an answer song. While in the Army, he recorded "Are You Lonesome Tonight?" and his smoldering voice made the most of the spoken narration. During the answer songs fad, the song offered an obvious temptation, and both Thelma Carter and Dodie Stevens gave the obvious answer, "Yes, I'm Lonesome Tonight." (What else could a girl say to Elvis?)

The point is that Dylan's "I'll Be Your Baby Tonight" is an answer song, probably the last one ever written. Dylan recorded it so long after the answer song fad died out that it sounds fresh and innovative. More specifically, it answers the girl group classic "Be My Baby." Sung by the Ronettes and released in August 1963, "Be My Baby" went to #2 on the charts. It was produced by Phil Spector, and is considered a classic example of Spector's "Wall of Sound." As such, it has been covered by many singers, including John Lennon, but no one except Dylan has ever answered it. He made the title more specific than that of the original because "Be My Baby" begins "The night we met." The Ronettes promise "I'll make you happy," and Dylan refers to this promise when he asks the girl to "make him smile."

And with all these other great singers on his mind, Dylan could not forget Elvis, of course. "One More Night" is a response—something like an answer song—to "One Night with You," which Elvis sang on his comeback special in 1968. It is impossible to imagine that Dylan did not watch this show, which featured Elvis in a black leather outfit and remains the most overwhelming display of pure star power ever seen on American television. Even as he acknowledges Elvis's greatness, he swerves from it. If Elvis's voice throbbed with such longing on "One Night with You" that he made women squirm in their seats, Dylan adopts a quieter tone, tinged with regret.

Something similar is going on in "Pledging My Time" on *Blonde on Blonde*, which is written against "Pledging My Love," a hit for rhythm and blues singer Johnny Ace in early 1955. Love, the principal concern of teenagers, is contrasted with commitment, the principal concern of married men like Dylan. The connection between the songs offers considerable interest.

We can guess that Dylan heard "Pledging My Love" on WLAC 1510, the other clear-channel radio station in Nashville in addition to WSM 650. A little-known and less-understood aspect of early rock and roll was that AM radio played a key role in disseminating music styles. WSM played white artists like Hank Williams, Ernest Tubb, and Eddy Arnold; they were great artists but they were white, and played "white music." WLAC, on the other hand, had bold disc jockeys who played what was then called "race music." In the 1950s, this was often the first black music white teenagers had ever heard. Young white boys especially loved songs with suggestive lyrics like "Work with Me Annie," which Hank Ballard and the Midnighters recorded in 1954.[5] What matters here is that it was probably on WLAC that the young Bobby Zimmerman heard Chuck Berry, Fats Domino, and Little Richard for the first time—as well as Johnny Ace.

And, finally, there's the salacious "Country Pie." People who take this song at "face (mouth?) value" miss the intertextuality because it contains Dylan's only use of Shakespeare. In Act 3, Scene 2, of *Hamlet*, Hamlet instigates the following passive-aggressive dialogue with Ophelia in which Shakespeare puns on "country." Hamlet asks Ophelia if he can lie in her lap and she says no. Then he asks if he can lay his head on her lap. She responds affirmatively. He asks, "Do you think I meant country matters?" She says, "I think nothing," and then he says, "That's a fair thought to lie between maids' legs." Dylan has so much fun with the song "Country Pie" that you can practically hear him grinning as he sings his lines that are filled with exuberant wordplay. In "Country Pie" he created something like the ultimate antithesis of "Blowin' in the Wind." How far he had come in about five years!

6

"Putting a Certain Orderliness to the Chaos"

In 1955, Allen Ginsberg wrote these words in "Howl":

I saw the best minds of my generation destroyed by madness, starving hysterical naked, dragging themselves through the negro streets at dawn looking for an angry fix, angelheaded hipsters burning for the ancient heavenly connection to the starry dynamo in the machinery of night...[1]

And so it goes, on and on, creating a long orgasmic spurt of words in the most famous single text of the Beat Generation. The run-on lines of Beat poetry (Ginsberg) and prose (Jack Kerouac) expressed their alienation from everything that Disneyland, which also opened in 1955, stood for. West coast versus East coast, or conformity versus rebellion. In short, the basic cultural conflicts of the 1950s.

"Howl" is a key starting point for Dylan's mature work in its surrealistic images, its attack on English syntax and so forth. However, and it is a big however, Dylan is a genius, and Ginsberg was not; he was talented, but no more than that. Various videos and accounts of his behavior confirm that impression. My guess is that Dylan had a similar reaction. (He spent a good deal of time with Ginsberg and Lawrence Ferlinghetti and the other Beat poets.) Dylan is so laconic that he has never said so, but his songs offer clear evidence that he rejected the stream-of-consciousness writing of the Beats, and the self-indulgent attitude that it implied. Dylan's masterpieces of the 1960s take the wild, associative images that he found in the Beat poets and their predecessors and put them into the most amazing stanza forms ever created by an American songwriter.

In analyzing anything relating to Dylan, such as his stanza forms, for example, it is often helpful to start with the New York art scene. Here is what one critic said about it: "In the midst of the grim turmoil of the '60s, moods shifted quickly. One could speculate that the chaos in public life induced many to seek order in the categories of art."² Perhaps a few brave souls on the front lines of the civil rights movement had a more vivid experience of "the chaos in public life" than Dylan, but there were not many. And nobody as introverted as Dylan deals well with the chaos of public life. By 1964, if not earlier, he needed order in his life.

In *Chronicles*, Dylan says something very relevant for this opposition of chaos and order. He says that in the early 1960s when he started drawing, he felt like he was "putting a certain orderliness to the chaos around...."³ "Orderliness" is not a word that most people associate with Dylan, but that is because people have not paid appropriate attention to the formal structures of his songs.

Dylan himself paid very careful attention indeed to the formal structures of his songs, and in doing so he was following the lead of no less than Hank Williams. In *Chronicles*, Dylan wrote something startling about what he learned from listening to Hank Williams:

> In time, I became aware that in Hank's recorded songs were the archetype [sic] rules of poetic songwriting. The architectural forms are like marble pillars and they had to be there. Even his words—all of his syllables are divided up so they make perfect mathematical sense. You can learn a lot about the structure of songwriting by listening to his records, and I listened to them a lot and had them internalized.⁴

"Archetype rules of poetic songwriting"? "Marble pillars"? The received wisdom from critics about Dylan is that he *broke* the rules of songwriting. Is it possible that his admirers and his critics alike have missed something essential about his songs—something that was right there in the readily available lyrics of his songs?

An analysis of Dylan's use of stanza and rhyme forms not only enriches our understanding of his great songs, it also enables us to orient his work in the evolution of American popular song and to understand Dylan's relationship with other great songwriters. Dylan is many things, and one of them is the link between Tin Pan Alley and rock and roll. We can thus connect these two great eras of popular song by putting Dylan's contributions in the middle. In this way, we can understand in a concrete way something that people have sensed only vaguely. I have in mind the matter of Dylan's influence on songwriters in the 1970s and 1980s, which is nowhere more apparent than in their use of his rhyme schemes.

If we ask what Dylan started with, the answer is easy. He started with the music he grew up with, the music of the 1950s, which ran the gamut from the magical to the maudlin, like the music of every decade. These songs, however, were meant to be played on AM radio. AM radio stations put time limits on songs, and thus songs had to be short and snappy, and that meant that their lyrics were written in couplets. An exceptionally pure example of couplets in 1950s rock and roll is Chuck Berry's "Maybelline." Each verse consists of couplets and can be represented for the sake of convenience as **aabbcc** (hill/ville, road/Ford, ninety-five/side by side—approximate rhymes as sung) or **aaaabc** (hill/pill/grille/hill). Each verse is followed by the three-line chorus, which can be represented as **aaa** (true/true/do).

If "Howl," and the work of the Beat poets in general, seemed too diffuse and self-indulgent to Dylan, "Maybelline" and the lyrics of 1950s rock and roll seemed too limited and restrictive for a songwriter who had little interest in AM airplay, and thus he concentrated on songs for live performances and albums. We understand something essential about Dylan, and about his creative drive in general, when we understand that his great songs represent a middle way, a synthesis of Allen Ginsberg and Jack Kerouac on one hand and Hank Williams and Chuck Berry on the other. (And those are only his contemporaries. He could never forget Shakespeare and Dante.) Dylan took the freedom of Ginsberg's and Kerouac's surreal images and combined them with the formal discipline of Williams and Berry. The results changed American popular music forever. The songs had "vague traces" (to use a phrase from "Mr. Tambourine Man") of all four of these artists, but did not imitate anything that anyone else had ever written.

By the time Dylan started writing, the couplet had been the standard songwriting form for so long that everybody unconsciously assumed that it was the only way to write songs. The possibility of other choices, and of the many other possible verse forms, had been erased from the consciousness of many.

This possibility was not erased from the consciousness of Dylan. He knew that his listeners had heard hundreds, if not thousands, of songs written in couplets, so he made his songs edgy because he usually avoided couplets as the sole rhyme form. It is essential to understand that Dylan's songs achieve their mesmerizing effect not just because of their startling imagery. They also lingered in the consciousness of listeners because they frustrated their expectations—expectations that were all the more powerful for remaining unconscious. His listeners expected that the first line would rhyme with the second line, and that the third line would rhyme with the fourth line, and so forth. The couplet tradition—if indeed it was a tradition, and not a dogma—offered little stimulus to his imagination, and most of Dylan's songs have different stanza forms. In English prosody, the technical word for such a stanza form is a nonce form—that is to say, a form created by the poet. (As opposed to a traditional form such as a sonnet, for example.)

We can best understand the techniques by which Dylan accomplished this by following the evolution of his stanza forms in the 1960s. We notice the remarkable variations in his stanza forms shown in the lists in Tables 3 and 4, which provide the material for the discussions in this chapter.

Table 3. Rhyme Forms in Dylan's Songs of the Early 1960s

Albums and Songs	No. of Stanzas	Stanza number: Rhyme forms
The Freewheelin' Bob Dylan (1963)		
"Blowin' in the Wind"	3	All: **abcbdb** Chorus: **aa**
"Girl of the North Country"	5	1, 2, 3, 5: **abab** 4: no rhymes
The Times They Are a-Changin' (1964)		
"The Times They Are a-Changin'"	5	1, 4: **abcdedfdf** 2: **abcbdefef** 5: **abcbcbdbd**
"Only a Pawn in Their Game"	5	1: **abccbdeb** 2: **abbcbbcdbcc** 3: **abcccdeffebb** 4: **abccddeffggg** 5: **abccdefgf**
Another Side of Bob Dylan (1964)		
"All I Really Want to Do"	6	1, 4: **aaaaaa** 2: **aabbaa** 3, 5: **aabbb** 6: **aabbcc**
"Chimes of Freedom"	6	1, 2, 3, 5: **abcbdddb** 4: **abcdeeef** 6: **abcbddde**
"My Back Pages"	4	All: **abcbdefe**
"It Ain't Me, Babe"	3	1, 3: **abcbdefeg** 2: **ababcdedf** Refrain: **aaa**
Bringing It All Back Home (1965)		
"Subterranean Homesick Blues"	4	1: **abaacdddeeffgfhfif** 2: **aaabccccddeeeeeeefe** 3: **aaaabcccdefgfhhif** 4: **abc(c)defgfhhiijjkklj**
"Bob Dylan's 115th Dream"	11	1: **abcbdefgehiji** 11: **abcbdefeghig** (3 rhyme sets in each stanza)
"Mr. Tambourine Man"	4	1: **aabccd** 2: **aabcdef** 3: **aabcddc** 4: **abcdefgd** Chorus: **abab**

6. "Putting a Certain Orderliness to the Chaos"

Albums and Songs	No. of Stanzas	Stanza number: Rhyme forms
Highway 61 Revisited (1965)		
"Like a Rolling Stone"	4	1: **abcbddeef** 2, 3: **abcbddde** 4: **abcdeeffg** Chorus: **aabcc** or **aabcbb**
"Highway 61 Revisited"	5	1,2: **aabbccc** 3: **ababccc** 4: **aaaabbb**
"Desolation Row"	10	1, 4, 5, 6, 10: **abcbdefeghih** 3, 7, 8, 9: **abcbdefghiji**

Table 4. Rhyme Forms in Dylan's Songs of the Late 1960s

Albums and Songs	No. of Stanzas	Stanza number: Rhyme forms
Blonde on Blonde (1966)		
"Rainy Day Women #12 & 35"	5	1: **aabccc** 2, 3, 4: **aabbcc** 5: **abccaa**
"Pledging My Time"	5	All: **abcbdd**
"Visions of Johanna"	5	1: **aaabcbcdd** 2: **aabacdccee** 3: **aabaccdee** 4: **aabcddddee** 5: **aabcaddddeeff**
"Stuck Inside of Mobile with the Memphis Blues Again"	9	1–3, 5, 6, 8: **abcbdefe** 7: **abbbcdef** 9: **abcdcefe** Chorus: **aba**
"Sad-Eyed Lady of the Lowlands"	5	1–4: **aaabcccb** 5: **aaabcdcb** Chorus: **abbcc**
John Wesley Harding (1967)		
"John Wesley Harding"	3	1: **abcdbef** 2: **abcdebfd** 3: **abcdbefd**
"The Ballad of Frankie Lee and Judas Priest"	11	All: **abcbdefe**
"Dear Landlord"	3	All: **abcbdefe**
"I Pity the Poor Immigrant"	3	1, 2: **abcdefgf** 3: **abcbdeae**
"Down Along the Cove"	3	All: **ababcb**

Albums and Songs	No. of Stanzas	Stanza number: Rhyme forms
John Wesley Harding (1967)		
"I'll Be Your Baby Tonight"	4	1, 2, 4: **aab** 3: **abcbb**
Nashville Skyline (1969)		
"To Be Alone with You"	4	1, 2: **ababcaca** 3: **abcbdede** 4: **abab**
"I Threw It All Away"	4	All: **abccb**
"Peggy Day"	5	1,2,4,5: **aaa** or **aaaa** 3: **aabcb**
"Lay Lady Lay"	4	1: **aabb** 2: **abbcc** 3: **abcdc** 4: **aabba**
"One More Night"	4 plus	1: **abaab** 2, 4, 5: **abccb**
"Country Pie"	6	1, 2, 4, 6: **aabb** 3: **abcb** 5: **abab**
"Tonight I'll Be Staying Here with You"	5	1, 2, 4, 5: **abccb** 3: **aabb**

"Girl of the North Country" offers an obvious example of how Dylan began. He wrote the song with rhyming verses, with a few approximate rhymes, such as ends/winds and prayed/day, and it seems conventional enough until we realize that it has no chorus. Although it satisfied listeners' expectations for rhymes in verses, it frustrated their expectation that a chorus would follow the verse, as it does in "Maybelline" and so many other songs. This feature of "Girl of the North Country" gives us the first indication of how Dylan would experiment with the verse and chorus structures of American popular songs throughout the 1960s.

We find another resolution of the problem of the verse and chorus structures in "Blowin' in the Wind." This great anthemic song has a rhyme scheme of **abcbdb**, which is to say, the verse has no couplets at all, but has 3 alternating lines that rhyme. It must have satisfied him to deny expectations with a verse that began in this way, because he used it throughout the 1960s. The **abcb** beginning appears not just in "Blowin' in the Wind," but also in songs such as "Bob Dylan's Blues," "The Times They Are a-Changin'," "With God on Our Side," "Chimes of Freedom," "Bob Dylan's 115th Dream," "Gates of Eden," "Like a Rolling Stone," "Desolation Row," and "Dear Landlord." The fact that he rarely uses it in the stanzas in songs on the *Nashville Skyline*

6. "Putting a Certain Orderliness to the Chaos"   109

album indicates just how much stylistic change that remarkable album represents.

Certain songs in Dylan's work mark major changes, and "Only a Pawn in Their Game" is one of them. Although people expected that Dylan would have nothing but anger for the killer of Medgar Evers, he wrote it not as an anger song but as a compassion song and sings it, thoughtfully and slowly, as a compassion song. The first and second lines do not rhyme, but the third and fourth ones in four of the five stanzas do. And then he writes three rhyming lines in a row in the third stanza. This turns out to be excessive, even for Dylan, and he cannot quite maintain it. He cannot maintain the structure in the fourth stanza, but he is committed to stretching it—quite literally. The third line of the second stanza runs to all of 14 syllables—something unimaginable for Chuck Berry.

Emboldened by the powerful effect that he achieved in "Only a Pawn in Their Game," he tried a one-time experiment in "All I Really Want to Do," in which the first and fourth stanzas feature no less than six lines that rhyme: **aaaaaa**. Dylan cannot sustain this, either—I suppose he realized it too late, and the rhyme scheme breaks down in the second, third, fifth, and sixth stanzas. The sixth stanza consists of three couplets.

After these early experiments, he figured out how he could avoid the structural cliché of a verse written in couplets followed by a chorus written in couplets, and he did so in "Chimes of Freedom." As we know, he debuted it at the 1964 Newport Folk Festival, and sang it with the assurance that he had lacked the year before. We also know that it is a breakthrough song because of its use of synesthesia; now we notice that its stanza form, **abcbdddb**, enabled him to avoid couplets in two different ways. He defies his listeners' expectations of two couplets that constitute a verse by rhyming the first four lines as **abcb** in five of the six stanzas; he then goes to the opposite extreme by following the first four lines with triple rhymes: **ddd**. (In prosody the formal term for a triple rhyme is a tercet.) It had taken him three years in New York and a couple of albums, but he was on his way.

Rather than consolidate and refine this discovery, as any other songwriter would have done, he tried experimenting with various extremes—mostly, one supposes, just to see what would happen. So "Subterranean Homesick Blues" features what is surely the longest stanza form in the history of American popular song—it has 18 lines in stanzas one and four! To keep the stanza from falling apart at this extreme length, he imbeds multiple couplets, tercets, and an internal rhyme. One stanza has 6 lines that rhyme ("tiptoes"/"No-Doz"/"those"/"hose"/"nose"). The tercet pattern recalls the stanza form in "Chimes of Freedom." When he performs this audaciously raucous song he also stresses the rhymes ("pave*ment*"/"govern*ment*") in the first stanza so that his listeners will be only partially bewildered.

He went to the opposite extreme in another raucous song, a companion piece to "Subterranean Homesick Blues," namely, "Rainy Day Women #12 & 35." (Both songs make paranoia seem funny.) In "Rainy Day Women #12 & 35" he uses mostly couplets, as though he could now write several stanzas in the **aabbcc** form that he used in stanza 6 of "All I Really Want to Do." He does the same thing in "Highway 61 Revisited," another loud, up-tempo song.

As a crisis ode, "Mr. Tambourine Man" has a verse and chorus structure, and a fairly conventional one at that. The first verse has two couplets (**aabccd**), and the **abab** chorus is the same one that he used as the stanza form in "Girl of the North Country." One has the sense that he is gathering his forces.

And that brings us to "Like a Rolling Stone." He did not want or need a chorus in the songs with very long stanza forms, but it is obvious that the relationship between verse and chorus was still bothering him. Since the **abcbdddb** form worked so well in "Chimes of Freedom" he retained the first six lines of that structure (**abcbdd**) in the first three stanzas. Then—and here one imagines him sitting at the typewriter with a cigarette hanging out of his mouth—he puzzled over what to do about the chorus. (I suspect that the chorus came to him before the verse.) He realized that he could break down the separation of the verse and the chorus by blending them together, just as a painter might blend two colors at the edge of a form. Then, he made the final line of each stanza end with a word that rhymed with "feel," the last word in the first line of the chorus (meal/deal/steal/conceal).

"Like a Rolling Stone" is unique. Dylan must have sensed this, because later he did not blend verse and chorus in quite the same way. In fact, he seemed not to like choruses, and the two rare examples of major songs that have choruses are "Sad-Eyed Lady of the Lowlands" and "Stuck Inside of Mobile with the Memphis Blues Again."

"Visions of Johanna" has what might be called a vestigial chorus, in that Dylan repeats the title of the song in the last line of every stanza. All the stanzas begin with a couplet or tercet. Only Dylan could have thought it up, and only Dylan could have sustained it for five stanzas. In the last two stanzas, the couplets come after four or five rhyming lines, which produces an appropriately incantatory effect. Only after these multiple rhyming lines does Dylan let himself end the stanza with couplets—perhaps as another aspect of the vestigial chorus, or perhaps as something suggested by the Shakespearean sonnet, which also ends with a couplet.

Once he had committed himself to the rigor of this format, he could let it hold the song together. As a result, he felt feel free to write lines of wildly varying length. "Visions of Johanna" has some short lines—two with five syllables and two with six syllables. At the other extreme, it has five lines with 15 syllables, two with 16 syllables, four with 17 syllables, and one with 22 syllables! This line, line two of the fifth stanza, is longer than anything in "Subterranean Homesick Blues"—and is probably the longest single line in the history of American popular song.

The authoritative statements and didactic tales in the album *John Wesley Harding* needed no complex stanza forms, and for once Dylan found a pattern **abcbdefe** that satisfied him enough so that he could use eight-line stanza form for five songs on the same album. These five songs have no couplets. For once, Dylan used a rhyme scheme with historical precedents. No less an eminence than Emily Dickinson used it in her "I Cannot Live with You." Because the last four lines repeat the rhyme scheme of the first four, this is sometimes called a mirror rhyme.

If we consider the stanza forms of *Nashville Skyline*, and compare them to those of the preceding albums, we again get the impression that Dylan is swerving from his own achievements of the 1960s. If "Visions of Johanna" is the prime example of those achievements, with a phenomenally difficult rhyme scheme rigorously sustained, then "Lay Lady Lay," "One More Night," and "Country Pie" constitute an opposite extreme. In so disciplined a writer as Dylan, each stanza in "Lay Lady Lay" has a different rhyme scheme. However, "Lay Lady Lay" begins with the easiest rhyme scheme of all, two couplets: **aabb**. This, of course, is the rhyme scheme of "Maybelline," and one of the most popular poems ever written by an American, Joyce Kilmer's "Trees."

Analyzing Dylan's rhyme schemes thus reveals some important things about his now legendary songs, but it has more significance than that. Analyzing the way Dylan organized words into lines, and lines into songs, is as fundamental an exercise as there is, both for itself and for what it leads to. This especially applies to the startlingly distinctive feature of his lyrics, the triple rhyme or tercet, as opposed to the couplets that he had grown up with, and which so many great performers had used to such great effect. Although Dylan's triple rhymes were as revolutionary as anything else in the arts in the 1960s, only the historically uninformed believe that they were unprecedented.

One understands why people say that Dylan put an end to Tin Pan Alley, but what they really mean is that Dylan put an end to the genteel tradition of songwriting, which featured lots of references to love, accompanied by the sound of lush violins. McLuhan would have said that electricity obsolesced gentility, which is to say that it redefined it.

The larger point is that revolutions, no matter how radical, usually have significant precedents that can be found if one knows where to seek them. This generalization especially applies to triple rhymes, which serve as yet another of the Ariadne threads in Dylan's work. And when we follow this particular Ariadne thread, we find that it takes us to an unexpected destination—Tin Pan Alley.

Tin Pan Alley is a generic name for the (usually Jewish) songwriters who wrote so many great hits from the 1930s to the 1950s that their work has come to be known as the Great American Songbook. Tin Pan Alley included some of the greatest songwriters of all time, such as Cole Porter and Irving Berlin, and some of the greatest songwriting teams of all time, such as Richard Rodgers and Oscar Hammerstein and George and Ira Gershwin. In his book *The Poets of Tin Pan Alley*, Phillip Furia cites a key principle for all of them: "As Doris Day puts it to Danny Thomas in the film biography of lyricist Guy Kahn, 'Gus, ya gotta learn to say "I love you" in thirty-two bars.'"[5] Furia goes on to comment, "Little wonder, then, that between 1920 and 1940, 85 percent of the popular songs were love songs—a substantially greater proportion than one finds in the nineteenth-century song or even in contemporary songs."[6] The poets of Tin Pan Alley achieved greatness within the conventions of their times, as great artists usually do.

When people say that Dylan broke with the Tin Pan Alley tradition, what they mean is that he expanded the thematic range for American popular song—and he certainly did that. However, as the lyricists of Tin Pan Alley wrote love songs in 32 bars, they showed that they were consummate wordsmiths. The melodies of their songs and relatively slow tempos (many of the songs are waltzes) allowed them to show off their dazzling wordplay.

In fact, the thematic restrictions of Tin Pan Alley songs gave the lyricists a certain freedom to experiment with the verse and chorus arrangement— and these experiments often appeared in the use of triple rhymes that anticipate what Dylan did in the 1960s. Table 5 shows a more or less random sample of Tin Pan Alley songs with triple rhymes.

Table 5. Examples of Triple Rhymes in Tin Pan Alley Song Lyrics

Song	Writer	Date	Rhymes
"Anything Goes"	Cole Porter	1934	clock/shock/rock
"Cheek to Cheek"	Irving Berlin	1935	speak/seek/cheek
"I'm Beginning to See the Light"	Hodges/James/ George/Ellington	1944	park/dark/park
"Teach Me Tonight"	Sammy Cahn/ Gene de Paul	1953	Clear my love/near my love/here my love

The time span of the four songs in Table 5 over two decades gives an indication of the durability of triple rhymes as a key marker of Tin Pan Alley songs.

More specifically, one songwriter, Cole Porter, created a body of work that significantly anticipates Dylan's songs, and enables us to make a connection between the 1930s and the 1960s, and between Tin Pan Alley and rock and roll. As Midwesterners (Porter was born in Indiana), Dylan and Porter

6. "Putting a Certain Orderliness to the Chaos"

used Manhattan as a base, but never "inhabited" it as Berlin and the Gershwins did. Richard Rogers once made a telling comment about the way Porter was in, but not of, Tin Pan Alley: "It is surely one of the ironies of the musical theatre that despite the abundance of Jewish composers, the one who has written the most enduring 'Jewish' music should be an Episcopalian millionaire who was born on a farm in Peru, Indiana."[7] To cite one of Porter's most felicitous neologisms, he was socially the "tinpantithesis" of Tin Pan Alley. As a Jew, Dylan has an affinity to Tin Pan Alley, but his Jewish origins made him an outsider among the folkies because folk music was both historically and socially a WASP (white Anglo-Saxon protestant) interest. (Think of Woody Guthrie, Burl Ives, and Pete Seeger.) Porter's homosexuality made him an outsider among his Tin Pan Alley friends, or at least distanced him from them as much as his inherited wealth and Midwestern WASP origins did.

Although Porter (1891–1964) lived a long, productive life, his great decade was the 1930s, and he had very much the same significance for the 1930s as Dylan had for the 1960s. If Dylan kept wanting to transcend the limitations of the various songwriting styles of his time, so did Porter. For all the success of *Anything Goes* and his other musicals culminating in the star-studded movie *High Society,* his songs with their delight in wordplay for its own sake and inventive melodies now seem more like self-contained experiences than part of a dramatic whole. These songs do not advance the story and reveal character as much as the songs of Rodgers and Hammerstein, for example. If one of Dylan's albums rarely sounded like the preceding one, Porter also commanded a variety of styles, from pseudo country and western ("Don't Fence Me In") to pseudo Viennese operetta ("Wunderbar").

If "Sad-Eyed Lady of the Lowlands" shocked record executives as well as listeners with its length of more than eleven minutes, so did Porter's "Begin the Beguine." Furia says that "at a whopping one-hundred and eight measures [it is] one of the longest popular songs ever written."[8] Dylan's and Porter's songs disturbed people both because of their length and also because the artists pushed at the limits of what middle-class Americans would accept. (Dylan might have said they transcended the thematic limits.)

If Dylan proclaimed "Everybody must get stoned" to a cheering studio audience on "Rainy Day Women #12 & 35," Porter's songs again and again incited people, if not to try drugs then to give themselves over to licentious behavior. This is the point of any number of Porter's songs, such as "Experiment," "Anything Goes," "Let's Do It," "Let's Misbehave," and "It's De-Lovely." And only Porter's catalogue, in his time and ours, has songs that let a hooker and a gigolo unapologetically describe their lives to straight society in "Love for Sale" and "Just a Gigolo."

Not surprisingly, Porter's songs offended the censors of the 1930s. For example, Porter's biographer William McBrien says about "But in the Morning No," a song from the musical *DuBarry Was a Lady*: "For many years, 'But in the Morning No' could not be sung on the air."[9] Naturally, things were worse in Boston. When *Out of This World* was being put together in 1939, "a female censor in Boston issued a 'de-sexing order' which stipulated in nine points the changes required for the show to continue."[10]

In short, the numerous analogies between Porter and Dylan, these two Midwestern prodigies, offer the possibility of connecting the 1930s and the 1960s, and thus beginning a holistic understanding of American popular music that is not broken up into discrete periods. Any such holistic understanding must connect Dylan to the songwriters who came after him as well as to those who came before him, and it is to this matter that we now turn.

The matter of Dylan's influence on subsequent songwriters recalls the old saw about the weather—everybody talks about it, but nobody does anything about it. The general wisdom is that Dylan was the most influential songwriter of his generation, and that he revolutionized American popular song and so forth. But most people cannot identify any major performers whom Dylan influenced except Bruce Springsteen. Moreover, Dylan's influence cannot be a matter of protest songs, which died out in the mid-1960s, or of songs of transcendence, which only Dylan wrote. So where do we find it?

The best way to investigate Dylan's influence on subsequent songwriters is to investigate their use of triple rhymes. It stands to reason that, if rock songs in the 1950s were written in couplets and then Dylan offered alternative stanzas that featured triple rhymes and then we find triple rhymes in the songs of later songwriters, these songwriters were assimilating what Dylan had done and finding out what they could do with it. Table 6 shows representative examples of what some American songwriters did with Dylan's triple rhymes from the late 1960s into the 1980s.

Table 6. Triple Rhymes or More in Some American Songs (1968–1984)

Song	Writer	Year	Rhymes
"Games People Play"	Joe South	1968	"to ya"/"halleluya"/"to ya"
"Sunday Morning Coming Down"	Kris Kristofferson	1970	"hurt"/"dessert/"shirt"
"Miss American Pie"	Don McLean	1973	"pie/"dry"/"rye"/"die"/"die"
"Ramblin' Man"	The Allman Brothers	1973	"Can"/"understand"/"man"
"Lyin' Eyes"	Don Henley/Glen Frey	1975	"eyes"/"disguise"/"realize"

6. "Putting a Certain Orderliness to the Chaos" 115

Song	Writer	Year	Rhymes
"The Pretender"	Jackson Browne	1976	"in"/"again"/"amen"
"We Are the Champions"	Freddy Mercury	1977	"face"/"disgrace"/"place"
"Texas in My Rearview Mirror"	Mac Davis	1980	"control"/"roll"/"soul"
"Jump"	Eddie Van Halen/ David Lee Roth	1984	"machine"/"seen"/"mean"
"Faux Commercial for Powdermilk Biscuits"	Garrison Keillor	?	"tried 'em"/"satisfied 'em"/ "item"

In the first song listed, "Games People Play," Joe South took up Dylan's early theme of hypocrisy and treated it in something like a light-hearted way. Encouraged by Dylan's cultural references, he took as the title the name of a pop psychology bestseller by Eric Berne, and used the phrase "sock it to ya" popularized on the TV comedy revue "Laugh-In." He uses the unusual, and ambitious, **aaab** stanza form.

Still more ambitious is Kris Kristofferson's "Sunday Morning Coming Down," a powerful song that, like his classic "Me and Bobby McGee," deals with irreparable loss. A former Rhodes Scholar, Kristofferson was one of the few songwriters of the time who could appreciate not just Dylan's references, but also the aesthetic that informed them. He created something like Dylan's weird sense of alienation in his song "Sunday Morning Coming Down," which probably bears some relationship to Dylan's "One Too Many Mornings." Nevertheless, it is a brilliant, original song, in part because Kristofferson understood the way Dylan had used painting and adapted it for his own purposes. In writing his song, Kristofferson turned for inspiration not to Picasso, but to Edward Hopper, and specifically to Hopper's painting "Early Sunday Morning" (1930), which daringly evokes loneliness by showing no people at all—just a brick building on a street. In a way that is reminiscent of Dylan's use of Picasso, Kristofferson translated Hopper's sense of cultural emptiness into words in his brilliant song.

Kristofferson was also inspired by Dylan's experimentation with stanza forms. The stanzas of "Sunday Morning Coming Down" begin with the **abcb** quatrain that Dylan often used in the mid–1960s. Then, he added additional rhymes in the remaining lines of the stanzas (for example, **abcbdbef**), with the rhyming words giving it a very effective unity. He also uses the **abcbdefe** rhyme form used by Dylan in songs recorded on his *John Wesley Harding* album.

Don McLean has not had Kristofferson's long, multi-faceted career, but he did write "Miss American Pie," the definitive song of the early 1970s. It stayed on the charts for most of 1973—much longer than any of Kristofferson's songs. This now classic song documents a historic moment, the inward turn of popular music after the violence that occurred during a Rolling Stones concert at the Altamont Racetrack in California and after the deaths of Jim

Morrison, Jimi Hendrix, and Janis Joplin. In "Miss American Pie" McLean takes from "Desolation Row" the idea of using references to create thematic unity. (And, one suspects, McLean reached beyond "Desolation Row" to "The Waste Land," which has a similar despondent tone.) But if Dylan's references deal with consciousness, McLean's deal with history. They deal with the sadness and sense of loss that people felt in the aftermath of the violence and assassinations of the 1960s, and in the midst of the Watergate crisis. And naturally these references include Dylan as "the jester."

Perhaps emboldened by Dylan's reach in "Desolation Row," McLean wrote "Miss American Pie" with so many stanzas that the recording lasts almost nine minutes. He begins with a stanza form of **abcddc**, and then uses the usual stanza form, whose couplets evoke the earlier era of good times—**aabb**, which is used throughout the song along with triple rhymes. In the chorus, he goes so far as to use a quintuple rhyme—**aaaaa** (see Table 6)—reminiscent of Dylan's "Subterranean Homesick Blues."

The Allman Brothers never had any anxieties about going electric. They even had twin electric lead guitars! They were one of the bands that made it in the 1970s, that great decade of rock and roll, and "Ramblin' Man" was probably their biggest hit. It sounds nothing like any Dylan song, of course, and shows what happened to his style as musicians assimilated what he had done. Triple rhymes were too hard to sustain in the verse, so they got relegated to the chorus in "Ramblin' Man" and in many other songs.

The Eagles's great songwriting team of Don Henley and Glen Frey sensed in the 1970s that the theme of loneliness had often recurred in country music and could be adapted with great effect in what became known as "soft rock." In the mid-1970s, The Eagles produced one hit after another, taking Dylan's version of country music on *Nashville Skyline* as a point of departure and enriching the sound with sweet country harmonies. The triple rhymes of classics such as "Lyin' Eyes" show their connection to Dylan's songs of the mid-1960s. Perhaps no other major group made such creative use of the connection between the 1960s and 1970s. Significantly, their great hit "Hotel California" sounds like a West Coast version of "Desolation Row."

Jackson Browne's "The Pretender" was the classic lament of the baby boomers in the 1970s, and it was a song that anticipated the movie *The Big Chill* (1983). It is a more personal statement by a man who has outgrown the singles scene implied in "Hotel California." He has settled down and gotten a job, and that occupies his days and his energy. He has given up his rock and roll dreams—Browne makes the most of the rhyme "pretender"/"surrender"—and has therefore fallen from cultural, if not religious, grace. "The Pretender" is something like a version of Dylan's "Drifter's Escape"—without the escape. It is primarily the triple rhyme of "in"/"again"/"amen" that links "The Pretender" to Dylan and the 1960s.

6. "Putting a Certain Orderliness to the Chaos"

The 1970s saw the beginning of the mega-concert era, when tours by Led Zeppelin, The Rolling Stones, and other super groups took on the quality of legend. Not surprisingly, songwriters started writing songs about bands and life on the road such as Willie Nelson's "On the Road Again." This topic did not interest Dylan, so when Paul McCartney and Wings recorded "Band on the Run," and when Queen recorded "We Are the Champions," the sound of the music and the spirit of the lyrics had little in common with Dylan. However, the writers did understand the effectiveness of the triple rhyme, but rather than integrating it into the stanza, as Dylan did, they used the traditional verse and chorus structure and relied on triple rhymes to punch up the chorus. Mac Davis in "Texas in My Rearview Mirror" and Van Halen in "Jump" did much the same thing.

It remains for me to comment on one very curious song. Although Garrison Keillor is a prolific writer of pretty much everything, he is not thought of as a major songwriter, and certainly not a rock and roll songwriter. (The music in his radio program "A Prairie Home Companion" is usually limited to acoustic music, and, in any case, he does not have the budget to afford rock groups.) Still, he has written some very clever songs for the program, and none of them is cleverer than his faux commercials, such as the one for the imaginary product Powdermilk Biscuits, as though one could buy biscuits in "the big blue box"! When he wrote his commercial for Powdermilk Biscuits, Keillor put his tongue deeply in his cheek and came up with the delightful triple rhyme "tried 'em"/"satisfied 'em"/"item" (as an homage to his fellow Minnesotan?)

By the 1980s, the post-disco era of the Reagan presidency, the cultural and media environments of the 1960s had changed so rapidly that songwriters could not use any of Dylan's devices and styles to respond to the world around them. Dylan continued to write, record, and tour, of course, but the fate that overtook Picasso in the 1930s, the fate that awaits most successful creative artists, had overtaken him. He had become a classic.

7

Dylan and Springsteen

Bruce Springsteen spoke for us all when he said "Thanks, Bob" after singing "The Times They Are a-Changin'" to Dylan, Lauren Bacall, and other assembled dignitaries, including President Bill Clinton and First Lady Hilary Rodham Clinton in the Kennedy Center. The date was August 12, 1997, and Dylan had just received the Medal of Freedom at that event.

We are all thankful to Dylan, of course, but Springsteen has more reason to be thankful than most of us. The multi-leveled precursor/ephebe relationship between Dylan and Springsteen as it has evolved over several decades is the most interesting, the most exciting, and the most productive personal dynamic in the entire history of American popular music.

Springsteen has said of Dylan's songs, "It's the greatest music ever written, to me. The man says it all, exactly the right way. Incredibly powerful. You don't get no more intense."[1] More generally, we can best understand the anxiety of influence from Dylan that Springsteen is expressing here, and what this extraordinary relationship means for rock history by relating it to markers of creativity as well as to something larger—the New Jersey Syndrome.

It is common knowledge that Springsteen's creative biography started in New Jersey, where he still lives. Like most great rock stars, he is a firstborn. He has two younger sisters, and his relationship with them helped him to function so effectively as the leader of the E Street Band. Although he does not belong to an ethnic minority, he experienced intense cultural marginality in working-class New Jersey. He had a famously conflicted relationship with his father. At a concert in 1976, he said that he would have late-night conversations with his father, which rapidly degenerated: "…then he'd start asking me where I was getting my money from … who I was going out with, what I thought I was doing with myself … and we'd end up, we'd end up screaming at each other, my mother'd end up running in from the front room … trying to keep us from fighting with each other, pulling him off me…."[2] As with Willie Nelson and Eric Clapton—and Barack Obama, for that matter—before him, whatever nurturing he got came from his grandmother. Like other talented boys with abusive and/or inadequate fathers, he looked outward for a father figure, and he found the usual "suspects."

On the night of January 6, 1957, at the tender age of eight, Bruce (and millions of other Americans) saw Elvis on the Ed Sullivan show, and it changed his life forever. It was not just that he wanted to be Elvis. He later said, "I couldn't imagine anyone not wanting to be Elvis Presley."[3] Such an intense relationship with a precursor at such an early age indicates what psychologists would call a lack of identity. His challenge, then, was to create an identity for himself, or as he put it, "My whole life was this enormous effort to become visible."[4] And so, as Clapton and Dylan had done before him, he fell into the ephebe's paradoxical but stimulating situation of creating an identity for himself by giving in to the hero worship of someone else.

Springsteen's relationship to Dylan amounts to the rock equivalent of Sinatra's relationship to Bing Crosby. In both cases, the younger man from a working-class town in New Jersey grew up when the older man was at the height of his popularity. At first the younger man imitated him, and then gradually grew out of imitation to establish himself as a major star in his own right. Just as Sinatra eventually performed with Crosby on his television show (and in the movie *High Society*), Springsteen eventually shared the stage with Dylan on various occasions. In an undated concert video that I found on YouTube, Dylan introduced him as "Mr. Bruce Springsteen." Let us pause for a moment to notice what an unprecedented tribute this was. Springsteen was publicly accepted as an equal that night. Coming from the laconic Dylan, that "Mr." is equivalent to five minutes of lavish praise from anybody else. Dylan does not refer to anybody else on stage as "Mr.," even as he (as the first among equals) is performing on the same stage with Eric Clapton, Mick Jagger, or Paul McCartney.

As someone who began recording in the aftermath of the 1960s, in the aftermath of Woodstock and of the murders at Altamont, and at a time when Sinatra, Elvis, and Dylan were all touring, Springsteen has an intense historical consciousness. In the early 1970s, he knew in his bones that he came after giants.

His contemporaries knew it, too. When he began work on his first album, *Greetings from Asbury Park*, Don McLean's "Miss American Pie" was riding high on the singles charts. Springsteen did what ephebes with an awareness of the past often do; he began proving himself by doing just what Dylan had done. On May 2, 1972, he auditioned for John Hammond, in Hammond's office, in the same office where Dylan had auditioned a little over a decade earlier. He came in with nothing but an acoustic guitar, which he did not even have a case for.[5]

It is true but inadequate to say that Springsteen was "influenced" by Dylan. We can understand Springsteen's career much better if we say that he was also energized by Dylan. He used Dylan's masterpieces of the 1960s very much as T. S. Eliot recommended that poets use tradition. Much of the internal dynamics of Springsteen's evolution come from his need to define himself against Dylan, the musical father who replaced his own inadequate, mentally unstable biological father (very much as Robert Johnson replaced Eric Clapton's absent father) and thus to outgrow the label "the new Dylan." Of course, the very fact that he took on this challenge suggests his heroic quality; his music has a certain tragic intensity that we never hear in Dylan. Dave Marsh said of Springsteen that "despite the legitimate claims of others to be taken seriously, Bruce Springsteen often seems like the last rock star, or at least the last one innocent of cynicism."[6] I would prefer to say that he is the last major star who rose to worldwide fame before the advent of cable TV and the internet, which redefined and reconfigured American entertainment.[7]

Springsteen's early albums chronicle the extraordinary process of overcoming his anxiety of influence from Dylan. Springsteen shows breathtaking audacity in engaging Dylan directly, as he does on *Greetings from Asbury Park*. The album is a postcard from Springsteen to Dylan in which Springsteen says, "I'm here!" On *Greetings from Asbury Park*, as well as in his later work, he refers again and again to the effects of what we might call the New Jersey Syndrome, which is a major element of American cultural geography.

The New Jersey syndrome is created by the perceived center-margin relationship between New York (i.e., Manhattan) and the surrounding area. Springsteen grew up in an area of intense cultural marginality with the sense of cultural inferiority that goes with it, and thus his situation contrasted sharply with Bobby Zimmerman's situation in Hibbing. The Hibbing people probably thought that their town was a perfectly fine place to live, despite the cold winters. Even if people in New Jersey do not share the belief that their state is in the provinces (the realm of the "losers" who cannot make it in New York), they have an awareness that lots of people do hold this belief. It is a belief intensified by the fact that many New Jersey people commute to New York to work. This set of beliefs about New Jersey and New Jersey people exacerbates Springsteen's anxiety of influence. For him, New York was not just the Big Apple, allegedly the capital of the world and so forth; it was the site of Dylan's triumphs, the city that he had claimed as no rock star ever had before, or ever would again.[8] Springsteen's songs, such as "It's Hard to be a Saint in the City," "Tenth Avenue Freezeout," "Meeting Across the River," "Incident on 57th Street," and "New York City Serenade," are all about the relationship between New Jersey and New York, and also about Springsteen's need to encroach on Dylan's territory and stake a claim to it, or at least part of it.

The immensely creative paradox of the Dylan/Springsteen relationship appears on *Greetings from Asbury Park*, when Springsteen announces himself as an artist to Dylan in "Growin' Up," a song that derives from "Chimes of Freedom" and "Visions of Johanna." Springsteen's "For You" has echoes of Dylan's "Like a Rolling Stone." Even "Spirit in the Night," the first expression of the mature Springsteen, showing as it does the liberated spirit of post–Altamont rock and roll, owes a lot to "Desolation Row," as do the cultural references in "It's Hard to be a Saint in the City." That song has a reference to Casanova, someone far removed from Springsteen's cultural experience and thematic range, because Casanova makes a brief appearance in "Desolation Row."

"Born to Run," Springsteen's breakout song, richly deserves its status as a rock classic—in part because it is a response to the Judy Garland classic "Somewhere Over the Rainbow." Although it is a song for the ages and thus transcends the year when it was recorded (1975), the date has great significance. As Louis Masur says, "Ten years had passed since Bob Dylan revolutionized music with 'Like a Rolling Stone.'"[9] And twenty years had passed since Elvis burst upon the scene, dominating the singles charts with "Hound Dog" and "Don't Be Cruel." Apparently, it takes us Americans ten years to absorb the psychic effects of one great star and prepare ourselves for the next one. Elvis in 1955, Dylan in 1965, and Springsteen in 1975 marked three cultural eras, as only the greatest performers can. This mighty triumvirate defines the core of American rock and roll.

With exceptional self-awareness, Springsteen once said, "Working on *Born to Run* was a very scary thing. I was born, grew old, and died making that album."[10] That is to say, the ephebe in him was not just "growin' up" anymore. The ephebe in him did battle with the demons that told him that he would never be as good as Dylan, that he would always be a no good, unloved guitar punk stuck forever in the death trap of cheap south Jersey seaside bars. In the process of recording *Born to Run*, his genius rode forth and slew those demons, and the ephebe in him died in this process of creative death and creative resurrection. The intensity of this battle explains the exceptional amount of time and effort that it took for him to record the album—some four months. He compiled fifty pages of notes just for the lyrics of the title song.[11]

Fortunately, he had an ally in this epic battle, and a very powerful one at that—Elvis. Masur points out that in the iconic photograph on the cover of the album that shows Springsteen leaning on the shoulder of Clarence Clemons, he has an Elvis Presley fan club pin on his guitar strap.[12] Although Springsteen has said again and again that seeing Elvis on *The Ed Sullivan Show* changed his life, the fact remains that Elvis was 14 years older than Springsteen, and at the dizzying pace of change that rock and roll experienced, that is several lifetimes. Taking Elvis as a role model (audacity again!), Springsteen figured out a way to swerve from Dylan. As opposed to what I have called Dylan's minimalist performance style—he just stands there when he is on stage—Springsteen is as physical on stage as Elvis was. He hops; he dances; he runs around; he exchanges quips with members of the band, Clarence and Steve. He even bends down and touches the outstretched hands of his adoring fans, as Elvis did. The dynamic that begins, like so much else in America, with Elvis and then goes through Dylan and to Springsteen, encapsulates half a century of rock and roll history. No one can hope to understand postwar America without it.

With all due respect to the stupendous importance of "Born to Run," I want to examine "Jungleland," also on the album *Born to Run*, as a key song that shows how an ephebe comes to terms with a great precursor, thereby achieving greatness in his own right. American culture does not offer—and has never offered—an experience more intense than seeing Springsteen and the E Street Band perform "Jungleland" live.

Rock songs exist as sound, and the sound of "Jungleland" is bigger than anything that Dylan ever recorded, and it matches Springsteen's active physical presence. The E Street Band includes not just guitars, drums, and bass, but also saxophone, piano, and organ. These massed instruments give "Jungleland" an orchestral sweep. The various soloists, such as Clarence Clemons on saxophone, come on between verses. The range of the sound is remarkable, too. Springsteen brings the band to its full, awesome thunder during the apocalyptic moments, and then quiets it to a murmur for the intimate lines.

This big sound represents more than Springsteen's assimilation of Phil Spector's wall of sound, and thus his swerve from Dylan's smaller band and smaller sound, although it is both of those things. It also indicates something more general—the pervasive difference between Dylan's intensive genius and Springsteen's extensive genius. Where Dylan concentrates and intensifies, Springsteen reaches out and extends. If a key word for Dylan is "transcendent," a comparable key word for Springsteen is "epic."

Performance style again indicates a key difference between them. In his now legendary, epic concerts, Springsteen quite literally reaches out to his audience. When he comes to the key lines of songs that he knows everybody knows, he extends the microphone toward the screaming fans and lets them sing them. When Dylan and Baez and the others sang "Blowin' in the Wind" at Newport in 1963, Dylan knew that everybody in the audience knew the lyrics, but it never occurred to him to extend the microphone toward them. One cannot imagine Dylan doing such a thing.

Jungleland, as a symbolic place and a state of mind, obviously derives from Desolation Row, which is also a symbolic place and a state of mind. Everyone on Desolation Row, as well as those who want to "escape" to Desolation Row, is stuck in place—even "Lady and I." As an extensive genius, Springsteen is too grounded in the E Street Band and in the New Jersey-New

York dynamic for transcendence. One of the anonymous listeners in *Bruce Springsteen's America* stated the difference between them like this: "He's the poet [Dylan], like the Boss is, but he's not the guy who's grounding your factory life, in the traveling salesman's life, in the working life of American people all over the country."[13]

The cosmic quality of "Jungleland" does not appear immediately because the reference to Harlem in the evocative opening line grounds the song in the urban jungle. (It also shows his mastery of Dylanesque alliteration. This reference begins the theme of fighting, and thus shows the song's debt to the New York saga of the Sharks and the Jets in the musical and movie *West Side Story* (1961), when Dylan was still a complete unknown. In particular, the way Springsteen repeats "tonight ... in Jungleland" throughout the song echoes "Tonight," Tony's first song in *West Side Story*. Springsteen substitutes guitars for switchblades and bands for gangs so that the situation resembles the "cutting" contests between jazz bands on the streets of New Orleans. The idea of heroism in a street fight late at night is essential to both *West Side Story* and "Jungleland." Ultimately, this street fight is a duel between Springsteen and Dylan, of course.

Only in the final stanza does Springsteen give us the key to the song in the phrase: "The poets down here." It is the poets "down here" (i.e., in New Jersey) who matter, as opposed to That Poet Up There in New York City, who does write and in fact will not stop writing. "Jungleland" is an inclusion song, an equivalent to Dylan's compassion songs. Just as Springsteen includes his fans in his concerts, he also includes himself as one of a group of ephebes, the poets who came after Dylan. These poets are "down here" and feel inferior because they have the New Jersey Syndrome. Stuck inside of New Jersey, they look up to Dylan, both literally and metaphorically, but making a stand leaves them wounded. (New York is due north from Asbury Park.)

Bloom cites a comment from an unlikely source, the German poet Goethe, which helps immensely in understanding the symbolic structure of "Jungleland" and this reference to being wounded and not even dead, in particular. Goethe once commented that "every talent must unfold itself in fighting."[14] In "John Wesley Harding," Dylan's statement of his own poetic strength, the hero "makes a stand," and Springsteen picks up this phrase to refer to what the ephebe must do in the process of becoming a precursor in his own right.[15] He must make a stand, even if it is in New Jersey.

Wounded by the dominating power of their precursors, ephebes lament that they are "not even dead," because death would offer a release from their anxiety, from their greatest fear, which is that they are not as talented as their precursors. The only release from this nagging fear is to prove that they are as talented. Springsteen's song "Prove It All Night" suggests how desperately ephebes need to do this. These poets (i.e., Springsteen) state their worst fear, that they "don't [can't?] write"—that is to say, they do not write anything significant in comparison with what Dylan did. Rather, they swerve from the precursor by just letting it all be. In "Jungleland," Springsteen incorporates "it all." He overcomes the New Jersey Syndrome by including both New Jersey and New York in his cosmic embrace. The song ranges from street gangs in New York to a couple in bed in New Jersey. Springsteen's reach in "Jungleland" achieves cosmic proportions because it embraces extremes. (There is exceptionally effective alliteration in "Jungleland.") It is no wonder that one of his admirers said, "This Springsteen is an American Dante."[16]

Putting Springsteen's name together with that of Dante gives Springsteen a very fine compliment indeed, but Springsteen lacks the spirituality that is essential for Dante, and which attracted Dylan to the Italian poet. It makes more sense to emphasize Springsteen's affinity with Whitman, another warm-hearted genius whose work also has a cosmic scope. The contrast between Springsteen and Dylan is instructive, and for once it works in Springsteen's favor. For all of Dylan's admiration for Whitman, he is too much of an intensive genius to extend himself as Springsteen does.[17]

Springsteen's cosmic sense also appears in his writing style. Whereas Dylan contained his transcendent images in tightly structured stanzas with complicated rhyme schemes, Springsteen broke away from such discipline. He wrote "Jungleland" in free verse, with only occasional rhymes like "pants"/"romance" and "stand"/"Jungleland." Unlike the regular 12-line stanzas of "Desolation Row," the stanzas of "Jungleland" vary widely in length; its six stanzas are 9, 8, 15, 5, 8, and 8 lines long.

As Dylan had done in "Stuck Inside of Mobile with the Memphis Blues Again," Springsteen took his anxiety of influence, his gnawing anxiety that he was not good enough—that he never would be good enough—and turned it into art. When an ephebe can turn anxiety into high art, as Springsteen did in "Jungleland," he has matched his precursor's strength with a strength of his own. It is no wonder Dylan introduced him as "Mr. Bruce Springsteen."

And where, we may ask, did Springsteen get this cosmic vision that makes "Jungleland" such a breathtaking achievement? It is not something that he picked up in the pizza joints and amusement parks of south Jersey—that is for sure. We find one source in "Chimes of Freedom," a very rare example of a Dylan song that Springsteen considered especially significant because he covered it. Springsteen issued his version of "Chimes of Freedom" on a 4-track extended play (EP) in 1988. He sang it at a concert in Ireland in the same year, and called it "the most powerful song about freedom ever written." The lists of people for whom the chimes are tolling amount to an embryonic version of the people who engage him as an artist.

Springsteen gave a more general answer to this question during a concert at the Memorial Coliseum in Los Angeles on September 30, 1985. In his spoken introduction to Woody Guthrie's "This Land Is Your Land," which I found on YouTube, he said, "I guess this is about the greatest song ever written about America.... It gets to the heart of the promise of what our country is supposed to be about." When Springsteen spoke those words about Dylan's first precursor, he was standing alone on a stage with only a harmonica rack and acoustic guitar, and he looked very much as Dylan had looked when he stood on the stage of the Royal Albert Hall twenty years earlier. Yes, to some extent he was imitating Dylan, and quite consciously too; yet he was also defying Dylan, or at least Dylan's pervasive skepticism about the value of political activism, and specifically this legendary song. Dylan had written in *Tarantula*, "...this land is your land & this land is my land-sure-but the world is run by those who never listen to music anyway."[18] One of the ways to understand Springsteen's role as our national poet, which is what he is, is to say that he moved into the void that Dylan created when he retreated from civil rights activism and from the world in general.

Springsteen has a complex relationship with Guthrie's signature song, since it is mediated by Dylan's looming presence. On one level, though, he was reaching back beyond Dylan to Dylan's roots. Springsteen could do this because Dylan, impelled and compelled by the relentless imperatives of his genius as he was, kept moving on and not looking back. One result of evolving so rapidly is that he has abandoned musical styles before taking full advantage of them. Springsteen sensed, probably unconsciously but no less powerfully, that since he could not escape Dylan he might as well work the situation to his advantage. He sensed that he could define himself as an artist not just in relation to Dylan but also in relation to America—to the American Dream— by revisiting and energizing the folk classics of Dylan's acoustic period with a rock and roll sensibility. For these reasons, "This Land is Your Land" offers the beginning of an Ariadne's thread, and if we follow it, it will show us how Springsteen, in "Jungleland" and elsewhere, is connected to a grand American tradition.

"This Land Is Your Land," in which Guthrie's vision extends from California to New York, derives from, and amounts to, a populist response to "America the Beautiful," especially the phrase "from sea to shining sea." As it happens, the lyrics to "America the Beautiful" were written by Katharine Lee Barnett after a visit to Pike's Peak in 1893. Only a decade before the Wright brothers' first flight, no one at the time could imagine a better view of America than what she had on that day.

What Barnett saw on that day was nature, and not just nature, but nature as her background in New England Transcendentalism prepared her to see it—nature as American destiny made manifest.[19] (Barnett was born in Falmouth, Massachusetts.) "God shed His grace on thee," she wrote, and in doing this she was in turn giving a typically optimistic American response to the lines in the preface to William Blake's poem "Milton": "And did the Countenance Divine/Shine forth upon our clouded hills?"[20] Over the years, Barnett's vision of untamed, untouched nature as a symbol of the purity of America's divine mission became what Springsteen in 1985 called "the promise of America." (The first American painting to be exhibited and praised in Europe was Frederic Church's "Niagara" [1857], which symbolized the power and grandeur of America.)

It is a long way from Niagara Falls—both the painting and the place—to Asbury Park, but the key point is that Springsteen, like the great American nineteenth-century painters, lets it all be. That is to say, he does not compete with Dylan in the use of fancy imagery or complicated structures. In this respect, the Springsteen-Dylan relationship has an important precedent in English poetry. We can say that Springsteen is playing Wordsworth, with his promise of simple language and heart-felt sentiments, to Dylan's John Donne, with his convoluted language and complex concepts.

Springsteen has an acute awareness of the promise of life, liberty, and the pursuit of happiness that nature represented to nineteenth-century Americans. As a kid from south Jersey, though, Springsteen had no interest in nature as such. "The purple mountains' majesty" had, and has, no resonance for him. What he saw as he looked around him was not epic natural grandeur, but people with their all too human lust and greed.

The American tragedy informs the emotional lives of his people on "Thunder Road." (The title refers to the 1958 film *Thunder Road*, a movie about running moonshine in the South that starred Robert Mitchum.) He understands more profoundly than any other living American artist that America has "promises to keep," in Robert Frost's famous phrase. Yet the boy has to admit that "all the promises'll be broken." And "all the promises" are America's promises of life, liberty, and the pursuit of happiness. In his introduction to "This Land Is Your Land" in 1985, Springsteen grouped them all together as "the promise" of America. It is the grandiose promise of America, and all the little promises, too, that will be broken. It is America's failure to keep those grandiose promises that constitutes the subtext of "This Land Is Your Land" and attracts him so powerfully. To put it more generally, it is the tension between the promises of America as the land of the free and the home of the brave, and her failure to keep those inspiring promises, that animate his work and move it toward cosmic tragedy.

When Springsteen was starting out in the early 1970s, Vietnam and Watergate made America's failure to keep her promises undeniable; they made Springsteen's people restless. Thus, there is the slow, deeply felt song "Racing in the Streets," which offers motion for the sake of motion as the only outlet for these social tensions. He lets them all be and makes them visible by channeling them into his songs. In the last stanza of "This Land Is Your Land"

Guthrie has a phrase that sums up Springsteen's cosmic consciousness of America: "I see my people." Springsteen sees America's people steadily and he sees them whole.

Unlike the nineteenth-century transcendentalists, though, Springsteen cannot see the purple mountains' majesty from any vantage point in south Jersey. What he sees is what Tony Soprano sees in the signature montage of *The Sopranos*—cramped houses, discount stores, and pizza parlors. South Jersey has no epic grandeur; what it has is people, with their all too human failings. Springsteen has compassion for all of them, as the early Dylan did. But Springsteen's compassion grounds him in the land and, as he has evolved, he has reached out to more and more of the American land.

Springsteen's consciousness of the contrast between the squalor of south Jersey and the vastness of America imaged in Church's painting of Niagara, in Barnett's "America the Beautiful," and in Guthrie's "This Land Is Your Land" led him to do two seemingly contradictory things. No doubt with Dylan in mind, he disbanded the E Street Band and stripped down his music to the acoustic guitar and the harmonica of Dylan's acoustic period, and he also broadened the scope of his vision. In 1982, he reached out far beyond New Jersey to a radically different place, a Midwestern state just south of Minnesota in his album *Nebraska*. It was as though the extraordinary achievements with the E Street Band had taken him as far as he could go, and he needed to do what Dylan had done in reaching out beyond New York with *Nashville Skyline*. Both artists needed to consolidate and rethink their music.

Nine years after "Born to Run," Springsteen reached even beyond Nebraska, and matched the scope of "This Land Is Your Land" with "Born in the USA." It was easy for people who did not know and love the whole song to take the heroic title phrase as the simplistic patriotism of a cockeyed optimist. The verses, though, include those who "live with the sadness," in that wonderful phrase from "Born to Run."

This progression from "Born to Run" and "Jungleland" to "Born in the USA" helps us to understand why Springsteen was the artist America needed most after the 9/11 attacks in the year 2001. America's tragedy hit home for him because it reversed the New York-New Jersey dynamic that he had grown up with and that shaped his career in a variety ways. New York had always been the Big Apple, the Promised Land that held the holy grail of fame and fortune. Springsteen's album *The Rising* (2002) makes the victims of 9/11 visible by giving voices to those who simply disappeared in the inferno.

If the buildings went down, then hope will bring them up again. And if the buildings do not come up literally, he will bring the awesome force of his empathy and compassion to bear on America's bleeding wound. He will make the victims visible by giving them voices. Springsteen, in the voice of a gospel preacher, calls on America to "rise up."[21] He adopted the voice and diction of a gospel preacher in his post–9/11 concerts, when he calls his audience back to life.

If previously he had responded to the needs of those who felt the effects of America's failed promises, he responded even more strongly to the needs of the victims of 9/11 and their families, to whom America's promises were denied. And, of course, what is implicit in his song "The Rising" is another promise, a promise even more grandiose than the promise of America—the promise of resurrection. By invoking the promise of the resurrection, he makes a promise of his own: to lift up the spirits of those who grieve.

The Rising established Springsteen as America's actual, if not official, poet laureate. In this capacity, he could sing to America during halftime at the Super Bowl on February 1, 2009, and sing "This Land Is Your Land" with Pete Seeger at the Lincoln Memorial on the eve of Barack Obama's inauguration.

In 2002, Springsteen had recorded the album *We Shall Overcome: The Seeger Sessions*, and in his sixtieth year, unchallenged as America's spokesman, he hosted a grand event in a grand venue. On May 3, 2009, he led a celebration for Pete Seeger's ninetieth birthday in Madison Square Garden. Lots of the old folkies showed up for the occasion, including, of course, Joan Baez, Arlo Guthrie, and Richie Havens. Rockers like Roger McGuinn and John Cougar Mellencamp paid tribute to this talented man who had written or arranged so many folk standards, and who represented the continuity of 1930s populism and 1960s liberalism. There was, however, one old folkie, a former folkie we might call him, who was never mentioned, and who was conspicuous by his absence—Bob Dylan. Only Springsteen had the authority to bring together these diverse generations and musical styles.

On December 7, 2009, Springsteen received the Medal of Freedom at the Kennedy Center. He sat in the Presidential Box with a Democratic President (whom he had helped to elect), some twelve years after Dylan had sat there with a different Democratic President.

8

The Real Revolution of the 1960s

This chapter presents the culmination of the "Dylan and..." theme that has informed various chapters of *Decoding Dylan*, such as the previous chapter. This chapter discusses Dylan, not in connection with the various artists who affected his songs, or the various artists whom his songs in turn affected, but in connection with two performers who are his contemporaries and who belong to the very small group of his peers: Woody Allen and Barbra Streisand.

It is immediately obvious that Dylan, Allen, and Streisand have little in common if we think only of their themes and performance styles. Nevertheless, they all started at about the same time, in the early 1960s, in the same place, Greenwich Village. And from there they went on to have three of the most extraordinary careers in the history of American popular culture. If ever there were any performers who were overachievers, whose work enjoyed widespread popularity among diverse audiences for decade after decade, it was Bob Dylan, Woody Allen, and Barbra Streisand. And there is another factor that they share in addition to starting out at the same time in the same place and then going on to conquer the world. It is not just that they are each geniuses in their different ways. They are *Jewish* geniuses, and thus their careers gain larger significance when we consider them in relation to the issues of immigration and assimilation that have done so much to make America what it is.

We can relate Dylan, Streisand, and Allen to major patterns in American history that play themselves out over long periods of time by applying to them the principle that immigration historian Marcus Hansen developed in his influential book *The Problem of the Third Generation Immigrant*. (In this connection, one cannot avoid thinking of Dylan's song "I Pity the Poor Immigrant.") In effect, Hansen applies the thesis-antithesis-synthesis progression to the process of immigration and assimilation in America. He describes a pattern in which the grandfather comes to America, the son prospers and assimilates, and the grandson becomes a major achiever. This is what happened with Dylan, Streisand (a granddaughter, not a grandson, obviously), and Allen.

Their story, like the stories of so many eminent Jews in America, begins in the Eastern European possessions of the Russian Empire in the nineteenth century. At that time, Jews lived under many onerous restrictions. They could only live, for example, in certain designated areas called the Pale of Settlement. Considering the extraordinary array of talent that came out of the Jewish villages, or shtetls, as they were called, we may consider the relevance of the markers of creativity that I discussed earlier, and when we do we realize that, for Eastern European Jews, ethnicity and cultural marginality tended to merge. They were forced to live in a deliberately created area of cultural marginality simply because they were Jews. They also could have sung the song that I have mentioned before, "We Gotta Get Out of This Place" (a song by Eric Burden and the Animals). And get out they did, in very large numbers. It is estimated that between 1882, the year after Tsar Alexander II was assassinated, and 1914, when World War I broke out, approximately two million Jews left Eastern Europe for America. The Jewish flight from Eastern Europe for America has had, and continues to have, exceptionally important implications for America and American culture. It is also the theme of two movies: Barbra Streisand's *Yentl* (1983) and *An American Tale* (1986), which was produced by Steven Spielberg's Amblin Entertainment.

For our purposes here, it matters that Dylan's grandfather Zigman Zimmerman left Odessa in 1906, in the aftermath of the disastrous 1905 revolution, which made Jews especially vulnerable.[1] Streisand's grandfather Isaac Streisand left Lvov in 1898.[2] Zigman Zimmerman settled in Duluth, where his son Abraham Zimmerman was born; Isaac Streisand settled in the Lower East Side of New York.[3]

Each of the three generations of Jewish immigrants produced its prodigies. To begin with, Irvin Berlin (1888–1989) was born Israel Baline in a shtetl near Mogilyov in what is today Belarus. He came to America in 1893, after the Cossacks burned his family's house. George Gershwin (1898–1937) and his brother Ira Gershwin (1896–1983) (born Jacob and Israel Gershovitz) were born about a decade later in Brooklyn. Irving Berlin and the Gershwins wrote songs that make up the heart of the Great American Songbook.

It is the next phase of the immigration saga that brings it up to the present. A certain element of survival of the fittest operated in Jewish immigration. The trip from Odessa or Lvov to Ellis Island was arduous and expensive, and only the bravest and hardiest survived it. Those who did make it, such as Isaac Streisand, had what it took to work hard and prosper. It was prosperity that made it possible for him and his wife to move to Brooklyn in 1920.

8. The Real Revolution of the 1960s

At the time, Brooklyn was expanding rapidly, and a great amount of new housing was being built. In the 1920s and 1930s, Brooklyn proved so attractive that many Jewish families moved from the Lower East Side as soon as they could afford it. Elliot Willensky, author of *When Brooklyn Was the World, 1920–1957*, says, "For Brooklyn, the years from 1920 through 1957 represent a kind of golden age," and adds that it was during these years that the subway system linked Brooklyn, even Coney Island, to Manhattan.[4] This move from the Lower East Side to Brooklyn anticipated the more general move from the cities to the suburbs that so radically transformed American life in the 1950s.

This large-scale move to Brooklyn created a Brooklyn Syndrome, a counterpart to the New Jersey Syndrome. Brooklyn and New Jersey, the two areas on the periphery of Manhattan, have produced major performers out of all proportion to their population, whereas Manhattan itself has produced very few. Brooklyn is east of Manhattan, and New Jersey is west of Manhattan, so it appears that talented kids in unlikely places such as Hoboken and Park Slope could "see" Manhattan, the city of their dreams, from where they lived, as they built up the determination to go there.

The Brooklyn Syndrome, as I propose to call it, explains the remarkable group of celebrities in entertainment and communication (in addition to Streisand and Allen) who have come from Jewish communities there. Some of them changed their names, and some did not. A partial list includes actress Lauren Bacall (Betty Perske); writer-director-actor Mel Brooks (Melvin Kaminsky); composer Aaron Copland (Kaplan); sportscaster Howard Cosell (Howard Cohen); record executive Clive Davis; singer Neil Diamond; entertainment executive David Geffen; actors Elliott Gould (Streisand's first husband), Jeff Chandler (Ira Gossel), Richard Dreyfuss, and Danny Kaye (David Daniel Kaminsky); singer-songwriter Carol King (Carol Klein); talk show host Larry King (Lawrence Harvey Zeiger); singer Barry Manilow; comedian Joan Rivers (Joan Rosenberg;); movie executive Irving Thalberg; and comedian Adam Sandler. The list of politicians among Brooklyn-born Jews includes senators Charles Schumer and Bernie Sanders.

It is this critical mass of talent concentrated in Brooklyn's Jewish communities that gives us the context for Allen and Streisand. Yet "Brooklynites" rarely ventured into Manhattan,[5] so they felt no less marginalized than Bobby Zimmerman did in Hibbing. And, speaking of cultural marginality, let us notice a contrast between what Dylan, Allen, and Streisand did with what the Lost Generation had done earlier. The artists of the Lost Generation, who suffered terribly from the little town blues and fled to Paris, were mostly writers (Ernest Hemingway) and composers (Aaron Copland). They were able to develop their talents in Paris because they did not need an audience to do so. Dylan, Allen, and Streisand did need audiences, so they went to New York, not Paris.

Another long-term pattern deserves mention here. It appears that the grandparents' origins are related to the grandchildren's place of residence. Streisand's and Allen's grandparents came from land-locked northern Europe, where people had limited opportunities to move inside the Pale of Settlement. After they made the enormous move to New York, they settled down. Isaac Streisand moved to Brooklyn in the 1920s, but his granddaughter moved from Brooklyn back to Manhattan in 1959, right after she graduated from high school. And then she moved once more from Manhattan to Los Angeles, when she went there to make the movie version of *Funny Girl*. Woody Allen moved only once, from Brooklyn to Manhattan. Although he has had various apartments in the city, he has famously refused to live anywhere else.

Unlike Streisand's and Allen's grandfathers, Dylan's grandfather came from the southern edge of Eastern Europe, from Odessa, a cosmopolitan port on the Black Sea. People who live in ports are accustomed to movement and travel, and the Zimmerman men have been moving and travelling ever since 1906, when Zigman Zimmerman left Odessa for Duluth. Abraham Zimmerman was born in Duluth, as was his first-born son Bobby. The Zimmermans moved to Hibbing in 1946, and after Bobby Zimmerman graduated from high school there he left Hibbing for Minneapolis in 1959, and then left Minneapolis for New York in 1961. He left New York for Woodstock in 1966, moved briefly back to New York in 1969, and in 1973 bought property in Point Dome, in the Los Angeles area. After he and Sara divorced in 1977, he has lived in various places.

Like Dylan, Allen and Streisand were born into observant Jewish homes. Unlike Dylan, Allen and Streisand never suppressed their ethnicity. In fact, Allen and Streisand made it essential to their personas. On the other hand, Allen has never made a pilgrimage to Jerusalem in a yarmulke. Whatever meaning Judaism has had for them at various stages of their lives, it created the ambience that they were familiar with, and so they replicated it in their private lives and in their careers. It is true for all three of them that their first spouses and first business managers were Jewish.

Like Dylan, Allen and Streisand had impaired relationships with their fathers. As young men, both Allen Konigsberg and Bobby Zimmerman seem to have had a similar disdain for their fathers and how they lived their lives. Allen's biographer Marion Meade says of Allen's father, "Marty drifted from one line of work to another: salesman, pool hustler, bookmaker, bartender, egg candler, jewelry engraver, and cabdriver."[6] Allen's one enduring memory of his parents' marriage was that they argued—endlessly. Meade says, "The household pathology was, as Woody remarked years later, 'there all the time as soon as I could understand anything.'"[7]

If Dylan and Allen had problematic relationships with their fathers,

Streisand had a painfully impaired relationship with her father, because he died when she was a year old. She has often referred to this crucial, lasting trauma in her life, and has said that the song "Papa Can You Hear Me?" from *Yentl* (1983) has great autobiographical meaning for her. It may well be that, for her, as for great male performers such as John Lennon and Eric Clapton, this enduring trauma of fatherlessness opened her up to the world and to its grief, thereby increasing her emotional range as a performer.

Like Dylan, Allen is a first-born with a younger sibling. (He has a sister, Letty, eight years his junior, with whom he remains close.) Technically, Streisand is a second-born, because she has a brother, Sheldon Jay. Significantly, however, he is seven years older. This age gap means that the birth order patterns started all over again with her, so that she is what psychologists call a virtual first-born. She has shown the determination and perfectionism of a first-born throughout her life. In effect, then, Dylan, Allen, and Streisand are all "first-borns."

Unlike so many others who have had the same dreams, they found both fame and fortune in abundance. They gained experience as performers (Dylan and Streisand as singers, Allen as a standup comedian) in the same place, Greenwich Village, at about the same time, the early 1960s. And, in the process of creating their most extraordinary careers, they revolutionized American entertainment. What we know about Dylan's evolution in the 1960s gives us a context for a broader understanding of what Allen and Streisand did. In turn, this understanding leads to a broader understanding of what the three of them have meant, and still mean, for the evolution of American popular culture—and especially for the significance of New York in American popular culture.

We can best compare their careers if we compare them not by the calendar year in which they achieved certain things, but by their ages. Table 7, which compares the beginnings of the adult careers of Bob Dylan, Barbra Streisand, and Woody Allen, will serve as the basis for further discussion.

Table 7. Chronologies of Early Successes of Dylan, Barbra Streisand and Woody Allen by Approximate Age

Age	Bob Dylan b. May 24, 1941	Barbra Streisand b. Apr 24, 1942	Woody Allen b. Nov 1, 1935
18		Wins talent contest at Lion Nightclub; regular engagement at Bon Soir nightclub (1960)	1st published joke in Earl Wilson's newspaper column (1953)
19		Caucus Club, Detroit. On PM East, Mike Wallace's radio show (1961)	Writes jokes for Herb Shriner and others (1954)

Age	Bob Dylan b. May 24, 1941	Barbra Streisand b. Apr 24, 1942	Woody Allen b. Nov 1, 1935
20	Performs at Gerde's Folk City; signs contract with Columbia Records (1961)	Wins New York Drama Critics' Circle Award; signs contract with Columbia Records; appears on *The Tonight Show*; *The Judy Garland Show*; *The Bob Hope Comedy Special* (1962)	Writer on *The Colgate Comedy Hour* (1955)
21	1st album *Bob Dylan* (1962)	*The Barbra Streisand Album* wins a Grammy (1963)	
22	Solo concerts at Town Hall & Carnegie Hall (1963)	Rave reviews for *Funny Girl*; album *People* wins second Grammy (1964)	
23	Albums *The Times They Are a-Changin'* and *Another Side of Bob Dylan* (1964)	"My Name is Barbra" gets a 35.6 audience share (1965)	
24	Albums *Bringing It All Back Home* and *Highway 61 Revisited* (1965)		Writer on *The Garry Moore Show* (1959)
25	Album *Blonde on Blonde* (1966)	Sings to largest crowd in history (in Central Park) for solo performer (1967)	Does standup comedy (1960)
26	Album *John Wesley Harding* (1967)	Movie version of *Funny Girl* (1968)	
27		Oscar for role in *Funny Girl* (1969)	*The Ed Sullivan Show* (1962)
28	Album *Nashville Skyline* (1969)	Albums *On A Clear Day You Can See Forever* and *The Owl and the Pussycat* (1970)	
29			*What's New Pussycat* (1964)
30	Albums *Self-Portrait* & *New Morning* (1971)	*Up the Sandbox* (1972)	Play *Don't Drink the Water* (1965)

Both Dylan and Streisand began singing in small clubs in the Greenwich Village area, and "power brokers" in the music business recognized their talent right away. By the time they were 20, they had signed contracts with Columbia Records, which then had the most prestigious label in the music business. They did amazing things over the next five years. By the time they were 25, they had become major stars, and had recorded their signature songs (Dylan's "Blowin' in the Wind" and Streisand's "People"[8]).

More generally, what did their careers mean for the performing arts in New York and in America? What the Russian anarchist Mikhail Bakunin once said has relevance here: "The creative act is also a destructive act." Dylan and Streisand rose to fame by singing in traditional venues—folk clubs and Broadway theaters. They had such creative power (and represented seismic historical changes in American entertainment) that there was also a destructive quality in what they did. Although we cannot say that Dylan destroyed

8. The Real Revolution of the 1960s

American folk music by taking up the electric guitar at the Newport Folk Festival in 1965, we can say that after him, American folk music lost its creative drive. No major folk singers appeared to continue the legacy of Pete Seeger. As we know, it is Bruce Springsteen, not Dylan, who has made common cause with Seeger and appeared with him at important public events. Similarly, no female folk singers have appeared to carry on the glorious tradition of Joan Baez.

McLuhan uses the verb "obsolesce" to describe what happens when the introduction of one medium transforms another medium, and that verb aptly describes what Dylan did to folk music. After he began to transcend its stylistic limitations with "Chimes of Freedom," he obsolesced it as a form. Although people continue to write and perform folk songs, they lack major creative energy.

Similarly, Streisand obsolesced the Broadway theater as a star-making venue. To understand how she did this, we need some context. By the age of 19, she possessed a marvelous vocal instrument, over which she had complete control (and this was without a single voice lesson.)[9] As Elvis did in the more modest ambience of the Sun Records studios, Streisand dominated the theater from the moment she set foot on stage. As Miss Marmelstein at the age of 20 in *I Can Get It for You Wholesale*, "she was hilarious. She was touching. She mugged. She belted. At that moment—9:35 PM on the fourth Thursday in March 1962—Barbra Streisand became a Broadway star."[10]

Audiences reacted in the same way, only more so, when she played Fanny Brice in *Funny Girl*. Shana Alexander wrote in a profile for *Life*, that "when Barbra opened on Broadway [on March 24, 1964] the entire gorgeous, rattle-trap show business Establishment blew sky-high."[11] When she won her Oscar for best actress (a co-winner with Kathryn Hepburn) for her performance in the film *Funny Girl* in 1969, she was the youngest performer who had ever won an Oscar.[12] She belongs to the very exclusive club of EGOTs—performers who have won an Emmy, a Grammy, an Oscar, and a Tony. She has also won a Golden Globe Award, a Directors Guild of America Award, the National Medal of the Arts, France's Legion d'Honneur, the American Film Institute's Lifetime Achievement Award, and the Kennedy Center Honors. In short, she has won most everything that show business and America have to award.

Ethnicity remains relevant, even in her glittering successes that have received such well-deserved awards. Although Streisand was the fourth Jewish actress who won an Oscar, she was the first performer widely known to be Jewish who had won for playing an explicitly Jewish character.[13] Streisand's win signaled the beginning of one of American film's greatest decades, the 1970s, in which Jewish performers like Streisand and Allen would play overtly Jewish characters. In an equally unprecedented way, Italian directors like Francis Ford Coppola and Martin Scorsese would direct Italian actors like

Robert DeNiro and Al Pacino in epoch-making films about Italian-Americans. Mario Puzo has said that *The Godfather* is not exactly about assimilation, but the failure of assimilation, in America.

It matters that Streisand was the first Jewish performer to win an Oscar for playing a Jewish character because it marks a major change in American show business. Ever since the 1920s, Jewish writers and executives had been involved in some of the most important movies ever made.[14] Beginning in the 1960s, though, these creative Jews did not remain behind the scenes, as they had done in the past.

Streisand changed Broadway in another way as well. Since the 1920s, the Broadway theater had been a place where stars were born. These especially included female singers such as Fanny Brice, Ethel Merman, Mary Martin, and many other gifted women. After Streisand, the connection between popular songs and dramatic narrative, always tenuous in America, began to give way. The national and international popularity of rock and roll swept everything before it. The next generation of female singers, such as Janis Joplin, Judy Collins, Joni Mitchell, and Carly Simon, who became stars did so by singing at concerts and in recording studios, not theaters.

After Streisand obsolesced the Broadway musical, it continued to thrive, of course, but it thrived in a transformed way. She transformed Broadway from a star-making venue into a songwriter's venue, as the careers of Stephen Sondheim and Andrew Lloyd Webber abundantly attest. After Streisand, Broadway has not produced a single great singer of national importance, and probably never will again.

After making it in New York, Dylan and Streisand left, never to return except for occasional visits. Dylan left in search of privacy. Streisand left for Los Angeles in search of further fame in Hollywood. Dylan and Streisand thus represent one version of the "little town blues." In their version of this great American story, they leave their homes, their indifferent parents, and their less gifted siblings for the Big City. The Big City serves them well; it is there that they establish their creative personas. But, because of their records, concerts, and movies, their personas have such power that they transcend the Big City and any other place. Stars who are big enough can take that persona wherever they like.

Woody Allen represents a different version of the "little town blues," of course. After he left Brooklyn, he briefly worked in Los Angeles, where he wrote for some television comedy shows, but he really never left the City. His biography Eric Lax says Allen once told him:

> "I first came to the city in 1941 with my father [at the age of six]," he says. "And I was in love with it from the second I came up from the subway into Times Square. You can't believe what a thing that is to suddenly look up and see it—remember, this was before it degenerated.... I was just stunned by it all.... It was just absolutely astonishing."[15]

8. The Real Revolution of the 1960s

For Allen, Manhattan remains what Henry James called The Great Good Place, which he found at an early age. It has never occurred to him to live anywhere else.

Yet Allen too has changed his chosen medium, movies, although his unique situation may limit the significance of the change. Historically, the movie business has been split between Hollywood, where the talent is, and New York, where the money is. In the spirit of integration that has also characterized the careers of Dylan and Streisand, Allen has integrated the two. He has remained in New York, and made his movies there (and in Europe). He has managed to do this because his producers Jack Rollins and Charles Joffe (also Brooklyn Jews) can fund his modestly budgeted movies without recourse to the Hollywood studios, whose role is limited to the distribution of the finished product.

Spirituality and tradition go together in Jewish life, and they inform the careers of Dylan, Allen, and Streisand in various ways. With Dylan, we recall that it is not enough to say that he is an introvert, although that is certainly true. More importantly, a part of his psyche simply does not belong in this world. Although Streisand made a wonderful album of spiritual songs, *Higher Ground* (1997), she devotes much more of her time and energy to social activism than to spirituality. As for Allen, he once declared that his parents' values were God and carpeting, thereby implying that they equated the two. As an artist, he has no apparent interest in spirituality at all.

However, tradition trumps spirituality. Jewish children raised in observant homes cannot escape an awareness of tradition, even though they grow up to be non-observant adults. (Tradition is so much a part of the consciousness of Jewish artists that even Steven Spielberg sang "Tradition.... Tradition!" the chorus of the famous song from the movie and musical *Fiddler on the Roof* during his interview on the television show *Inside the Actors Studio*.) Although Dylan, Allen, and Streisand have an abiding interest in tradition, they have secularized their parents' commitment to Jewish tradition, and have turned it into the secular tradition of art. Since they have a cosmopolitan orientation, they have an abiding interest in European cultural traditions that their WASP counterparts often lack.[16] Naturally, they are interested in different aspects of that tradition and use it in different ways.

The one thing—aside from his genius, which is a given—that sets Dylan apart from other rock stars, both American and British, is his endlessly inventive adaptation of the heritage of High Modernism in its glory days—Picasso and all that. Previously, I have shown how Eliot and Picasso affected his great songs of the mid-1960s. He continues to study art and art history. In his *Rolling Stone* interview with Douglas Brinkley, he spoke with passion of Rembrandt and Caravaggio[17] as few other musicians would. His own experience of painting enables him to look at museum exhibits with a practitioner's eye.[18]

Although Dylan's respect for, and use of, European high culture makes him unique among 1960s rock stars, we realize that it forms part of a larger pattern when we notice Streisand's and Allen's analogous engagement with European culture.

Streisand's engagement with European culture began at home, or perhaps it would be better to say that it began as a reaction against home. She grew up in a visually incoherent environment, one without a sense of style that resulted from the difficulties that Jews faced once they got to the New World. Not all of these difficulties were financial. Playwright David Mamet has commented that "none of the [Jewish] homemakers knew quite what a home was supposed to look like. They had no tradition of décor, the adoption of which would be anything other than arbitrary. When our grandparents left the shtetl they brought nothing with them."[19] When Streisand mentions her love of fine design in her aptly named book, *My Passion for Design*, she adds, "I also have intense relationships with furniture, because we had practically none when I was growing up."[20] Then she adds something that Dylan and Allen could say as well about the motivation that cultural marginality gives to gifted people: "When you don't like your surroundings, you have to use your imagination to create a world you do like." Surprisingly, perhaps, she connects this cultural marginality to the early death of her father. "Sometimes I think it's all connected to the loss of a parent because you'd do anything to get that mother or father back. But you can't ... yet with objects, there's a possibility."[21]

Streisand's reaction to this lack of style was to turn herself into a world-class connoisseur and collector of European decorative arts, emphasizing Art Nouveau. "With the first money I made on Broadway, I began to buy Art Nouveau furniture." It is not just furniture, either. "Aesthetically, I would prefer wearing period clothes."[22] Her preferred clothing and her preferred décor are all of a piece. In the extraordinary multi-building compound that she has created in Malibu, depicted in the photographs in *My Passion for Design*, there is no artwork or decorative item created after 1940. Moreover, her passion for traditional design from the past is matched only by her passion for the traditional music.

On December 31, 1999, Streisand gave a gala concert at the MGM Grand in Las Vegas to welcome the new millennium, and she released *Timeless*, a DVD of the concert. In one of her several monologues on *Timeless*, she comments, as a matter of fact, "You don't know where you're going until you know where you've been." It seems as obvious to her as it did to Eliot that artists benefit greatly from studying tradition, not necessarily Jewish tradition, however.

Streisand's deep, life-long engagement with cultural tradition began with *Funny Girl*, and then continued with her next movie *Hello, Dolly!* (1969). Her most important films after that were also set in the past: *The Way We Were* (1973), *Funny Lady* (1975) (two of the major period pieces of the 1970s), and *Yentl* (1983).

Yentl offers an exceptionally successful example of the way artists keep tradition alive by innovating. In the film, Streisand plays a Jewish girl in Poland who wishes to study. But only boys can study in this tradition-bound society, so she disguises herself as a boy. Like so many Jews in the shtetls, she has the little town blues, and so she innovates in the most radical way possible. She leaves the shtetl and comes to America. Her dialectical relationship with tradition, in which she both destroys tradition and preserves it, and which has informed so much of her career, appears with particular clarity here.

Streisand's multi-faceted engagement with the past continues with the songs on her albums. On her greatest hits album, she included two overtly Jewish songs in the style of the 1920s, "Second-Hand Rose" and "Sam, You Made the Pants Too Long." Throughout her career, she retained her love of, and respect for, musical tradition. She included songs from the Great American Songbook on *The Broadway Album* (1985), which enjoyed such success that she followed it up with *Back to Broadway* (1993). Her choices of material for both albums indicate the same creative mixture of tradition and innovation that the girl/boy in *Yentl* has.[23] *The Broadway Album* includes Broadway classics and contemporary songs by Stephen Sondheim. (When you listen to the heart-stopping perfection of her version of "Send in the Clowns," you think that nobody has ever sung it before, and if they do, that subsequent versions will pale in comparison.) The point to remember is that it never occurred to Streisand or anyone else that she would actually *perform* in any of Sondheim's great shows. She had not only obsolesced Broadway theater; she had transcended it. Still, she had a deep appreciation for Sondheim's genius and she took the songs from their dramatic context, and used that fabulous voice of hers to establish them as independent entities.

Streisand herself wrote the cover notes for *Back to Broadway*, and they reveal how her collaboration with Sondheim worked. Of "Everybody Says Don't," from *Anyone Can Whistle* (1964), she writes, "*I didn't hear this piece arranged in a conventional Broadway style, but more as the classical sound of anger expressed in the music of Bartók and Stravinsky*" (emphasis added). This revealing comment shows how much the heritage of the musical modernists, such as Bartók and Stravinsky, has affected her musical sensibility. This is very much analogous to how much Eliot and Picasso affected Dylan's musical sensibility.

Another revealing comment refers to Sondheim's "Children Will Listen," from *Into the Woods* (1986). She says that she liked it, but that it was never performed as a complete song. "*So I asked Stephen Sondheim if he had anything that was cut from the score that I might use to complete it. As it turned* out, he had these marvelous quatrains and we used them to create a verse and a bridge" (emphasis added). Thus, the song "Children Will Listen" exists separately from the dramatic production, and in fact has little to do with it. Here we have a specific example of how she fulfills her historic role as the destroyer of the star-making potential of the Broadway tradition, and simultaneously as the conservator of its heritage—reconfigured as individual hit songs.

Woody Allen's use of tradition offers a striking contrast to that of Dylan and Streisand, but is equally pervasive in his work. Dylan fearlessly and unconsciously assumed that he could engage the great creative spirits of the past—creative spirits as different as Hank Williams and Picasso, to refer again to the obvious extremes—and assimilate what he could learn from them. In fact, he made learning from them an explicit part of his work by the use of intertextuality. In Dylan's cultural references in "Desolation Row" and elsewhere he acknowledges his sources while adapting them for his own purposes.

Allen uses intertextuality, too, and understanding all the jokes and references in his work requires readers and viewers to bring an enormous amount to it. It is not enough, though, to say that Allen uses intertextuality. He takes it to such extremes that it is an essential part of his significance for film history. Quite simply, he is the most intertextual artist in the entire history of American culture. No other American artist even comes close to him in his creative use of intertextuality in his prose and movies. Two other Jewish writer-directors associated with Manhattan are known for their comedies that use intertextuality: Mel Brooks and Nora Ephron. Thus, we have a key pattern in the history of film comedy in America, and we may surmise that Jews as outsiders in WASP America both acknowledged their cultural heritage while also using it as a source of humor.

The use of intertextuality requires knowledge of cultural tradition that is—in several senses of the word—foreign to American culture, yet a defining feature of European culture. This fact explains a comment by John Baxter: "It's not surprising that Allen should find his greatest appreciation among foreigners, since he has always presented himself as one. As his official biographer Eric Lax acknowledges, Allen's influences are 'an amalgam of old Europe and New York.'"[24]

However, the aspects of European tradition on which he draws on so successfully differ noticeably from those that engage Dylan and Streisand. Unlike them, Allen hardly has any interest in poetry, painting, or design. Movie tradition is the only artistic tradition that matters to him.[25] If Dylan assimilates tradition, Allen reacts to it overtly, as the paradigmatic case of Ingmar Bergman shows. He once told Eric Lax that Ingmar Bergman is "probably the greatest film artist, all things considered, since the invention of the

8. The Real Revolution of the 1960s 141

motion picture camera."[26] This is precisely how ephebes speak of precursors. (Notice how much Allen speaking about Bergman sounds like Springsteen speaking about Dylan.) Allen's comment about Bergman epitomizes his attitude toward the great (WASP) artists of film.

It seems odd for a comedian to choose Bergman as a precursor because it takes considerable imagination to respond with comedy to Bergman's intense Scandinavian dramas. If Bergman made *Scenes from a Marriage* (1973) and filled it with Scandinavian angst, Allen reacted to it, and swerved from it, by filling *Scenes from a Mall* (1991) with American farce. In fact, reacting to, and against, movie tradition is essential to Allen's creative process, and he has been doing this from his earliest years.

Allen was first exposed to movies at an early age when his cousin introduced him to movie magazines, and he could not get enough of them. Unlike other kids his age, he did not just look at the pictures; he read the articles and remembered what he had read. As an artist, Allen is, above all, someone who knows tradition. The image of the Huck Finn–like innocent that Dylan used as a persona during his early days in New York is meaningless to Allen. He knows movie tradition and high culture as well. What makes him distinctive is that he incorporates what he knows into his work more than any other filmmaker ever has.

In this regard, his mentor, instead of precursor, is probably Groucho Marx, who once said, "I wouldn't belong to any club that would have me as a member."[27] Allen's spin on this self-putdown is to incorporate tradition into his writing by inventing comic ways to keep it at a distance. In his short stories, he takes a serious subject or a serious figure from high culture and swerves from it by presenting it in the ambience of Jewish Brooklyn for comic effect. A classic example of this comic swerve from high culture is his short story, "If the Impressionists Had Been Dentists," which is presented as a series of letters from Vincent van Gogh to his brother Theo. It begins: "Will life never treat me decently? I am wracked by despair! My head is pounding! Mrs. Sol Schwimmer is suing me because I made her bridge as I felt it and not to fit her ridiculous mouth!"[28] By using his reaction as an American outsider to European high culture for comic purposes in this way, Allen aligns himself with the tradition established by Mark Twain.

His more immediate source, though, was probably the radio comedy shows of the 1930s and 1940s such as "The Jack Benny Program" and "Fibber McGee and Molly." These radio classics often made fun of high culture. In one episode of "Fibber McGee and Molly," Fibber wins a poetry contest and awaits a visit from his muse, which he pronounces as "moose."

Allen follows this pattern of acknowledging the WASP tradition in popular culture, and then swerving from it for comic effect again and again in the pervasively intertextual trilogy of films that he made in the 1970s: *Play*

It Again, Sam (1972); *Annie Hall* (1977); and *Manhattan* (1979). In the first scene of *Play It Again, Sam*, he sits in a movie theater watching Humphrey Bogart say goodbye to Ingrid Bergman in the legendary ending of *Casablanca*. As he leaves, he frets about his inferiority to Humphrey Bogart. As the movie progresses, Bogie begins to appear to him, not as an intimidating precursor, but as a kindly mentor in the person of a Bogart impersonator who gives Allen sage advice about women. One could say that Bogart is to the Woody Allen character as Picasso was to the real Dylan.

A major change, which signals Allen's full maturity as a filmmaker, occurs in *Annie Hall* and *Manhattan*. In these and later films, the woman learns about high culture, often after the Woody Allen character encourages her to do so. She becomes more confident and experiences professional growth as a performer that causes an emotional rift between them, followed by a physical separation. In the film *Manhattan*, the Allen character even separates himself from the City and distances the audience from it by shooting in black and white and by using George Gershwin's music from the 1930s as a sound track.

With regard to *Manhattan* in Allen's evolution, we can adapt one of McLuhan's key principles, namely that each technology turns the previous technology into an art form. Thus, it was only after the arrival of industrialization that rural life became an interesting subject for art. This principle applies to *Manhattan* because it is balanced between the past (black and white images; Gershwin sound track) and the present (neurotic New Yorkers at major New York institutions). He was in the process of turning the present, which New York symbolizes for him, into an art form.

Just as Dylan's only significant movie, *Pat Garrett and Billy the Kid*, and Streisand's most important films were set in the past, Allen made a remarkable sequence of period pieces, as they are called in Hollywood. These included *A Midsummer Night's Sex Comedy* (1982) set at around the early nineteenth century, *Zelig* (1983) set in the 1920s, *The Purple Rose of Cairo* (1985) set in the 1930s, and *Radio Days* (1987) set around 1942. Another of his films, *Hannah and Her Sisters* (1986), might be considered an exception, but it amounts to a reworking of Chekhov's play *The Three Sisters*. As Streisand did with Broadway songs, respecting them while making them new again, Allen made Chekhov new again as well.

There is a curious correlation in the reaction of fans to Dylan's and Allen's use of tradition. The more an artist uses tradition to go beyond the immediate circumstances of his biography to create "impersonal art," in Eliot's sense of the term, the more people seek autobiographical explanations for their creations. Allen tempts his fans to interpret his films as autobiographical because he wears the same clothes and has the same body language as in real life. Nevertheless, Allen believes in impersonal art as much as Dylan does.

8. The Real Revolution of the 1960s

During another conversation with Eric Lax, he made a strong case for his movies not as autobiographical, but as impersonal:

> When I made *Stardust Memories* I didn't feel I was a much adored filmmaker whose life was miserable and all around me things were terrible. I thought I was a respectable moviemaker and the perks of success—as I said in my film *Celebrity*—actually outweighed the downside. I was never blocked, conflicted much, or steeped in gloom—although I often played that character.... Of course, the public doesn't know me—only the character I present to create conflict and laughs.[29]

For all of Dylan's differences from Allen, and there are many, he too could say "the public doesn't know me." And the reason that the public does not know Allen and Dylan is that Allen and Dylan do not want the public to know them—as is usually the case with introverts.

In the most general sense, Dylan, Streisand, and Allen did what Caesar did: they came, they saw, they conquered. They came to Manhattan (as they had wanted to do from an early age), they saw the possibilities that it offered, and they conquered it as no performers ever had before. They did so in large part because, as it usually happens with major innovators, historical circumstances gave them the opportunity to show the world what they could do.

In his early days in New York, Dylan immersed himself in the cultural triangle of folk music, modernist poetry, and modern painting. The folkies with whom Dylan sang had little if any interest in painting, and artists with whom he drank coffee listened to jazz, not folk music. Dylan created by synthesizing, and synthesized by creating.

Streisand also had a cultural triangle—not of interests, but of gifts. No American actress of her generation could sing as well as she could, and no American female singer of her generation could act as well as she could. And none of them had her infallible comic touch. She synthesized these diverse gifts into one astoundingly creative persona. To this day no one has ever done as many things as well as she has.

Allen also has three talents; he is a screenwriter, a comic performer, and a director. He did not experience the more or less instant success of Dylan and Streisand because it took him a longer time to integrate these talents. As a depressed introvert, he thought that he would stay behind the scenes and write gags for others. But, like Dylan, he also wanted to transcend the limits of the art form in which he started out, which was writing gags. He was not so much like Dylan in that Dylan had wanted to perform as soon as he could stand. Allen said of his early experiences doing standup comedy, "It was unspeakably agonizing."[30] After several fitful starts with screenplays, Allen integrated the gags, which he had been able to write since his early teenage years, into a Broadway play, *Don't Drink the Water*, which opened in 1966.

Only in 1972, at the age of 37, did Allen succeed in integrating his talents as writer, director, and actor into a single film, *Play It Again, Sam*. One reason integrating his talents took so long is that his managers, Jack Rollins and Charles Joffe, had to push him along every step of the way. "Rollins and Joffe envisioned Woody, as Rollins puts it, 'as the first triple-threat man since Orson Welles.': someone who could write, perform, and direct his own material."[31] Since Rollins and Joffe thought only in terms of film, they did not realize that Dylan and Streisand were also triple threats, and that as time passed more and more performers would become triple threats because the new oral age was conducive to integrated forms of creativity.

As they matured, Dylan, Allen, and Streisand did indeed become double and triple threats, or hyphenates, in Hollywood jargon. Dylan is a singer-songwriter-arranger. Allen is a writer-director-actor. And Streisand? She is a singer-actress-director-producer, and occasional writer. (She adapted "Yentl, a Yeshiva Boy," a story by Isaac Balshevis Singer, as the script for *Yentl*.) When performers are this important (the most important performers of their time, who sustain their creative output as hyphenates at a very high level for half a century), we may ask what it all meant for American popular culture. We can conclude by turning to McLuhan for help with an answer to this question.

McLuhan comments that "we actually live mythically and internally, as it were, but we continue to think in the old, fragmented space and time patterns of the pre-electric age."[32] "Fragmented space and time patterns" aptly characterizes the popular culture establishment as Dylan, Allen, and Streisand found it. In the music business, one writer wrote the lyrics and another writer wrote the melody. They gave the finished song to an arranger, who wrote an arrangement. They took the arrangement to a studio, where the singer came in, sang, and went home. Then the record company handled production and marketing. This arrangement produced Sinatra's great albums, among others, and functioned superbly. The same fragmented arrangement operated in drama, comedy, and musicals, whether on Broadway or in Hollywood. Writers wrote, performers acted and sang, and directors directed. Although some great shows and great movies were produced, its time was coming to an end.

As McLuhan wrote, "The aspiration of our time for wholeness, empathy, and depth of awareness is a natural adjunct of electric technology."[33] Understanding how this aspiration for wholeness manifested itself, and how Dylan's songs satisfied it, requires a brief digression on the evolution of sound technology in the 1950s and 1960s.

As usually happens, technological change accompanied (drove?) social change in the 1960s. It first took the form of the TR-63, a transistor radio that Sony introduced in the United States in December 1957, which was immortalized in "Transistor Sister," Freddy Cannon's hit song in 1961. Although the transistor radio made it possible for the first time to walk around and listen to music on the radio, it had two disadvantages that limited its popularity.

8. The Real Revolution of the 1960s   145

First, you had to hold it with one hand, and second, even if you held it right against your ear (which took some concentration and effort), the sound quality remained poor. Thus, transistor radios hardly outlasted the 1960s, in large part because they could not accommodate or compete with stereophonic sound.

The first stereophonic records were released in June 1958. The prosperity of the 1960s allowed people to buy these more expensive records, as well as the stereo equipment (record players and speakers) needed to play them. When a few FM stereo stations started broadcasting in stereo in 1961, they created a synergy with the newly available stereo records. The resulting split between FM and AM stations in the 1960s produced (or corresponded to, depending on the way one wants to say it) a corresponding split in musical styles for teenagers and college students.[34] Teenagers could listen to Motown and Sonny and Cher (and later the Monkees and the Association) on traditional AM stations with the fast-talking announcers who used a style that was perfected in the 1950s. Or they could listen to Dylan, the Doors, and Big Brother in stereo. Once they had heard these singers on the radio, they could, and usually did, go out and buy the albums. They could feel confident that AM stations would not play these acts, and that television programs would not book them. This sense of separateness from straight society, a more general version of the alienation of the Beat Poets in the 1950s, finds expression in Dylan's "Ballad of a Thin Man" and "Desolation Row." More importantly, in a historical sense, it corresponds to a particular stage of the evolving media complex.[35]

Another technological development that deepened the mystique of Dylan as it developed in the 1960s was the stereo headphones that John Koss developed in 1958 to be used with the new stereo records.[36] Stereo headphones produced an unprecedented and unappreciated change in the experience of listening to music, which is why the singer in "Ballad of the Thin Man" is told to put them on. Throughout human history until 1958, people who were listening to music had at least some awareness that a certain distance separated them from the performers of that music. Stereo headphones, however, abolished that distance for the first time. Never before did people listening to music have the sensation that it was being performed in the middle of their heads and the knowledge that no one else could hear it in that way in that moment. People could lie in bed in total darkness in the middle of the night and listen to "Like a Rolling Stone," knowing that they, *and only they*, could hear that song at that particular moment. It is no wonder, then, that they formed a deep attachment to Dylan's songs. They had the mesmerizing experience of listening to Dylan singing and playing a song that he had written. They had the fully justified belief that he was singing to them and nobody else in the world. Stereo sound and stereo records, as well as the "cool" (in

McLuhan's sense of low-definition) images of television, had created an "aspiration for wholeness," and Dylan satisfied that aspiration.

The effects of the innovations of stereo sound and of stereo headphones help to explain a great deal about the tumultuous decade of the 1960s, including the social tensions in society, which erupted into traumatic violence. And these effects help to explain the Baby Boomers' deep ongoing attachment to Dylan and the other great performers of the 1960s.[37]

People listening to "Like a Rolling Stone" with headphones had a radically different experience of music than people who sat in the Winter Garden Theater and listened to Streisand sing "People" in *Funny Girl*. When combined with the far-flung spaces of America, a battle ensued that can be understood as a battle between the private experience of listening to music on stereo headphones and the public experience of listening to music in a theater. Given Americans' long-standing preference for private space over public space, stereo headphones won the "battle."

To understand how this happened, we need to recall the popularity in the 1950s of sound tracks of Broadway musicals such as *My Fair Lady*. Throughout the 1950s, sound tracks found eager audiences among people who could not go to Broadway performances. Sound tracks, however enjoyable, were reminders one could not hear the real thing, as the wealthier and (presumably) more sophisticated people in New York could. But we know that after Elvis, records were the experience of music. "Hound Dog" sounded the same wherever you were. By dissolving the power of the center-periphery relationship, and making any place a center, Elvis thus used the light, cheap, portable 45 rpm records of the 1950s to set in motion a process of democratization of popular music that continues in mp3 downloads, and in other ways as well.

To put it graphically, stereo records and the changes that they created in listeners' habits and attitudes drained the creative energy from the Broadway musical. For about a decade, from Elvis's year, 1955, to the year 1965, as *Funny Girl* was settling into its long run, things seemed to continue as usual. But we know the end result of the process. Streisand was the last major star that Broadway produced, and she soon left New York.

In an odd way, Allen's devotion to living in New York and making movies there also provides evidence for the de-centralization of American entertainment. After making *Don't Drink the Water*, he had only wanted to make movies, which he was able to do while remaining in New York.

To bring it all back home, Dylan's departure from Minnesota for New York had far-reaching consequences for him and for the world. Like all great performers, he came along at the right time. When he arrived in New York, he found an urban environment and a media environment, as did Allen and Streisand, that allowed the specific features of his genius to find their fullest expression. America has never been the same because of interrelated and overlapping processes. The new electric media facilitated the collapse of the center-margin structure in American culture, which had made New York the place to make your dreams come true. In that center-margin structure, different people such as writers, singers, and directors had different functions. When it collapsed, not all at once, but steadily, those functions became integrated, as the careers of Dylan, Allen, and Streisand clearly demonstrate.

Conclusion: Dylan's Paradoxes

After listening to and thinking about Bob Dylan for more than 50 years, I have realized that there is one word that sums up his life and career better than any other word I know: paradox. Very little can be said about Dylan without sooner or later mentioning a paradox.

Dylan is one of the most charismatic performers of our time, an artist who has performed thousands of concerts before adoring fans, yet he is an introvert. Actually, he is more than an introvert; he is an obsessive recluse like other American artists of comparable achievement in whose company he belongs—artists such as Andrew Wyeth and Emily Dickinson. He intensely dislikes appearing in public anywhere except on a concert stage—so he doesn't.

Dylan is an American rock star, yet he has a profound, enduring respect for such intimidating representatives of European high culture as Pablo Picasso and Dante Aligheri. This attitude means that he has turned American individualism on its head. If American individualists usually assert their uniqueness by cutting themselves off from one aspect or another of the world, Dylan embraces the world. In this way he has in effect rebelled against the idea of rebellion. This is the most subversive thing he has ever done, and it has defined a great deal about his career. To put it another way, he has rebelled against a bedrock virtue of American culture—cultural innocence. Writers such as Mark Twain and Woody Allen were defending American innocence when they made clever jokes at the expense of European culture, but Dylan will have none of it.

Dylan's protean sensibility allows him to appreciate Hank Williams as well as Picasso, so he refuses to choose between European high culture and American popular culture. He balances himself between the two of them; it is no wonder that he once told an interviewer that he was an acrobat!

Dylan's refusal to choose between high culture and popular culture makes him a man in the middle, and thus he again and again places himself in transitional, luminal spaces in his songs. Significantly, this motif appears in his first song of his maturity, "Chimes of Freedom," with the reference to the doorway; it continues in "The Gates of Eden," "Mr. Tambourine Man," "Sad-Eyed Lady of the Lowlands," and in later songs like "Knockin' on Heaven's Door." And there is a visual equivalent of these transitional spaces in the cover of *Street Legal*, which shows him standing in a doorway looking out.

Dylan is an exceptionally prolific songwriter who has made dozens of albums and is generally considered to have revolutionized American popular music. It has become a cliché to say that his influence is incalculable. And yet when I surveyed people about his work, they often found it difficult to think of the titles of any of his songs other than "Blowin' in the Wind" and "Lay Lady Lay." These are the accessible songs that serve as bookends for the masterpieces *Highway 61 Revisited* and *Blonde on Blonde*. The hard truth is that in these albums Dylan makes exceptional demands on his listeners, especially in the extraordinary trilogy of songs about transcendence: "Mr. Tambourine Man," "Desolation Row," and "Visions of Johanna." These enigmatic songs are as puzzling as the spiritual journey itself. In this sense Dylan resembles an even more demanding poet, Wallace Stevens.

Dylan has written one great song after another that shows respect, even reverence, for what Goethe called "the eternal feminine." A first suggestion of the eternal feminine appears in his great compassion song "Girl from the North Country." Various equivalents of Dante's muse Beatrice appear in his songs. Yet in what we call real life, he treated the three women with whom he had relationships in the 1960s—Suze Rotolo, Joan Baez, and Sara Lowndes—very badly. But gifted women can turn their suffering into art, and Joan Baez did so in "Diamonds and Rust," her magnificent song about her relationship with Dylan.[1]

After performers live long enough, critics and reporters start calling them "legendary," and certainly Dylan is legendary. His Nobel Prize makes him even more legendary. Among musicians, he belongs with the two other legendary survivors of the 1960s, Paul McCartney and Mick Jagger. In America, only Harrison Ford has comparable stature and achievements.

As a fantastically wealthy and grizzled curmudgeon, and an artist who does whatever he wants without giving any consideration to other people's expectations, Dylan is now an Institution. He feels free to follow his muse wherever she leads him. In 2018, he was making iron sculptures. But anyone who has followed his career knows that he will continue to innovate as long as he is physically able to do so.

Chapter Notes

Preface

1. Quoted in Brinkley, "Bob Dylan's America," *Rolling Stone*, 45.
2. www.nobelprize.org. See the statement under "All Nobel Prizes in Literature."
3. Greenblatt, *Will in the World*, 11.
4. Eliot, *The Sacred Wood*, 28.

Chapter 1

1. Dylan, Bob, *Don't Look Back*, 1967. This documentary film has recently been re-released on DVD/Blu-Ray by the Criterion Collection.
2. Baez, *And A Voice to Sing With*, 91.
3. *Ibid.*, 23
4. Sounes, *Down the Highway*, 193.
5. *Ibid.*, 371-2. Sounes was the first investigator who brought these facts to light.
6. For a discussion of Dylan's films, see Lee, *Like a Bullet of Light: The Films of Bob Dylan*.
7. Marcus, *The Basement Tapes*, xiii.
8. See "Socio-Ethnic Origins of the Performers and Entrepreneurs," *Rock Eras*, 52–59.
9. Simonton, *Greatness: Who Makes History and Why*, 167.
10. See Slezkine, *The Jewish Century*.
11. Quoted in Sounes, *Down the Highway*, 230.
12. *Ibid.*, 234.
13. Dylan, *Chronicles*, 49.
14. Sounes, *Down the Highway*, 16.
15. *Chronicles*, 108.
16. Sounes, *Down the Highway*, 232–3.
17. *Chronicles*, 107.
18. Another example of autobiographical interpretations of popular songs is the endless speculation about which of Carly Simon's lovers she was thinking about when she wrote "You're So Vain."
19. Heylin, *Revolution in the Air*, 294.
20. *Ibid.*, 295.
21. Dylan responds strongly to visual images, so it is possible that a painting played a certain role in the creation of "Highway 61 Revisited." I have in mind Giovanni Tiepolo's "The Sacrifice of Isaac," which Dylan could have seen in the Metropolitan Museum.
22. Cott, *The Essential Interviews*, 129.
23. See also Wurzer, *Tales of the Road*, and *Highway 61 Revisited*.
24. Cott, *The Essential Interviews*.
25. See Dylan, "2016 Nobel Lecture in Literature," *Youtube*. https://www.youtube.com/watch?v=6TlcPRlau2Q
26. *Chronicles*, 229.
27. *Ibid.*, 65. Although Dylan enrolled in and attended the University of Minnesota, he did not take his studies seriously and did not graduate.
28. *Ibid.*, 96.
29. Quoted in Sounes, *Down the Highway*, 27.
30. *Ibid.*, 125.
31. Brinkley, "Bob Dylan's America," 49.
32. Elvis fans know that he had a twin brother who did not survive.
33. In Southern speech, "Mobile" is stressed on the first syllable, not the second one, so that the names of the cities are like a drumbeat: "MO-bile" and "MEM-phis."
34. Bloom, *A Map of Misreading*, 106.
35. *Ibid.*, 3.
36. Ong, *Fighting for Life*, 78.
37. *Ibid.*, 85.
38. Brothers, *Louis Armstrong's New Orleans*, 204.
39. *Ibid.*, 207.
40. Bloom, *The Anxiety of Influence*, 66.
41. *Ibid.*, 87. Bloom's emphasis.
42. Simonton, *Greatness*, 146.
43. Leman, *The New Birth Order Book*, 18.
44. *Ibid.*, 137.
45. Sounes, *Down the Highway*, 180–181.
46. See https://www.youtube.com/watch?v=t4nA3QwGPBg for the full interview, complete with several songs that Dylan sang live.

Chapter 2

1. Fitzgerald's biographer, Matthew Broccoli, says in *Some Sort of Epic Grandeur*, "Although *This Side of Paradise* now seems tame, it was received in 1930 as an iconoclastic social document—even as a testament of revolt," 117.
2. Dylan, *Chronicles*, 9.
3. Sounes, *Down the Highway*, 81.
4. Feinstein, et al., *Early Dylan*.
5. See also the pictures of Rotolo and Dylan together in *Early Dylan*, 20, 47.
6. Rotolo, *A Freewheelin' Time*, 158.
7. Dylan, *Chronicles*, 8.
8. Sounes, *Down the Highway*, 88–89.
9. Rotolo, *A Freewheelin' Time*, 92.
10. *Chronicles*, 226.
11. *Ibid.*, 35.
12. *Ibid.*, 36–39.
13. Quoted in McGregor, ed., *Bob Dylan: A Retrospective*, 84.
14. Hemingway, *A Farewell to Arms*, 284.
15. Guthrie, *Bound for Glory*, 217.
16. *Ibid.*, 218.
17. Carman, *A Race of Singers*, 129.
18. Brinkley, "Bob Dylan's America," 49.
19. Bloom, ed., *Walt Whitman: Selected Poems*, 127.
20. *Ibid.*, 11.
21. The lines from Mick Jagger's lyrics for the Rolling Stones classic "Satisfaction" that refer to watching television were probably inspired by "I Shall Be Free." Dylan's influence on British rock and roll is a major unexplored topic.
22. Marcus, *Like A Rolling Stone*, 48.
23. Dylan, *Chronicles*, 34.
24. The Dylan-Baez relationship resembles that of Frank Sinatra and Lauren Bacall; Sinatra and Dylan treated these talented women very badly. The Dylan-Baez relationship curiously anticipates the relationship between Robert Redford as a creative writer and Barbra Streisand as a politically engaged woman in *The Way We Were* (1973). Both on the "big screen" and what we call real life, the man continues to write, and gets married; the woman continues her political activities.
25. Curtis, *Rock Eras*, 155.
26. Sounes, *Down the Highway*, 143–144.
27. For Baez, the personal subtext of her introduction might be—"Well, really, he's mine, but I'm going to share him with you."
28. *Chronicles*, 267–8.
29. Quotation of Van Ronk in Scaduto, *Bob Dylan*, 217.
30. *Chronicles*, 59.
31. *An Anthology of French Poetry*, 21.
32. *Ibid.*, 22.
33. *Ibid.*, 113.
34. *The Essential Interviews*, 65.
35. Pete Seeger's "The Bells of Rhymney" may also have some relevance for "Chimes of Freedom." In 1959, Seeger had taken a poem by this name by the Welsh poet Idris Davies, and written music for it. The Byrds recorded a folk-rock version of "The Bells of Rhymney" in 1965.
36. *Chronicles*, 31–2.
37. Donne, *The Complete Poems*, Coffin, ed., 441.
38. Sometime in the 1960s I read a review in the *New York Times Book Review* that began, "Mississippi is this generation's Spain...."
39. Dylan stands in a doorway looking out on the cover of *Street Legal*, for instance. When he is in the doorway, he is both inside and outside, and thus that space illustrates his sense that he lives in two different time periods—AD and BC. In general, his cultural identity has a certain ambiguity, with roots in the private arts of music and painting on one hand and the public arts of singing and acting on the other. In "Chimes," the doorway may hint at the ambiguity of his attitude toward the civil rights movement. After his first rush of enthusiasm, he was both in it and out of it at the same time.
40. McLuhan, *Understanding Media*, 64.
41. *Ibid.*, 65.
42. *Ibid.*, 16.
43. *Ibid.*, 50.
44. *Ibid.*, 53.
45. *Ibid.*, 54.
46. Dylan, *Writings and Drawings*, 182.
47. *Ibid.*, 158.
48. "Ballad of a Thin Man" probably owes something to Eliot's "The Hollow Men," from 1925, especially these lines, which occur toward the end:

Between the idea
And the reality
Between the motion
And the act
Falls the Shadow

The excessive self-awareness of the hollow men paralyzes them; the thin man does not know what to do, either, because he is clueless, i.e., literate (Eliot, *The Complete Poems and Plays, 1909-1950*, 58).
49. Marcus, *Like a Rolling Stone*.
50. Regarding this epoch-making performance, see Wald, *Dylan Goes Electric*.
51. For all the importance of "Like a Rolling Stone," I know of only one other song that mentions it by name: "Time Marches On," by Tracy Lawrence.
52. Eksteins, *Rites of Spring*, 15.
53. Marcus, *Like a Rolling Stone*, 180.
54. Cott, *The Essential Interviews*, 56.
55. West, *Novels and Other Writings*, 59.
56. *Ibid.*, 97.
57. *Ibid.*, 65.

Chapter 3

1. Dylan, *Chronicles*, 89.
2. *Ibid.*, 117.
3. Kafka, *Collected Stories*, 75.
4. *Chronicles*, 110.
5. Eliot, *The Sacred Wood*, 27.
6. *Ibid.*, 28.
7. Eliot, "Tradition and the Individual Talent," in *The Sacred Wood*, 31.
8. Eliot, "The Metaphysical Poets," in *The Sacred Wood*, 124.
9. Cott, *The Essential Interviews*, 129.
10. *Chronicles*, 84.
11. *Ibid.*, 86. My emphasis.
12. Eliot, "Tradition and the Individual Talent," *The Sacred Wood*, 28.
13. *Chronicles*, 20.
14. Greenblatt, *Will in the World*, 152.
15. Sounes, *Down the Highway*, 57–8.
16. *Chronicles*, 55.
17. Duncan, *Picasso's Picassos*, 79.
18. Rotolo, *A Freewheelin' Time*, 98.
19. *Ibid.*, 105.
20. Dylan probably also saw Marcel Duchamp's "L.H.O.O.Q." Duchamp defaced the Mona Lisa by drawing a mustache and beard on the most famous face in Western art.
21. Quoted in McGregor, ed., *Bob Dylan: A Retrospective*, 84.
22. Cott, *The Essential Interviews*, 64.
23. Quoted in FitzGerald and Boddewyn, *Picasso and American Art*, 285.
24. Quoted in *Ibid.*, 279.
25. *Ibid.*, 240. A little later in the book, Fitzgerald comments, "Over a period of fifteen years, Lichtenstein passed from dueling with Picasso over specific images to free folding Picasso's style into his own signature look" (262). What Fitzgerald does not say is that only after Picasso died in 1973 was Lichtenstein able to "pass from dueling with Picasso" into his mature style.
26. Quoted in Brinkley, "Bob Dylan's America," 48.
27. Cott, *The Essential Interviews*, 54.
28. Quoted in FitzGerald and Boddewyn, *Picasso and American Art*, 249.
29. The cover of the album "Bringing It All Back Home" is an assemblage very much in the spirit of New York Pop Art in the mid-1960s.
30. FitzGerald and Boddewyn, *Picasso and American Art*, 249.
31. *Chronicles*, 90.
32. Rotolo, *A Freewheelin' Time*, 181.
33. Dylan, *The Drawn Blank Series*.
34. Gilot, *Life with Picasso*, 120.
35. Quoted in Cott, *The Essential Interviews*, 97.
36. Gilot, *Life with Picasso*, 266.
37. *Ibid.*, 116.
38. Baez, *And a Voice to Sing With*, 93.
39. *Chronicles*, 146.
40. Gilot, *Life with Picasso*, 109.
41. Baez, *And a Voice to Sing With*, 95–6.
42. Richardson, *A Life of Picasso*, Vol. 2, 11. By now it has become clear that there is no point in asking Dylan how he writes his songs, but that does not mean that journalists have stopped doing it. On the CBS program *60 Minutes*, on December 2, 2004, Ed Bradley interviewed Dylan. He asked Dylan the same questions that interviewers had been asking him for forty years: "Where do you get your ideas? How do you write your songs?" Dylan showed exemplary patience with him, and referred to "that wellspring of creativity," and said that "those songs were almost magically written." Bradley's body language indicated that he was quite uncomfortable—probably because he could not accept the truth of what Picasso had said about such questions: "There is no answer."
43. Gilot, *Life with Picasso*, 84.
44. *Ibid.*, 98.
45. Richardson, *A Life of Picasso*, Vol. 1, 51.
46. *Chronicles*, 108.
47. Richardson, *A Life of Picasso*, Vol. 1, 145.
48. Sounes, *Down the Highway*, 35.
49. *Ibid.*, 66.
50. *Chronicles*, 19.
51. Richardson, *A Life of Picasso*, 164.
52. *Ibid.*, 32.
53. *Ibid.*, 15. See Richardson's reproduction of this painting.
54. *Ibid.*, 45.
55. *Ibid.*, 17.
56. Marcus, *Like a Rolling Stone*, 184.
57. Richardson, *A Life of Picasso*, Vol. 2, 52.
58. Baez, *And a Voice to Sing With*, 84.
59. Fitzgerald, *Making Modernism*, 137.
60. Richardson, *A Life of Picasso*, Vol. 2, 34.
61. Sounes, *Down the Highway*, 115.
62. Gilot, *Life with Picasso*, 366.
63. Baez, *And a Voice to Sing With*, 98.
64. Quoted in Gilot, *Life with Picasso*, 352.
65. See, for example, the photographs in Feinstein, et al., *Early Dylan*, 30–38.
66. It is a very curious thing that Dylan, so reclusive and so withdrawn, has a deep, if not close, connection with Baez, the committed social activist. She wrote one of the most exquisite songs of the 1970s, "Diamonds and Rust," about their relationship—and sang it on the Rolling Thunder tour as he watched from the wings.

Chapter 4

1. Dylan, *Chronicles*, 9.
2. *Ibid.*, 27.
3. McLuhan, *Understanding Media*, 3.
4. *Ibid.*, vii.

5. *Ibid.*, 5–6.
6. *Ibid.*, 487.
7. *Ibid.*, vi.
8. Bloom, *Walt Whitman: Selected Poems*, xviii.
9. *Ibid.*, xix.
10. *Ibid.*, 117–8.
11. *Ibid.*, 125.
12. *Ibid.*, 300.
13. The equivalent of Baudelaire in the 1960s was Andy Warhol, whose work Dylan also found sterile and lacking in spirituality.
14. Bloom, *Walt Whitman: Selected Poems*, 117.
15. Stevens, *The Collected Poems of Wallace Stevens*, 129–130.
16. Eliot, *The Complete Poems and Plays: 1909–1950*, 387.
17. *Ibid.*, 44.
18. *Ibid.*, 52.
19. McLuhan, *Understanding Media*, 54.
20. Eliot, *The Complete Poems*, 38.
21. Cole Porter's song is not to be confused with the great doowop song of the same name that was a big hit for the Five Satins in 1954.
22. "Dancing on the Ceiling" is a rare night song that can be sung by both men and women. Ella Fitzgerald included it in *Ella Fitzgerald Sings the Rodgers and Hart Songbook*, from 1956.
23. It has been said that the lonely Sinatra is the quintessential Sinatra. If that is so, then the night song is the quintessential Sinatra song. This may explain why he made "One for My Baby (and One More for the Road)" a standard in his repertoire. In that song, he is not in bed, but in a bar at 3:00 AM. Another of his standards, "Angel Eyes," has very much the same tone and feel.
24. Dylan, *Chronicles*, 81
25. Bloom, *The Anxiety of Influence*, 133.
26. Bloom, *Walt Whitman: Selected Poems*, 45.
27. It is highly unlikely that there would have been any country music stations on AM radio in New York in the 1960s, so we are probably dealing here with Dylan's memory of listening to Hank Williams late at night on the WSM radio station in Nashville.
28. The women speak of "escapades out on the D train." It has not been noticed in commentaries on "Visions of Johanna" that the D train of the New York subway has a stop that Dylan would have known well, at Washington Square and Fourth Street.
29. Musa, ed., "The Divine Comedy," in *The Portable Dante*, 598.
30. *Ibid.*, 599.
31. Gilbert, *Eat Pray Love*, 199–200.
32. Heylin, *Revolution in the Air*, 294.
33. *Ibid.*, 295.
34. Incidentally, such a relationship between a poet and a mentor is not one that Bloom ever considers.
35. Musa, ed., *The Portable Dante*, 618.

Chapter 5

1. Stevens, *The Collected Poems*, 131.
2. Dylan, *Chronicles*, 52–53.
3. "I Dreamed I Saw Joe Hill" has an instructive history. Various people have sung it over the years, but what matters here is the role it played in an exchange of songs between Dylan and Baez. After "I Dreamed I Saw St. Augustine" came out on *John Wesley Harding*, Baez sang "I Dreamed I Saw Joe Hill," the original, at Woodstock in 1969. Her husband David Harris was serving time in prison for resisting the draft, and she reported to the assembled masses that Davis had started "a very, very good hunger strike." Since "I Dreamed I Saw Joe Hill" was not part of her usual repertoire at the time, it seems reasonable to suppose that by singing it at Woodstock she was also replying to "I Dreamed I Saw St. Augustine." She was, in effect, saying to Dylan that she was singing at Woodstock, although he would not let her sing in England in 1965. If in his song Dylan announced that he had chosen spirituality over social activism, she was announcing that she had made the opposite choice in her choice of a song to sing at Woodstock. Then, after the Rolling Thunder tour in 1975, when he let her sing with him, as he had not done ten years prior, she wrote a bittersweet masterpiece about their relationship, "Diamonds and Rust." The deep bond between Dylan and Baez had long ago transcended their physical relationship, and will last as long as both of them are alive. This bond/connection/relationship between two great artists has no precedent in the history of American popular music.
4. Eliot, *The Complete Poems and Plays*, 53.
5. In the late 1940s and early 1950s, African American groups had code names that indicated that they were black. The Midnighters was such a name; other examples from the time include the Inkspots and the Penguins.

Chapter 6

1. Ginsberg, *Collected Poems*, 126.
2. Ashton, *American Art Since 1945*, 129.
3. Dylan, *Chronicles*, 270.
4. *Ibid.*, 96.
5. Furia, *The Poets of Tin Pan Alley*, 14.
6. *Ibid.*, 15.
7. *Ibid.*, 155.
8. *Ibid.*, 171.
9. McBrien, *Cole Porter*, 231.
10. *Ibid.*, 327.

Chapter 7

1. Quoted in Marsh, *Born to Run*, 51.
2. Quoted in Masur, *Runaway Dream*, 26. Masur's book does for Springsteen's signature song what Marcus did for Dylan in *Like a Rolling Stone*.
3. Quoted in *Ibid.*, 18.
4. Quoted in *Ibid.*, 23.
5. See Springsteen's own account of this momentous day in *Ibid.*, 34–5.
6. Marsh, *Born to Run*, 226.
7. The Rise of MTV meant that singers had to be dancers, like Michael Jackson, or filmmakers, not just singers. See "Michael Jackson and MTV," in *Rock Eras*, 324–339.
8. When Sinatra sings "New York, New York," you can practically hear him gloat as he sings the line about making it in New York. He knew whereof he spoke.
9. Masur, *Runaway Dream*, 2.
10. Quoted in *Ibid.*, 42.
11. *Ibid.*, 40.
12. *Ibid.*, 107.
13. Quoted in Coles, *Bruce Springsteen's America*, 193.
14. Cited in Bloom, *The Anxiety of Influence*, 52.
15. Something similar is going on in Elton John's "Saturday Night's All Right for Fighting."
16. Quoted in Coles, *Bruce Springsteen's America*, 203.
17. This may explain why Dylan told Douglas Brinkley that "I don't think the dream of Whitman has ever been fulfilled" (quoted in "Bob Dylan's America"). Perhaps what Dylan does not quite want to say is that the dream of Whitman will never be fulfilled by him.
18. Dylan, *Tarantula*, 88.
19. This larger vision of America also constitutes the subtext of Ansel Adams' photography.
20. Erdman, ed., *Complete Poetry and Prose of William Blake*, 95.
21. Dylan had done this before, when he toured with a gospel choir and sang "You Gotta Serve Somebody" during his Christian phase in the 1970s. But people perceived his use of gospel choruses as an individual choice, whereas Springsteen was responding to a deeply felt societal need.

Chapter 8

1. Heylin, *Bob Dylan: Behind the Shades Revisited*, 6.
2. Spada, *Streisand: Her Life*, 4.
3. I have been unable to find any information about Woody Allen's grandparents.
4. Willensky, *When Brooklyn Was the World*, 11.
5. Baxter, *Woody Allen*, 8.
6. Meade, *The Unruly Life of Woody Allen*, 26.
7. *Ibid.*
8. "People," a wistful song that Streisand's soaring soprano turned into a classic, is related to "You Gotta Have Heart," from the musical *Damn Yankees* (1955), by Richard Adler and Jerry Ross.
9. There are two other American singers of whom that statement can be made. They are Joan Baez and Elvis Presley. Joan Baez appeared at the Newport Folk Festival in 1959, and her pure, piercing soprano has remained unchanged ever since. She thus offers a curious example of stasis and change. While her voice and vocal style remained unchanged for half a century, she lived a life of utmost personal integrity in agitating for peaceful change in the world. Unlike Streisand, she never wanted to appear in the theater or in movies. That brings us back to the unmoved mover of so many trends in popular music: Elvis. In Streisand's extraordinary vocal gifts, in her spectacular rise to dizzying heights of success, and, in the way she changed American entertainment, she is to female singers as Elvis was, and still is, to male singers. Like Elvis, she combined early vocal maturity with an intense drive to succeed. Like him, she experienced no significant influences from any singer, male or female, and thus had no anxiety of influence to overcome.
10. Spada, *Streisand: Her Life*, 103.
11. Quoted in *Ibid.*, 149.
12. Marlee Matliln also holds that record; she won an Oscar for *Children of a Lesser God* in 1986 at the age of 21.
13. Paul Muni had won an Oscar for Best Actor in *The Story of Louis Pasteur* in 1937, and Walter Matthau had won Best Supporting Actor for *The Fortune Cookie* in 1966. After Streisand won in 1968, a series of Jewish actors won Oscars: Richard Dreyfuss for *The Goodbye Girl* in 1978; Dustin Hoffman for *Kramer vs. Kramer* in 1979; Michael Douglas in 1987 for *Wall Street*. Note that none of the characters that they created in these great performances were Jewish.
14. For example, Julius Epstein, Phillip Epstein, and Howard Koch wrote the script for *Casablanca*.
15. Quoted in Lax, *Woody Allen*, 20–21.
16. Steve Martin, a major art collector and author of the superb play *Picasso at the Lapin Agile*, is a rare WASP performer who has a significant commitment to European culture.
17. Brinkley, "Bob Dylan's America," 76.
18. Although Italian-American singers such as Sinatra and Tony Bennett had a serious commitment to painting, Dylan is the first major Jewish singer to share this commitment.

19. Quoted in Baxter, *Woody Allen*, 10.
20. Streisand, *My Passion for Design*, 20.
21. *Ibid.*, 24.
22. *Ibid.*, 218.
23. These choices probably represent a further development of her repertoire for night club acts in the 1960s.
24. Baxter, *Woody Allen*, 3.
25. I have found only one use of a visual idea from a painting in his work. During the final scene of *Everyone Says I Love You*, Allen and Goldie Hawn dance on the banks of the Seine in Paris. Then the classical realism of the scene becomes magical realism as Hawn gradually rises from the pavement. Allen turns slowly, holding on to her with an outstretched arm. As he does so, he replicates Chagall's "The Promenade" (1917–18).
26. Lax, *Woody Allen*, 23.
27. The analogies between Marx and Allen extend further. If Marx made suggestive remarks to Margaret Dumont, the epitome of WASP propriety, Allen made suggestive remarks to Diane Keaton, the epitome of WASP kookiness. It makes sense that in the third act of *Everybody Says I Love You* (1996), the Woody Allen character and the Goldie Hawn character wear Groucho Marx mustaches and attend a party where everyone wears a Groucho Marx mustache.
28. Allen, *The Complete Prose of Woody Allen*, 107.
29. Quoted in Lax, *Conversations with Woody Allen*, 231.
30. Quoted in Meade, *The Unruly Life of Woody Allen*, 50.
31. Lax, *Woody Allen*, 155.
32. McLuhan, *Understanding Media*, 4.
33. *Ibid.*, 5.
34. See "But What About AM Radio?," in Curtis, *Rock Eras*, 220–226.
35. The next stage of this evolution occurred in the 1970s. As FM radio became the industry standard for radio stations, nobody wanted to listen to music on monaural AM stations any more. The managers of AM stations then responded to this crisis in one of two ways. Either they converted to FM stereo, and revamped their music programming (programming formats proliferated during the 1970s), or they continued to broadcast in AM, gave up music altogether, and converted to talk formats. This changeover had enormous consequences in the 1980s and 1990s.
36. Here is another analogy between Dylan and Shakespeare: Just as the spread of the British Empire created the mystique of Shakespeare as the world's greatest writer, stereo headphones gave tremendous impetus to the mystique of Dylan. They also had to be geniuses; the thing to remember is the confluence of genius and social circumstances.
37. When the Sony Walkman was introduced in 1979, it created another unprecedented experience of music listening. For the first time, it was possible to walk around unencumbered while listening to stereo music. This experience of music proved to be a defining one for the children of Baby Boomers.

Conclusion

1. We will never know as much as we would like about the Dylan-Baez relationship, so we have to use whatever meager evidence she provides. (We may feel confident that he'll never say anything about it.) It's worth noticing that in "Diamonds and Rust" Baez refers to herself in the third person as "the Madonna." What I suspect—and I emphasize that this is only guesswork—is that when he was in love with her, he called her "Madonna." Her exquisite face and angelic voice made this a natural comparison. What matters, though, is that if he did call her "Madonna," it signaled the beginning of his engagement with the eternal feminine, and also the way painting creates a reference point in his psyche. It thus makes perfect sense that his fertile imagination turned the real Joan Baez into a heavenly Madonna. We may suppose that this transformation culminated in "Sad-Eyed Lady of the Lowlands."

Bibliography

Allen, Woody. *The Complete Prose of Woody Allen*. New York: Wings Books, 1991.
Arnheim, Rudolf. *Picasso's Guernica: The Genesis of a Painting*. Berkeley: University of California Press, 1962.
Ashton, Dore. *American Art Since 1945*. New York: Oxford University Press, 1982.
Baez, Joan. *And a Voice to Sing With*. New York: Summit Books, 1987.
Baxter, John. *Woody Allen: A Biography*. New York: Carrol & Graf, 1998.
Benson, Carl. *The Bob Dylan Companion: Four Decades of Commentary*. New York: Schirmer Books, 1998.
Bloom, Harold. *The Anxiety of Influence: A Theory of Poetry*. New York/Oxford: Oxford University Press, 1973.
Bloom, Harold. *A Map of Misreading*. New York: Oxford University Press, 1975.
Bloom, Harold, ed. *Walt Whitman: Selected Poems*. American Poets Project, 2003.
Blunt, Anthony. *Picasso, the Formative Years: A Study of His Sources*. Greenwich, CT: New York Graphic Society, 1962.
Boucher, David, and Gary Browning. *The Political Art of Bob Dylan*. New York: Palgrave Macmillan, 2004.
Bowden, Betsy. *Performed Literature: Words and Music by Bob Dylan*. Lanham, MD: University Press of America, 2001.
Brinkley, Douglas. "Bob Dylan's America." *Rolling Stone*, 14 May 2009.
Broccoli, Matthew. *Some Sort of Epic Grandeur: The Life of F. Scott Fitzgerald*. Columbia: University of South Carolina Press, 2002.
Brothers, Thomas. *Louis Armstrong's New Orleans*. New York/London: W.W. Norton & Co., 2006.
Carman, Bryan K. *A Race of Singers: Whitman's Working-Class Hero from Guthrie to Springsteen*. Chapel Hill/London: University of North Carolina Press, 2000.
Coles, Robert. *Bruce Springsteen's America: The People Listening, A Poet Singing*. New York: Random House, 2004.
Cornfield, Jack. *After the Ecstasy, the Laundry*. New York: Bantam, 2001.
Cott, Jonathan, ed. *Bob Dylan: The Essential Interviews*. New York: Wenner Books, 2006.
Curtis, James M. *Culture as Polyphony: An Essay on the Nature of Paradigms*. Columbia: University of Missouri Press, 1978.
Curtis, James M. *Rock Eras: Interpretations of Music and Society, 1954–1984*. Bowling Green, OH: The Popular Press, 1987.
Donne, John. *The Complete Poems and Selected Prose of John Donne*. Edited by Charles M. Coffin. New York: The Modern Library, 2001.
Duncan, David Douglas. *Picasso's Picassos*. New York: Harper, 1961.
Duncan, David Douglas. *The Private World of Pablo Picasso*. New York: Harper, 1958.
Dylan, Bob. *Chronicles*, Vol. 1. New York: Simon & Schuster, 2004.
Dylan, Bob. *The Drawn Blank Series*. Edited by Ingrid Mossinger and Kerstin Drechsel. New York: Prestel, 2007.

Dylan, Bob. *Lyrics: 1962–2001*. New York: Simon & Schuster, 2004.
Dylan, Bob. *Tarantula*. New York: St. Martin's Press, 1966.
Dylan, Bob. *Writings and Drawings*. New York: Alfred E. Knopf, 1973.
Eksteins, Modris. *Rites of Spring: The Great War and the Birth of the Modern Age*. Boston/New York: Houghton Mifflin, 1989.
Eliot, T.S. *The Complete Poems and Plays, 1909–1950*. New York: Harcourt, Brace & World, 1971.
Eliot, T.S. *The Sacred Wood and Major Early Essays*. Mineola, NY: Dover Publications, 1998.
Erdman, David, ed. *The Complete Poetry of William Blake*. Berkeley: University of California Press, 1982.
Feinstein, Barry, Daniel Kramer, and Jim Marshall. *Early Dylan*. Boston/New York/London: Little, Brown & Co., 1999.
FitzGerald, Michael C. *Making Modernism: Picasso and the Creation of the Market for Twentieth-Century Art*. New York: Farrar, Straus and Giroux, 1995.
FitzGerald, Michael C., and Julia May Boddewyn. *Picasso and American Art*. New York: Whitney Museum of American Art, 2007.
Flores, Angel, ed. *An Anthology of French Poetry from Nerval to Valery in English Translation*. New York: Anchor Books, 1958.
Furia, Phillip. *The Poets of Tin Pan Alley: A History of America's Greatest Lyricists*. New York/Oxford: Oxford University Press, 1990.
Gabler, Neil. *An Empire of Their Own: How the Jews Invented Hollywood*. New York: Anchor Books, 1989.
Gilbert, Elizabeth. *Eat Pray Love*. New York: Viking, 2006.
Gilot, Françoise, and Carlton Lake. *Life with Picasso*. New York: McGraw-Hill, 1964.
Ginsberg, Allen. *Collected Poems, 1947–1980*. New York: Harper and Row, 1984.
Gray, Michael. *The Bob Dylan Encyclopedia*. New York: Continuum, 2006.
Gray, Michael. *Song and Dance Man: The Art of Bob Dylan*. London/New York: Cassell, 2000.
Greenblatt, Steven. *Will in the World: How Shakespeare Became Shakespeare*. New York/London: W.W. Norton, 2004.
Guthrie, Woody. *Bound for Glory*. New York: E.P. Dutton, 1968.
Hajdu, David. *Positively 4th Street: The Lives and Times of Joan Baez, Mimi Baez Farina and Richard Farina*. New York: Farrar, Straus and Giroux, 2001.
Hansen, Marcus. *The Problem of the Third Generation Immigrant*. Rock Island, IL: Augustana Historical Society, 1938.
Harvey, Todd. *The Formative Bob Dylan: Transmission and Stylistic Influences, 1961–1963*. Landham, MD/London: Scarecrow Press, 2001.
Hemingway, Ernest. *A Farewell to Arms*. New York: Scribner's, 2012.
Heylin, Clinton. *Bob Dylan: A Life in Stolen Moments: Day by Day, 1941–1995*. New York: Schirmer Books, 1996.
Heylin, Clinton. *Bob Dylan: Behind the Shades Revisited*. New York: William Morris, 2001.
Heylin, Clinton. *Revolution in the Air: The Songs of Bob Dylan, 1957–1973*. Chicago: Chicago Review Press, 2009.
Jaffe, Hans, and Ludwig C. *Pablo Picasso*. New York: H.N. Abrams, 1964.
Kafka, Franz. *Collected Stories*. New York/Toronto: Alfred A. Knopf, 1993.
Lax, Eric. *Conversations with Woody Allen: His Films, the Movies, and Moviemaking*. New York: Alfred A. Knopf, 2009.
Lax, Eric. *Woody Allen: A Biography*. New York: Alfred A. Knopf, 1991.
Lee, C.P. *Like a Bullet of Light: The Films of Bob Dylan*. London: Helter Skelter Publishing, 2000.
Leman, Kevin. *The New Birth Order Book: Why You Are the Way You Are*. Grand Rapids, MI: Fleming R. Revell, 1998.
Lévi-Strauss, Claude. *Structural Anthropology*. Translated by Claire Jacobson and Brooke Grundfest. New York: Anchor Books, 1963.
Marcus, Greil. *Invisible Republic: Bob Dylan's Basement Tapes*. New York: Henry Holt, 1997.
Marcus, Greil. *Like a Rolling Stone: Bob Dylan at the Crossroads*. New York: Public Affairs, 2005.
Marqusee, Mike. *Wicked Messenger: Bob Dylan and the 1960s; Chimes of Freedom*. New York: Seven Stories Press, 2005.

Marsh, Dave. *Born to Run: The Bruce Springsteen Story*. New York: Dell Books, 1981.
Marshall, Lee. *Bob Dylan: The Never Ending Star*. Cambridge, UK: Polity, 2007.
Masur, Louis P. *Runaway Dream: "Born to Run" and Bruce Springsteen's American Vision*. New York/Berlin/London: Bloomsbury, 2009.
McBrien, William. *Cole Porter: A Biography*. New York: Alfred A. Knopf, 1998.
McGregor, Craig, ed. *Bob Dylan: A Retrospective*. New York: William Morrow, 1972.
McLuhan, Marshall. *Understanding Media: The Extensions of Man*. New York: McGraw-Hill, 1964.
Meade, Marion. *The Unruly Life of Woody Allen*. New York: Open Road Media, 2014.
Musa Mark, ed. *The Portable Dante*. New York: Penguin Books, 1995.
Negus, Keith. *Bob Dylan*. Bloomington: Indiana University Press, 2008.
Olivier, Fernande. *Picasso and His Friends*. Translated by Jane Miller. London: Heinemann, 1964.
Ong, Walter. *Fighting for Life: Contest, Sexuality, and Consciousness*. Ithaca/London: Cornell University Press, 1981.
Ong, Walter. *The Presence of the Word: Some Prolegomena for Cultural and Religious History*. New Haven/London: Yale University Press, 1967.
Ong, Walter. *Rhetoric, Romance, and Technology: Studies on the Interaction of Expression and Culture*. Ithaca/London: Cornell University Press, 1971.
Richardson, John R. *A Life of Picasso, Vol. I: 1881–1906*. New York: Random House, 1991.
Richardson, John R. *A Life of Picasso, Vol. II: 1907–1917*. New York: Random House, 1996.
Richardson, John R., ed. *Picasso: An American Tribute*. New York: Public Education Association, in cooperation with Chanticleer Press, 1962.
Ricks, Christopher B. *Dylan's Visions of Sin*. New York: Ecco Books, 2004.
Riley, Tim. *Hard Rain: A Dylan Commentary*. New York: Da Capo Press, 1999.
Rotolo, Suze. *A Freewheelin' Time: A Memoir of Greewich Village in the Sixties*. New York: Broadway Books, 2008.
Santelli, Robert. *The Bob Dylan Scrapbook, 1956–1966*. New York: Simon & Schuster, 2005.
Scaduto, Anthony. *Bob Dylan*. New York: Grosset and Dunlap, 1968.
Simonton, Dean Keith. *Greatness: Who Makes History and Why*. New York/London: The Guilford Press, 1994.
Slezkine, Yuri. *The Jewish Century*. Princeton: Princeton University Press, 2006.
Smith, Larry David. *Bob Dylan, Bruce Springsteen, and American Song*. Westport, CT: Praeger, 2002.
Smith, Larry David. *Writing Dylan: The Songs of a Lonesome Traveler*. Westport, CT: Praeger, 2005.
Sounes, Howard. *Down the Highway: The Life of Bob Dylan*. New York: Gove Press, 2001.
Spada, James. *Streisand: Her Life*. New York: Crown Publishers, 1995.
Starr, Larry, and Christopher Waterman. *American Popular Music: From Minstrelsy to MTV*. New York/Oxford: Oxford University Press, 2003.
Stevens, Wallace. *The Collected Poems*. New York: Vintage Books, 1990.
Streisand, Barbra. *My Passion for Design*. New York: Viking, 2010.
Varesi, Anthony. *The Bob Dylan Albums: A Critical Study*. Toronto/Buffalo: Guernica, 2002.
Wald, Elijah. *Dylan Goes Electric: Newport, Seeger, Dylan, and the Night that Split the Sixties*. New York: Dey Street Books, 2015.
Webb, Stephen H. *Dylan Redeemed: From Highway 61 to Saved*. New York: Continuum, 2006.
West, Nathaniel. *Novels and Other Writings*. New York: Penguin Books, 1997.
Wilentz, Sean. *Bob Dylan in America*. New York: Anchor Books, 2011.
Willensky, Elliot. *When Brooklyn Was the World, 1920–1957*. New York: Harmony Books, 1986.
Williamson, Nigel. *The Rough Guide to Bob Dylan*. London: Rough Guides, 2004.
Wurzer, Cathy. *Highway 61 Revisited*. Minneapolis: University of Minnesota Press, 2009.
Wurzer, Cathy. *Tales of the Road*. St. Paul, MN: Minnesota Historical Society Press, 2008.

Index

Abel 84
After the Ecstasy, the Laundry 96
Alexander, Shana 135
Alexander II 130
"All I Really Want to Do" (BD song) 106; as a one-time experiment 109
All Quiet on the Western Front 17
Allen, Woody 5, 129, 131, 132, 136, 138, 146, 147; and impersonal art 142–3; on Ingmar Bergman 139–140; multiple gifts of 143; relations with parents 139–40; use of tradition and intertextuality 140ff.
The Allman Brothers 114, 116
Altamont Race Track 115, 119, 121
AM radio 104
Amblin Entertainment 130
America 98, 127, 133
"America the Beautiful" 125, 127
"The American Sublime" 95
"Angel Eyes" 88
"Angels in the Sky" 88
Annie Hall (WA movie) 142
Another Side of Bob Dylan (BD album) 30, 43, 106, 134
Anyone Can Whistle 139
answer songs 101–2
An Anthology of French Poetry from Nerval to Valery in English Translation 37
Anything Goes (musical) 113
"Anything Goes" (song) 113
The Apartment 60
"Apocalyptic Vision" 66
Apollinaire, Guillaume 36; "The Breasts of Tiresias" 85
Arabic 98
Aramaic 98
"Are You Lonesome Tonight?" 101
Ariadne 125
Arlen, Harold 12
Armstrong, Louis 56; and cutting contests 22–3
Arnheim, Rudolf 59
Arnold, Eddy 101

Artforum 60
Asbury Park, NJ 123, 126
The Association 145

Bacall, Lauren 131
Back to Broadway 139
Baez, Joan 20, 34, 61, 64, 67, 69, 70, 74, 128, 135; *And a Voice to Sing With* (memoir) 7, 63, 70
Bakunin, Mikhail 134
"Ballad of a Thin Man" (BD song) 43–44, 74, 78, 145
"The Ballad of Frankie Lee and Judas Priest" (BD song) 98–99, 107
"Ballad of Hollis Brown" (BD song) 31
Ballard, Hank, and the Midnighters 101
Ballets Russes 44
"Band on the Run" 117
The Barbra Streisand Album 134
Barcelona, Spain 65, 66
Barkely, Catherine 30
Barnett, Catherine Lee 125, 126
Bartók, Béla 139
The Basement Tapes (book){en}9
Baudelaire, Charles 11, 36, 37, 39, 77, 78, 79; "Correspondences" anticipates "Chimes of Freedom" 37
Baxter, John 140
"Be My Baby Tonight" 101
Beat poets 24, 43, 45, 103, 145
Beatlemania 39, 49
Beecher, Bonnie 18
"Begin the Beguine" 113
Belarus 130
Bellow, Saul 11
Bergman, Ingmar 140
Berlin, Irving 12, 112, 113, 130
Berne, Eric 115
Bernstein, Leonard 12
Berry, Chuck 34, 75, 102, 105, 109; "Maybelline" 43, 105, 108, 111
Betty Parsons Gallery 61
Beverly Hills Chihuahua (movie) 47

Index

Big Brother 145
The Big Chill (movie) 116
birth order 25–6
Black, Jeanne 101
Black Sea 132
Blake, William: "Milton" 126
Blonde on Blonde (BD album) 11, 24, 94, 95, 99, 107, 134
Bloom, Harold 59, 88, 89, 123; and "Mr. Tambourine Man" 75; tessera as completion 24; theory of the anxiety of influence 21
Bloomfield, Mike 12
"Blowin' in the Wind" (BD song) 2, 31, 33, 34, 35, 37, 50, 66, 71, 102, 106, 122, 134; verse and chorus structure 108–9
Blunt, Anthony 59
Bob Dylan (album) 134
Bob Dylan in America (book) 4
Bob Dylan: The Essential Interviews 64
"Bob Dylan's Blues" (BD song) 108
"Bob Dylan's 115th Dream" (BD song) 52, 74, 106, 108
The Bob Hope Comedy Special 134
Bon Soir (nightclub) 133
"Born in the USA" 127
Born to Run (BS album) 121
"Born to Run" (BS song) 121, 122
Boston, MA 114
Bound for Glory 31–2
Braque, Georges 69
Braoool 67
Breakfast at Tiffany's (movie) 27
Brice, Fanny 12, 136
"The Bride Stripped Bare by Her Bachelors, Even" 61
Bringing It All Back Home (BD album) 86, 106, 134
Brinkley, Douglas 32, 137
Broadway 138
The Broadway Album 139
Brooklyn 130, 131, 132, 136, 138
Brooklyn Syndrome 131
Brooks, Mel 131, 140
Brothers, Thomas 22
Browne, Jackson 115, 116
Bruce Springsteen's America 123
Buddha 97
Burden, Eric, and the Animals 130
"But in the Morning, No" 114
Byron, Lord 30

Cain 84
California 115
Camelot (musical) 83; and "Desolation Row" 83
Canal Street (New Orleans) 22
Cannery Row (novel) 82
Cannon, Freddie 144
Caravaggio 137
Carman, Bryan K. 32
Carmel, CA 63

Carnegie Hall 134
Carter, Thelma 101
Casanova, Giacomo Giralomo de Seingalt 81, 83, 84, 121
Caucus Club (Detroit, MI) 133
Central Park 134
Cézanne, Paul 30, 67
Chagall, Mark 71; BD's interest in 11–12
Chandler, Jeff 131
Charles, Ray 101
Charles I 83
Chelsea Hotel 14
Chicago, IL 27
The Chicago Daily News 45
"Children Will Listen" 139–40
"Chimes of Freedom"(BD song) 37, 50, 73, 75, 77, 93, 96, 106, 108, 109, 121, 124; and Baudelaire's "Correspondences" 37–38; obsolesces folk music; similarities to "If I Had a Hammer" 40; stanza form in 109; synthesis in 39–40
Christianity 75
Chronicles (BD's memoir) 13, 29, 30, 36, 51, 54, 60, 65, 71, 73, 79, 103; on method of songwriting 63; on T.S. Eliot 52
Church, Frederick 126
Cinderella 81–2, 84, 89
Cinderella (movie) 81
Clapton, Eric 25, 118, 119
clear-channel AM radio 19
Clear Lake, IA 17
Clemons, Clarence 121, 122
Clinton, Bill 13
Coburn, James 8
Cohen, John 15, 53
The Colgate Comedy Hour 134
Collins, Judy 136
Columbia Records 65, 133, 134
Coney Island 130
Cooper, Gary 98
Copland, Aaron 131
Coppola, Francis Ford 135
Coruña, Spain 64
Cosell, Howard 131
"Cotton Fields" 18
"Country Pie" (BD song) 102, 108
Creoles 22
The Crewcuts 88
Crosby, Bing 8, 119
Crusades 92
Cukor, George 49
Cubism 70, 75
Culture as Polyphony. An Essay on the Nature on Paradigms (book) 2
Curtis, Donna v

"Dancing on the Ceiling" 87, 88
Dante Alighieri 81, 82, 86, 92, 105, 124; referenced in "Tangled Up in Blue" 80
Davis, Bette 81–2, 85, 89
Davis, Clive 131

Index

Davis, Mac 115
Day, Doris,. 112
"Dear Landlord" (BD song) 99, 107, 108
"Le Dejeuner sur l'Herbe" (painting) 57
"Les Demoiselles d'Avignon" (painting) 66, 68, 69
DeNiro, Robert 136
Dennis, Carolyn 8
Dennis-Dylan, Desiree Gabrielle (daughter of BD) 8
"Desolation Row" (BD song) 5, 17, 40, 48, 52, 69, 71, 73, 74, 75, 77, 78, 80, 86, 89, 93, 107, 108, 116, 121, 122, 145; order in 82–3; and Picasso 58–9; and "The Waste Land" 82
Diaghilev, Serge 43
Diamond, Neil 131
Dickinson, Emily 8, 17
Dine, Jim 60
Dinning, Mark 88
The Divine Comedy 80
Dr. Strangelove (movie) 52
Donne, John 126; "Meditation XVII," 40
"Don't Be Cruel" 121
Don't Drink the Water (WA play) 134, 143, 146
Don't Look Back (movie) 7, 25
"Don't Fence Me In, " 113
"Don't Think Twice It's All Right" (BD song) 36
The Doors 145
"Dora Maar" 58
Dorfman, Bruce 11
Dostoyevsky, Fyodor 30
"Down Along the Cove" (BD song) 107
Down the Highway (book) 4
Dreyfuss, Richard 131
"Drifter's Escape" (BD song) 98, 116
DuBarry Was a Lady 114
Dubois, Blanche 28
Duchamp, Marcel 61
Duluth, MN 9, 64, 130, 132
Duncan, David Douglas 58, 59
The Duprees 81
Dylan, Bob (Robert Allen Zimmerman) 34, 44, 116, 117, 119, 121, 123, 124, 125, 127, 128, 131, 133, 137, 138, 140, 141, 142, 143, 144, 145, 146; affinities with Cole Porter 113–4; affinities with Duke Ellington 72; affinities with Pablo Picasso 57–71; as American artist 2; as Ariadne 3; arrives in New York 27; artistic genealogy 71–2; behavior during recording of "Like a Rollng Stone" 26; birth 9; as Bobby Zimmerman in Hibbing 13, 17, 20, 23, 26, 47, 63, 81, 83, 88, 120, 129, 131; comment on Lee Harvey Oswald 35–6; on connection between the 1960s and the Civil War 54; and the couplet tradition 105; in *Don't Look Back* 7; and European High Modernism 71–2; as a first-born 25; and folk music 135; historical sense 54–5; as Huck Finn 36; interest in Judaism 12, 13; Jewish heritage 10; and John Donne 126; lack of strong father figure 18; leaves New York 136; "Like a Rolling Stone" and "Hound Dog" 66–7; marries Carolyn Dennis 8; marries Sara Lownds 8; as mediator 77; minimalist performance style 25; personal and professional relations with Jews 68; on poet as synthesizer 53; reaction to Elvis Presley 25; reading program 29–30; reads the French Symbolist Poets 36; reads Hemingway 30; rhyme forms in songs 106–8; signs contract with Columbia Records 28; similarities to Jay Gatsby 27; statement about father 13; as synthesizer 72; theme of transcendence 73; visits Tupelo, MS 20; and *Understanding Media* 41–2; *see also individual song titles*
Dylan (née Lownds), Sara 7, 12, 68, 70, 92; divorces BD 132; as inspiration for "Sad-Eyed Lady of the Lowlands" 14
Dylan's Visions of Sin (book) 4

E Street Band 8, 118, 122
The Eagles 114, 116
Early Dylan (book) 28, 70
"Early Sunday Morning" 115
The Ed Sullivan Show 119, 121, 134
Edmiston, Susan 60
Edwards, Bobby 87
Einstein, Albert 11; in "Desolation Row" 85; and *Fiddler on the Roof* 85; "On the Electrodynamics of Moving Bodies" 85
Eliot, T.S. 4, 21, 37, 51, 71, 74, 79, 120, 137, 139; as elitist in "Desolation Row" 85; "The Metaphysical Poets" 53; "Traditional and the Individual Talent" 3, 53; "The Waste Land" 97, 116; "The Waste Land" and "Desolation Row" 82, 84, 85
Elliot, Ramblin' Jack 29, 57
Ephron, Nora 60, 140
Eric Burden and the Animals 130
Europe 140
Evers, Medgar 35, 108
"Everybody Says Don't" 139

Falmouth, MA 125
A Farewell to Arms 30
Fats Domino 101
Faulkner, William 30
"Faux Commercial for Powdermilk Biscuits" 115, 117
"Femme au chapeau" 60
Ferlinghetti, Lawrence 103
Fibber McGee and Molly 141
Fiddler on the Roof (musical) 85
Fighting for Life. Contest, Sexuality, and Consciousness 22
Fitzgerald, F. Scott 27, 99
Fitzgerald, Michael 67
Florence, Italy 9
Flores, Angel 37

"The Flower Seller" 58
FM Radio 145
Folk music 41
For Whom the Bell Tolls 40
"For You" 121
"Forever Young" (BD song) 99
The Formative Bob Dylan 57
France 92
Freedom Brigade 40
The Freewheelin' Bob Dylan (BD album) 29, 29, 68, 96, 106
French Symbolist poets 24, 41, 60, 77, 86
Freud, Sigmund 11
Frey, Glen 114, 116
"The Fruit Dish" 58
Funny Girl (movie) 138; BS wins Oscar for 134
Funny Girl (musical) 134, 145, 146
Funny Lady (movie) 139
Furia, Phillip 112

Gable, Clark 47
Gabler, Neal 12
La Galloise 69
"Games People Play" 114
Ganz, Sally 59
Ganz, Victor 59
Garfunkel, Art 25
Garland, Judy 121
The Garry Moore Show 134
"Gates of Eden" (BD song) 27, 74, 78, 83, 108
Geffen, David 131
Gene Vincent and the Blue Caps 81
Georgione 57
Gerde's Folk City 28, 133
Gere, Richard 7
Gershwin, George 12, 34, 112, 130, 144
Gershwin, Ira 12, 34, 112, 130, 144
Gilbert, Elizabeth 91-2
Gilot, Françoise 64, 69; and *Life with Picasso* 61-2
Ginsburg, Allen 37, 42, 43, 103, 105
"Girl from the North Country" (BD song) 31, 36, 80, 106, 108
"Girl with Rooster" 59
Goddard, Paulette 47, 48
The Godfather (movie) 49
Goethe, Johan Wolfgang 123; and the "eternal feminine" 80
Gogh, Theo 141
Gogh, Vincent Van 141
The Good Samaritan 85
"Got My Mojo Working" 67
Gould, Elliot 131
Grammy 134
"Great American Nude, No. 10" 61
Great American Songbook 130, 139
The Great Gatsby 27, 49, 99
Greatness 25
El Greco 66
Greenblatt, Steven: *Will in the World* 3

Greenwich Village 29, 37, 129, 134
Greetings from Asbury Park 119, 120
Grossman, Albert 12, 68
Grossman, Sally 96
"Growin' Up" 121
Guell, Eusebi 67
"Guernica" 58
Guggenheim Museum 11
Guthrie, Arlo 128
Guthrie, Woody 18, 28, 33, 38, 40, 57, 66, 71, 74, 113, 125, 127; as father figure for BD 19, 24; influence of Guthrie's *Bound for Glory* 31

Halen, Eddie Van 115
Hamlet 90, 102
Hamlet 102
Hammerstein, Oscar II 12, 112
Hammond, John 28, 119
Hank Ballard and the Midnighters 101
Hannah and Her Sisters (WA movie) 142
Hansen, Marcus 129
"A Hard Rain's a-Gonna Fall" (BD song); imagery 57; influenced by *Bound for Glory* 32; influenced by *A Farewell to Arms* 31
Harrison, Rex 49
Harvey, Todd 57
Hass, Joseph 45
A Hatful of Rain 89
Havens, Richie 128
The Hawks 8, 43, 45, 66
Hayes, Billy 56
Hays, Lee 40
Hebrew 98
"He'll Have to Go" 101
"He'll Have to Stay" 101
Hello, Dolly! (BS movie) 138
Hemingway, Ernest 30, 39, 40, 113, 131
Hendrix, Jimi 25, 116
Henley, Glen 114, 116
Henry, Frederick 30
Heylin, Clinton 14, 74, 91
Hibbing, MN 9, 13, 16, 18, 27, 29, 30, 71, 72, 73, 81, 120
High Noon 98
High Society 113, 119
Highway 61 15-16
Highway 61 Blues Museum 16
Highway 61 Revisited (BD album) 39, 69, 96, 107, 134; BD's liner notes 43
"Highway 61 Revisited" (BD song) 2, 14-16, 68, 107, 110
Hill, Joe 97
Hoboken NJ 131
Holly, Buddy 17-18
Hollywood 46, 136, 137
Holmes, Sherlock 46
Homer (Greek poet) 17
Hope, Bob 8
Hopper, Edward 115
"Hotel California" 116

Index

"Hound Dog" 34, 48, 66, 88, 12, 14
How the Jews Invented Hollywood (book) 12
"Howl" 103
Huck Finn 141
The Hunchback of Notre Dame (movie) 83
Hush, Hush, Sweet Charlotte (movie) 81

"I Couldn't Sleep a Wink Last Night" 87
"I Dreamed I Saw Joe Hill" 97
"I Dreamed I Saw St. Augustine" (BD song) 97
"I Pity the Poor Immigrant" (BD song) 99, 107, 129
"I Shall Be Free No. 10" (BD song) 33, 37; and Guthrie's "We Shall Be Free" 33–4
"I Shall Be Released" (BD song) 84
"I Threw It All Away" (BD song) 108
"The Idea of Order in Key West" 78–9, 95
"If the Impressionists Had Been Dentists" 141
"I'll Be Your Baby Tonight" (BD song) 96, 108
"I'll Keep It with Mine" (BD song) 99
"I'll Save the Last Dance for You" 101
"*I'm Not There*" (film) 8
immigration 129–20
Impressionists 30
"In the Still of the Night" 87, 88
"In the Wee Small Hours of the Morning" 87
In the Wee Small Hours of the Morning (Sinatra album) 88
"Incident on 57th Street" 120
"Independence Day" 16
Indiana 112
intertextuality 56
Into the Woods 139
Israel 98
"It Ain't Me, Babe" (BD song) 80, 81, 106
It Happened One Night (movie)
"It's All Right Ma, I'm Only Bleeding" (BD song) 60, 74
"It's De-Lovely" 113
"It's Hard to be a Saint in the City" 120, 121
Ives, Burl 113

The Jack Benny Program 141
Jackson, Michael 13
Jaffe, Hans 59
Jagger, Mick 25, 81, 119
"Jailhouse Rock" 24
James, Billy 28
James, Henry 137
Jewish Museum 61
Jews 130; and American popular culture 12
Jo, Tamita
Joel, Billy 13
Joffe, Charles 144
John Wesley Harding (BD album) 94, 95, 96, 100, 107, 108, 111, 134
"John Wesley Harding" (BD song) 97, 107, 123
Johns, Jasper 59
Johnson, Jay 56
Jolson, Al 12

Jones, Casey 100
Joplin, Janis 116, 136
Jordan, Robert 40
Judaism 75
The Judy Garland Show 134
"Jump" 115
"Jungleland" 122–3, 125; and "Desolation Row" 122; free verse 124
"Just Like Tom Thumb's Blues" (BD song) 31, 74

Kafka, Franz 4, 11, 51, 71, 74; "The Metamorphosis" as a liberating work 51–2
Kahn, Guy 112
Kahnweiler, Daniel-Henri 66, 68, 69
Kansas City 94
Kaye, Danny 131
Keillor, Garrison 115, 17
Kelly, Ellsworth 25
Kennedy, John F. 36, 39, 84
Kern, Jerome 12
Kerouac, Jack 103, 105
Khokhlova, Olga 70; Picasso's portrait 71
Kilmer, Joyce 111
King, Carol 131
King, Larry 131
King, Dr. Martin Luther, Jr. 11, 96
King, Peewee 81
Kings of Tyrus 93
Konigsberg, Letty (WA's sister) 133
Konigsberg, Marty (WA's father) 132
Kornfeld, Jack 96
Koss, John 145
Kristofferson, Kris 8, 114

The Lady and the Tramp 47
"Large Bathers" 67
Las Vegas, NV 24
Laugh-In 115
Lax, Eric 136, 140, 143
"Lay Lady Lay" (BD song) 2, 71, 108, 111
Leadbelly (William Huddie Leadbetter) 18
Led Zeppelin 117
Leman, Kevin 25
Lemon, Jack 60
Lennon, John 13, 25, 101
Leonardo da Vinci 10
Lerner, Alan Jay 83
"Let's Do It" 113
"Let's Misbehave" 113
"Let's Spend the Night Together" 100
Levelers 83
Lewis, Wyndham 42
Library of Congress 65
Lichtenstein, Roy 59; affinities with BD 60
Life with Picasso 61, 63, 64, 70
"Like a Rolling Stone" (BD song) 12, 21, 25, 37, 45, 50, 58, 66, 68, 69, 74, 81, 86, 90, 107, 108, 110, 121, 145; analogies with movies 46–7; as compassional song 48; as fairy tale 46; democratization and gender roles 47–8

Lincoln Memorial 128
Lion (nightclub) 133
Little Richard 20, 34, 102
Loewe, Frederick 83
London, England 10
"The Lonesome Death of Hattie Carroll" (BD song) 35
Longfellow, William Wadsworth 30
"Lord Randal" 57
Los Angeles 136
Lost Generation 131
Louis Armstrong's New Orleans 22
"Love Me Tender" 24
Lower East Side 131
Lvov 130
"Lyin' Eyes" 114, 116

Maar, Dora 70
Madison Square Garden 128
Maid in Manhattan 49
Making Modernism: Picasso and the Creation of a Market for Twentieth-Century Art 67
Málaga, Spain 64
Malamud, Bernard 11
Malibu, CA 138
Mamet, David 138
The Man in the Gray Flannel Suit 79
"Man with Mandolin" 69
Manet, Edouard 57
Manhattan 120, 131, 136
Manhattan (WA movie) 142
Manilow, Barry 131
A Map of Misreading 21
Marcus, Greil 9, 34, 43, 45
market segmentation 66–8
Martin, Dean 81
Martin, Mary 136
Mary 91
"Masters of War" (BD song) 34, 35, 43
Masur, Louis 121
"Maybelline" 43
McBrien, William 114
McBroom, Amanda 17
McCartney, Paul 25, 119; and Wings 117
McClure, Michael 11
McLane, Shirley 60
McLean, Don 114, 119; and "Miss American Pie" 115–6, 119
McLuhan, Marshall 30, 78, 85, 111, 135, 142, 144; BD and, 41–3; "Ballad of a Thin Man" and "My Back Pages" and 43–44; liberation theology 74–5; media theories 74–5
McQuinn, Roger 128
"Me and Bobby McGee" 115
Meade, Marion 132
Medal of Freedom 128
"Meeting Across the River" 120
Mellencamp, John Cougar 128
Melville, Herman 17
Memorial Coliseum (Los Angeles) 124
Memphis, TN 20

"Memphis Mafia" 8
Mercury, Freddy 115
Merman, Ethel 136
Michaels, Marilyn 101
Middle Ages 92
A Midsummer Night Sex Comedy (WA movie) 142
Minneapolis, MN 65, 132
Minnesota 26, 29, 31, 146
"Miss American Pie" 114, 119
Miss Lonelyhearts (novel) 46
"Mr. Tambourine Man" (BD song) 5, 73, 74, 77, 82, 86, 93, 105, 106; McLuhanesque qualities 75; as a shore-ode 76; stanza form in 110
Mitchell, Joni 135
Mitchum, Robert 126
"Mixed-Up Confusion" (BD song) 20
Moby Dick 17
Modern Times (BD album) 87
Mogilyov 130
"Mona Lisa" 58
The Monkees 68, 145
Morrison, Jim 25, 68, 116
Moscow 67
Moses 96
"Motorpsycho Nightmare" (BD song) 52
Motown 145
"Moulin de la Galette" 65
"My Back Pages" (BD song) 43, 74, 78, 106
My Fair Lady 48, 49, 146
"My Name Is Barbra" (TV special) 134
My Passion for Design (BS book) 138

Nashville, TN 19, 20, 55, 100
Nashville Skyline (BD album) 71, 94, 95, 100, 101, 108, 111, 116, 134
The Natural (movie) 11
Nelson, Willie 13, 117, 118
Nerval, Gerard 36
New Morning (BD album) 134
New Jersey 118, 120, 123
The New Jersey Syndrome 118 ff., 123, 124
New York City 9, 26, 27, 28, 29, 31, 36, 38, 41, 45, 50, 55, 65, 66, 71, 83, 100, 119, 120, 123, 127, 130, 131, 132, 134, 137, 140, 142, 146, 147; art scene 103–4; and popular culture 133
"New York City Serenade" 120
New York Drama Critics Circle Award 134
New York Public Library 54, 84
Newport, RI 36, 44, 65
Newport Folk Festival 28, 35, 39, 44, 70, 122
Newton, Isaac 13
"Niagara" (painting) 126
Niagara Falls 126
Nietzsche, Friedrich 91
"The Night Time's the Right Time" 101
9/11 attacks 127
No Direction Home (movie) 8, 10, 19, 29, 39, 43, 46
Nobel Prize Committee 1

Index

Notre Dame Cathedral 83

Obama, Barack 13, 118, 128
Odessa, Russia 51, 130, 131
The Odyssey 17
Oklahoma! 94
Old Testament 98
Oliver, Joe 22
Olivier, Fernande 59
On a Clear Day You Can See Forever (BS album) 134
"On the Road Again" 117
"On the Street Where You Live" 49
"One More Night" (BD song) 101, 108
"One Night with You" 101
"One Too Many Mornings:" (BD song) 115
Ong, Walter J. v 22
"Only a Hobo" (BD song) 40
"Only a Pawn in Their Game" (BD song) 35, 106, 109
Only the Lonely (Sinatra album) 99
Ophelia 81, 89, 102
Oswald, Lee Harvey 35–6, 45, 96
Out of This World 114
The Owl and the Pussycat (BS movie) 134
"Oxford Town" (BD song) 36

Pablo Picasso 59
Pacino, Al 136
Pale of Settlement 130, 131
"Papa, Can You Hear Me?" 133
Paris, France 45, 61, 65, 77, 131
Park Slope 131
"A Pastoral Concert" (painting) 57
Pat Garrett and Billy the Kid (BD movie) 8, 142
Paul McCartney and Wings 117
Peck, Gregory 79
"Peggy Day" (BD song) 108
People (BS album) 134
"People" (BS song) 134, 145
Peru, IN 113
Peter Paul and Mary 35
Peterson, Ray 101
Picasso, Pablo 4, 51, 57, 61, 71, 74, 75, 85, 90, 115, 117, 137, 139, 140; affinities with BD 57ff.; blue period 65–66, 68; rose period 66, 68
Picasso: An American Tribute 58
Picasso and His Friends 59
Picasso: The Formative Years: A Study of His Sources 59
Picasso's "Guernica": The Genesis of a Painting 59
Picasso's Picassos 58
Pike's Peak 125
Pilgrims 55
Play It Again, Sam (WA movie) 142, 143
"Pleasant Valley Sunday" 68
"Pledging My Love" 102
"Pledging My Time " (BD song) 102, 107

PM East (radio show) 133
Poe, Edgar Allan 30
Poets of Tin Pan Alley 112
Point Dome (Los Angeles) 132
Pop Art 43, 61
Porter, Cole 34, 112; triple rhymes 112–3
Portinari, Beatrice 80, 86
Portnoy's Complaint 11
Pound, Ezra 52, 86
Presley, Elvis 1, 8, 19, 20, 23, 24, 28, 34, 48, 56, 59, 60, 66, 67, 71, 101, 119, 121, 122; appears on *Ed Sullivan Show* 119; BD's reaction to 25; "Comeback Special" (1968) 101–2; recording of "Blue Christmas" 56
"The Pretender" 115
Pretty Woman 49
Price, Chilton 81
The Private World of Pablo Picasso 59
The Problem of the Third Generation Immigrant 129
"Prove It All Night" 123
The Purple Rose of Cairo (WA movie) 142
Pushkin, Alexander 30

Queen 117
"Queen Jane Approximately" (BD song) 61

A Race of Singers 32
"Racing in the Streets" 126
Radio Days (WA movie) 142
"Rainy Day Women #12 and 35" (BD song) 71, 107, 113
"Ramblin' Man" 114, 116
Randy's Record Mart 19
"Rat Pack" 8
Rauschenberg, Robert 60
Reagan, Ronald 117
Redford, Robert 11
Reeves, Jim 101
Reinhardt, Ad 25, 61
Remarque, Erich Maria 17
Rembrandt Harmenszoon van Rijn 137
Renaldo and Clara (BD movie) 8
Renoir, Pierre-Auguste 65
Revolution in the Air (book) 14, 74
"Rhapsody in Blue" 12
Richards, Keith 25
Richardson, John 58, 64, 66
Rimbaud, Artur 36, 37, 38, 39, 52, 77; influence of "Vowels" on "Chimes of Freedom" 38
The Rising (album) 127
"The Rising" (song) 128
Rivers, Joan 131
Robertson, Robbie 8
Robinson, Smoky 13
Rock and Roll Hall of Fame 25
Rock Eras 35
Rodgers, Richard 12, 112, 113
"Rollin' and Tumblin'" 87
Rolling Stone 137

168 Index

The Rolling Stones 81, 101, 115, 117; BD's imagery on cover of *Get Yer Ya-Ya's Out* 90
Rolling Thunder Revue (BD tour) 7
Rollins, Jack 144
Romeo 80–81
Ronk, Dave Van 29, 36, 37, 46, 68
The Ronnettes 101
"The Rose" 17
Roth, David Lee 115
Rothko, Mark 11
Rotolo, Suze 70; appears with BD on cover of *The Freewheelin' Bob Dylan* 28, 96; quoted 27; reads Gilot's *Life with Picasso* 61–4; takes BD to the Museum of Modern Art 58
Royal Albert Hall 7, 125

"Sad-Eyed Lady of the Lowlands" (BD song) 14, 24, 73, 74, 75, 80, 92, 94, 107, 110; length 113; and songs of courtly love 92–3
St. Bernard 91
St. Louis University v
"The Saltimbanque Family" 59
"Sam, You Made the Pants too Long" 139
Sanders, Bernie 131
Sandler, Adam. 131
"Save the Last Dance for Me" 101
Scaduto, Anthony 36
Scenes from a Mall (WA movie) 141
Scenes from a Marriage (movie) 141
Schumer, Charles 131
Scorsese, Martin 10, 19, 39, 43, 135
"Seated Woman" 60
"Second-Hand Rose" 139
Seeger, Pete 40, 43, 65, 66, 74, 113, 128, 135
Self-Portrait (BD album) 134
"Send in the Clowns" 139
Shahn, Ben 11
Shakespeare, William 2, 10, 23, 56, 105
Shchukin, Sergey 67
Shelly, Percy Bysshe 30
"Show Me" 49
Shrek (movie) 46, 47
Shriner, Herb 133
Simon, Carly 136
Simon, Paul 25
Simonton, Dean 9, 10, 25
Sinatra, Frank 8, 87, 101, 119; and evolution of night song 88
Sinatra: A Man and His Music 101
Slezkine, Yuri 11
"Somewhere Over the Rainbow" 121
Sondheim, Stephen 12, 139
"Songs for Passersby" (poem) vi
Sonny and Cher 145
Soprano, Tony 127
The Sopranos 127
South, Joe 114
Southern Methodist University, v
Spanish Civil War 40
Spector, Phil 101, 122
Spielberg, Steven 130

"Spirit in the Night" 121
Springsteen, Bruce 21, 99, 114, 123, 126, 127, 135, 141; difficulties with his father 118; recognized by BD 119; swerve from BD 121–2; and Whitman 124; and William Wordsworth 126
Stardust Memories (WA movie) 143
Starr, Ringo 25
stereo headphones 145–6
stereophonic records 145
Stevens, Dodie 101
Stevens, Wallace 78, 95, 96
Stewart, Redd 81
"Still Life #30" 60
"Still Life with Chair Caning" 69
Stratford-on-Avon, England 10
Stravinsky, Igor 44, 139
Street Legal (BD album) 77
A Streetcar Named Desire (movie) 28
Streisand, Barbra 5, 129, 130, 132, 137, 138, 140, 143, 144, 146, 147; achieves stardom in *I Can Get for You Wholesale* 135; and Art Nouveau furniture 138; changes the Broadway musical 135–6; early death of father 133; leaves New York 136; multiple gifts 143; wins Oscar for *Funny Girl* 134
Streisand, Isaac (BS's grandfather) 130
Streisand, Sheldon Jay (BS's brother) 133
"Stuck Inside of Mobile with the Memphis Blues Again" (BD song) 20, 23, 107, 110, 124; autobiographical elements 23–4
"Subterranean Homesick Blues" (BD song) 106, 110, 111; stanza form 109, 116
Sun Studios 28, 135
"Sunday Morning Coming Down" 114
Super Boel 128
Surrealists 61
Synthetic Cubism 69

"Talkin' World War III Blues" (BD song) 32
"Teen Angel" 88
"Tell Laura I Love Her" 101
"Tell Tommy I Miss Him" 101
Tennessee 92
"Tenth Avenue Freezeout" 120
Terkel, Studs 25
"Texas in My Rearview Mirror" 115
Thalberg, Irvin 131
Thatcher, Becky 30
"This Land Is Your Land" 31, 66, 125, 126, 127
This Side of Paradise 27
Thomas, Danny 112
"Three Musicians" 60
The Three Sisters (play) 1424
Thunder Road (movie) 126
"Thunder Road" (song) 126
Timeless (BS concert) 138
Times Square 136
The Times They Are a-Changin' (BD album) 69, 106, 34

"The Times They Are a-Changin'" (BD song) 34, 106, 108, 118
Tin Pan Alley 34, 103, 111–2, 113; triple rhymes 112
Tiresias 86; as man/woman 84–5
Titian 57
"To Be Alone with You" (BD song) 108
Tolstoy, Leo 30
"Tonight I'll Be Staying Here With You" (BD song) 101, 108
The Tonight Show 134
Top 40 stations 38
Toulouse-Lautrec, Henri de 65
Town Hall 134
tradition 137
transistor radios 144–5
"Transistor Sister" 144
Traum, Happy 16, 53
"Trees" 111
triple rhymes, use of by songwriters influenced by BD 114–177
Tubb, Ernest 87, 101
Tupelo, MS 1, 20
Twain, Mark 141

Understanding Media. The Extensions of Man 1, 41, 85; ideas in 41–2; impact on BD 74–5
University of Minnesota 18, 56, 65
University of Missouri–Columbia v
Up the Sandbox 134
Upanishads 84

Vietnam 126
Vincent, Gene, and the Blue Caps 81
Vinci, Italy 10
"Visions of Johanna" (BD song) 2, 24, 48, 58, 73, 74, 75, 78, 80, 82, 86, 94, 96, 100, 107, 111, 121; as completion of "Desolation Row" 88–9; as night song 87–88; as tessera 88; vestigial chorus 110
La Vita Nuova 93

"Walking the Floor Over You" 87
Wallace, Mike 133
"Walls of Red Wing" (BD poem) 31
Walter, Marie-Therese 70
Watergate 126
Waters, Muddy 67, 86
The Way We Were (BS movie) 139
"We Are the Champions" 115, 117
"We Gotta Get Out of This Place" (song) 129

Welles, Orson 144
Wesselman, Tom 60, 61
West, Nathaniel 46
West Side Story (movie) 12, 123
What's New Pussycat? (WA movie) 134
When Brooklyn Was the World 131
"When the Ship Comes In" (BD poem) 31
Whitaker, Dave 19
"White Christmas" 56
Whitman, Walt 32, 77, 78, 79; and "Mr. Tambourine Man" 76–7; significance of for BD 320–3; "Song of Myself" and "Visions of Johanna" 89–90
"The Wicked Messenger" (BD song) 77, 98
Will in the World: How Shakespeare Became Shakespeare 3
Willensky, Eliot 131
Williams, Hank 19–20, 23, 40, 71, 101, 103, 105, 140
Wilson, Brian 13, 25
Wilson, Earl 133
Winter Garden Theater 146
"Witchcraft" 101
"With God on Our Side" (BD song) 32, 36, 96, 108
WLAC 101
"Woman in Gray" 60
Woodstock, NY 9, 119, 132
Wordsworth, William 23, 126
"Work with Me Annie" 102
Worland, Rick v
World War I 67, 130
Wright Brothers 125
WSM (Nashville) 19, 101
"Wunderbar" 113
Wyeth, Andrew 8, 17

Yentl (movie) 130, 139
"Yes, I'm Lonesome Tonight" 101
"You Belong to Me" 81
Young, Neil 13
"Your Cheatin' Heart" 24
"You're the Reason I Can't Sleep at Night" 87

Zelig (WA movie) 142
Zimmerman, Abraham (BD's father) 9, 13, 132
Zimmerman, David (BD's brother) 9, 13
Zimmerman, Zygman (BD's grandfather) 51, 99, 130, 132

www.ingramcontent.com/pod-product-compliance
Ingram Content Group UK Ltd.
Pitfield, Milton Keynes, MK11 3LW, UK
UKHW042016140426
5217IPUK00015B/1205